AF600451

The Rise of the Diva on the Sixteenth-Century Commedia dell'Arte Stage

ROSALIND KERR

The Rise of the Diva on the Sixteenth-Century Commedia dell'Arte Stage

UNIVERSITY OF TORONTO PRESS
Toronto Buffalo London

Toronto Buffalo London
www.utppublishing.com

ISBN 978-1-4426-4911-8

Toronto Italian Studies

Library and Archives Canada Cataloguing in Publication

Kerr, Rosalind, 1941–, author
The rise of the diva on the sixteenth-century commedia dell'arte stage / Rosalind Kerr.

(Toronto Italian studies)
Includes bibliographical references and index.
ISBN 978-1-4426-4911-8 (bound)

1. Women in the theater – Italy – History – 16th century. 2. Actresses – Italy – History – 16th century. 3. Sex role in the theater – Italy – History – 16th century. 4. Commedia dell'arte – History and criticism. I. Title. II. Series: Toronto Italian studies

PN2672.W65K47 2015 792.02′8082 C2014-907709-2

This book has been published with the assistance of the Social Sciences and Humanities Research Council standard research grant. The author also acknowledges assistance from the Publication Subvention Program, Faculty of Arts and Office of the Vice-President (Research), University of Alberta.

University of Toronto Press acknowledges the financial assistance to its publishing program of the Canada Council for the Arts and the Ontario Arts Council.

Canada Council for the Arts Conseil des Arts du Canada

ONTARIO ARTS COUNCIL
CONSEIL DES ARTS DE L'ONTARIO
an Ontario government agency
un organisme du gouvernement de l'Ontario

University of Toronto Press acknowledges the financial support of the Government of Canada through the Canada Book Fund for its publishing activities.

To the memory of my daughter
Alexandra Currier (1973–1985)

someone will remember us
I say
even in another time
– Sappho, trans. Anne Carson

Contents

Illustrations

Acknowledgments

This book has been in gestation for a long time and owes so much to so many that it is impossible to express adequate thanks to everyone who contributed to its completion. It has undergone many incarnations since my supervisor Domenico Pietropaolo inspired me to research the early Italian commedia dell'arte actresses while I was a doctoral student at the Graduate Centre for the Study of Drama, University of Toronto, in the early 1990s. At the time gender and performance studies were opening up new approaches to the representation of women on the stage, and so this was an exciting topic to pursue, especially since the contribution of these actresses to the creation of Italian professional theatre in the sixteenth century was receiving increased attention from Italian and Anglo-American scholars. I was fortunate to have Ann Saddlemyer and the late David Trott as members of my dissertation committee for a thesis entitled "The Actress as Androgyne in the Commedia dell'Arte Scenarios of Flaminio Scala."

My research – then as now – is deeply indebted to the important commedia dell'arte scholars who have created a substantial body of work in English, including translations of documents, plays, and scenario collections that have become foundational to teaching and research in the field. The list that follows is by no means complete: Pamela Brown, Frances K. Barasch, Louise George Clubb, Christopher Cairns, Domenico Pietropaolo, Kenneth Richards, Laura Richards, Anne MacNeil, M.A. Katritzky, Robert Henke, Julie Campbell, Erith Jaffe-Berg, Richard Andrews, Thomas Heck, Anne Heck, and Tim Fitzpatrick.

During my years in the Department of Drama at the University of Alberta, I profited from the exchange of ideas relating to the theory and practice of commedia dell'arte in several graduate classes. Research assistants Kyna Hamill, Robin Whittaker, and Cassandra Silver deserve special mention, as does my graduate class of 2009, who adapted and performed Flaminio Scala's *The Fake Husband.*

Another very important stimulus to my research over the years has been my memberships in the Renaissance Society of America, the Canadian Society of Italian Studies, and the American Association of Italian Studies, at whose annual meetings I have interacted with notable scholars who have encouraged and inspired me, notably Guido Ruggiero, Laura Giannetti, Ian Moulton, Jane Tylus, Konrad Eisenbichler, Gianni Cicali, Laura Benedetti, Mary-Michelle DeCoste, Maria Stampino, Deanna Shemek, Meredith Ray, Elissa Weaver, Valeria Finucci, Eugenio Giusti, Gary Cestaro, Michael Sherberg, Carol Lazzaro-Weiss, Dana Renga, and Alexandra Coller.

Two particular such occasions stand out, the first when Laura Giannetti and Guido Ruggiero hosted the 2006 Medieval, Renaissance, and Baroque Interdisciplinary Symposium in Miami, Florida. The excitement generated on that occasion encouraged me to pursue my research into the formation of early modern sexual identities. The second and more recent occasion was the 2013 meeting of the American Association of Italian Studies in Eugene, Oregon, at which I gave a keynote address entitled "Circulating Endless Desire: The Rise of the Diva on the Sixteenth Century Commedia dell'Arte Stage," the gratifying response to which spurred me on to complete the manuscript that became this book.

I gratefully acknowledge permission to reproduce parts of this book that appear elsewhere. Parts of chapter 1 originally appeared as "The Italian Actress and the Foundations of Early Modern European Theatre: Performing Female Sexual Identities on the Commedia dell'Arte Stage," *Early Theatre* 11.2 (2008): 181–97, also available online at http://digitalcommons.mcmaster.ca/earlytheatre/vol11/iss2/10. Special thanks are due to M.A. Katritzky as contributing editor of the Issues in Review section, "New Developments in Commedia Research." Parts of chapter 4 were in gestation in "Transgressive Transvestism in Three Scala Scenarios," in *Gendered Contexts: New Perspectives in Italian Cultural Studies,* ed. Laura Benedetti, Julia L. Hairston, and Silvia M. Ross (New York: Peter Lang, 1996), 109–20. Parts of chapter 5 have been adapted from two articles: "Isabella Andreini, Comica Gelosa (1562–1604): Petrarchism for the Theatre Public," *Quaderni d'Italianistica* 27.2 (2006): 71–92; and "The Imprint of Genius: Tasso's Sonnet to Isabella Andreini," *Quaderni d'Italianistica* 22.2 (2001): 81–96. Another part of chapter 5, "Sex and the Satyr in the Pastoral Tradition: Isabella Andreini's *La Mirtilla* as Pro-feminist Erotica," is forthcoming in *Magic, Marriage, Midwifery: Eroticism in the Middle Ages and Renaissance,* ed. Ian Frederick Moulton (Turnhout: Brepols, 2014/2015).

My research has also been made possible by the generous funding I have received from the Social Sciences and Humanities Research Council of Canada, which has been exceptionally helpful and considerate. SSHRC post-doctoral and standard research grants allowed me to travel to England, France, and Italy to conduct my research and gather archival materials as well as supporting the hiring of editorial assistants to help with data collection, manuscript preparation, and copyediting. I am extremely grateful to Brianna Wells for her outstanding contribution and enthusiastic support. As well, Shane Riczu provided expert assistance in several areas, and I am indebted to Amyrose McCue Gill for her exceptional skills in all areas of manuscript preparation. I also gratefully acknowledge the support provided by the subvention program of the Faculty of Arts and the Vice-President (Research Office) of the University of Alberta.

I am also very thankful to those I dealt with at the University of Toronto Press: to the late Ron Schoeffel, who saw the manuscript through many of its stages; to readers for their invaluable commentary and detailed suggestions; to Suzanne Rancourt for taking me through the final writing process; to Anne Laughlin, for deftly steering the manuscript through production; and to Terry Teskey, my editor, for her keen eye and expert assistance.

Finally, I owe a great debt to family, friends, and colleagues who have generously supported me through this long process in many different ways. There are so many: my son Andrew and his family, Stefano Muneroni, Elena del Rio, Mary Polito, Piet Defraeye, Louise Turcotte, Robyn Mott, Sandra Nicholls, Susan Bennett, Patricia Demers, Bonnie Prentice, Donia Mounsef, Linda Rubin, Judy Sandbrook, Stephen Johnson, Anne Malena, Kate Weiss, Julie Brown, Connie Golden, Kim Laflamme, Kerri Calvert, Lois Harder, Michele Wilanowski, Patrizia Bettella, Enrico Musacchio, and Christine McWebb. To these and to others I have unwittingly forgotten to mention here by name, please accept my grateful thanks.

The Rise of the Diva on the Sixteenth-Century Commedia dell'Arte Stage

Introduction

This book explores the multifaceted significance of the emergence of the professional actress from the 1560s onwards in Italy.[1] It is intended to deepen English-speaking scholars' understanding of the impact this phenomenal change had on the development of early modern Western theatre. Although Shakespearean scholars have developed a large body of work dealing with the stage representation of erotic desire and its relationship to the formation of sexual identities in early modern culture, their work is generally restricted to an all-male theatre, since women were not permitted on the professional English stage until the 1660s.[2] Thinking about what it meant to have "real" women taking not only the female but also the transvestite heroine roles, as they did on the Italian professional stage, enriches our knowledge about theatrical practice and challenges some of the dominant assumptions about the performance of sexual identities in early modern Europe. In tracing the historical progression of the actress' materialization from her earliest appearance as a sideshow attraction to a revered diva, this work explores ways in which actresses used their appeal as sexual, cultural, and commodity fetishes to target their audiences' desires.[3] In addition to showing how the actresses' performances interrogate early modern female sexual identities, it traces the trajectory through which the most gifted stratum of actresses achieved celebrity status. This early appearance of celebrity culture, usually considered to be an eighteenth-century phenomenon in the English theatre, may also have been accelerated in Italy by the early arrival of the actress. Locating the unprecedented popularity of these actresses within the context of celebrity worship allows us to understand how their iconic status changed the acting profession and enhanced the importance accorded to women within it.

Reading the available documentation relating to the activities of such early actresses as Flaminia of Rome, Vincenza Armani, and Vittoria Piissimi brings into focus the complex interplay of factors that made their presence essential to the commercial and artistic success of the new professional theatre. The extensive archive left by the first great international diva, Isabella Andreini, makes it possible to authenticate her celebrity status and reveals ways in which she queried the boundaries defining female sexual identities.

My research builds on the evidence that the addition of the actress to the previously all-male troupes (established in the 1540s) was the marketing device that ensured the commercial success of this struggling new form of professional theatre. I have been greatly influenced by the evidence presented in the comprehensive document collections brought out by several notable Italian scholars as part of a renaissance in commedia dell'arte studies that began in the 1970s in Italy. This methodology informs the opening chapter, which examines the documentation concerning the emergence of marketplace theatre and the novel presence of female performers as an identifiable social group. In this instance my goal is to make a substantial number of the documents collected by Ferdinando Taviani in *La fascinazione del teatro*, volume 1 of *La commedia dell'arte e la società barocca* (1969), available as source materials, for their coverage of the well-known controversies the church raised in its opposition to the proliferation of theatrical entertainments. In revisiting the familiar objections the church raised against the theatre, I intend to pinpoint the particular qualities of stage performances that made them so offensive to the religious authorities, and to capture the reasons for the church's extra animosity towards the newly arrived female performer. What emerges from the documents is a strong sense of the church's awareness that the new commercial theatrical form posed a serious threat to the centrality of religious worship in the lives of the people. In particular, I cite from Roberto Tessari's *Commedia dell'Arte: la maschera e l'ombra* (1989) commentary on this loss of faith in the church and the turning towards earthly pleasures and secular entertainments as the ultimate happiness. The expansion of the period of Carnival when theatrical entertainments were permitted so that the commedia dell'arte eventually were able to perform all year round signalled that theatre had become a popular attraction in early modern Italy and that the church had lost some of its power to regulate people's lives.

Considered more globally, this loss of belief in the sacred led to the rise of what Simon During describes as "secular magic."[4] In order to experience the supernatural that had once been part of religious belief systems, people turned to the magic found in stage illusions, conjuring tricks, and special effects. During's study offers insight on the watershed event that took place as loss of religious faith left the populace with a new taste for secular entertainments that could be satisfied by the new commercial theatre with its mixture of acrobatics, conjuring tricks, enchantments, and displays of madness, all woven into a dramatic fiction. The magical effects that theatrical entertainment exerted over audiences led church officials to regard it with the kind of deep suspicion and unresolved ambivalence that is usually attached to a fetish object, according to cultural anthropologist William Pietz.[5]

While Pietz's work focuses on how the *fetisso* (fetish) proved particularly useful to the Inquisition as a means of controlling female sexuality, his definition of the term illuminates many of the underlying assumptions antitheatricalist clerics continually made about the demonic effects that theatre, as a human invention, had on viewers.[6] The term "*fetisso*" was first used by sixteenth-century Portuguese traders to describe the inability of their West African native partners to reduce the objects they were trading to a straightforward commercial value; the concept of the fetish's ambiguous value and irreducible materiality proves useful when applied to the novel display of female bodies on the commedia dell'arte stage. The cross-cultural origins of the fetish exhibit its properties as a "reified, territorialized historical object [that] is also 'personalized' in the sense that, beyond its status as a significant object, it evokes an intensely personal response from individuals."[7] Especially pertinent here is the church's condemnation of women's bodies as more dangerous than men's because of their innately sinful materiality. A close reading of antitheatricalist commentary captures the church's dismay at the controversial display of women's bodies, and their fears about the demonic effects of seeing women perform. If church officials fetishized women as demonic beings, they were also aware that when women performed they had a special appeal for audiences as sexual commodities. Although the commedia dell'arte operated some centuries before the rise of the mass consumerism usually associated with the commodity fetish, the techniques of advertising, marketing, and packaging the product can be discerned in the methods it used to sell its products. As the actress proved to be the biggest selling point in drawing audiences, her commodification was also closely tied to her sexual appeal. Lorraine Gamman and Merja Makinen in *Female Fetishism: A New Look* (1994) refer to this marketing of sex as a form of "consumer fetishism of the erotic."[8]

Chapter 1, entitled "The Early Female Performer as Marketplace Fetish," describes the rise of piazza entertainers, including the charlatan, mountebank, and early commedia dell'arte performers and the female entertainers who appeared with them. The central arguments advanced by church authorities concerning the extreme dangers posed by demonic female performers reveal the contours of the ideological warfare theologians were waging against the social upheaval they were powerless to quell. By considering examples of the kinds of activities these first female performers engaged in and the responses they evoked from their audiences, we can come to understand how their fetishized presence exerted an irresistible appeal over audiences. What becomes apparent from some of M.A. Katritzky's research on the women who appeared on the mountebank stages is that the antitheatricalists were right in their assessment that female bodies were put on display for the purposes of selling products and, over time, the theatrical entertainment itself. While the equation of the sexual with the commercial fetish in the form of the actress cannot be denied, it is also possible to show from the battle lines drawn between the church and the theatre apologists reveal that the actress could no longer be simply regarded as a disposable pawn by either camp. The real points of difference that come up in the fight between the actor/apologist Niccolò Barbieri in *La Supplica* and his Jesuit opponent, G.D. Ottonelli (who devotes considerable attention to Barbieri in two of the volumes of his massive *Della Christiana Moderatione del Theatro*), highlight the polarized ideological responses to the actress, who continued to be fetishized either as a negative demonic force or as a conduit to the divine.

Although Freudian theories referencing sexual differences based on the new family relationships that emerged from the rise of the bourgeois patriarchal household were only fully articulated some centuries later, Jon Stratton notes in *The Desirable Body: Cultural Fetishism and the Erotics of Consumption* that there is evidence of a new emphasis on female sexuality as early as the sixteenth century.[9] Freud's description of the formation of the fetish as a process whereby all women become phallicized objects in the eyes of men proves useful in exposing the different ways in which sexual differences are constructed through stage representations of female "others." The obsessive desire of the male characters to pursue female characters and their ever-present fear of being cuckolded are driving themes in most commedia dell'arte plots. While the maidservant's body parts are often exposed as pornographic fetishes, her sexual availability is juxtaposed to the apparent unobtainability of the *prima donna*, the classic Petrarchan love object.

Chapter 2, "Pornographic Bawds, Courtesans, and Maid Servants," looks at the roles taken by the courtesan/maidservant in order to show how she is contrasted to the *prima donna* by having lesser exchange value and greater sexual availability. It includes a close reading of the first recorded commedia dell'arte performance in Bavaria in 1568 to show the sexually promiscuous courtesan Camilla circulating among the male characters. Using Freudian theories explaining how the cuckolding joke works for the male spectator, it offers readings from Scala scenarios in which the maidservant plays a role that highlights her sexual availability: "Il vecchio geloso" (The Jealous Old Man, Day 6), "La fortunata Isabella" (Lucky Isabella, Day 3), and "Le burle d'Isabella" (Isabella's Tricks, Day 4).[10] It offers a socio-semiotic analysis of the key role taken by the maid Franceschina in the *Recueil Fossard* (1580s) as she points out to audiences the sexual hypocrisy of the early modern household. The chapter concludes with the maidservant Ruchetta's cynical speech on virginity from *Il finto marito* (1618) as an example of a maidservant who advocates for sexual pleasure.

Since the actresses actively participated in improvising their roles in the creation of the scenarios, they provide us with a unique opportunity to study – at least in theatrical representation – "the emergence of feminine subjects in the modern west."[11] As troupe members who helped to build the action by improvising their roles, they were positioned to acknowledge and dispute their objectification by voicing their own desires. In my search for examples of the actresses operating as active female subjects, I have found it useful to follow some of the strategies offered by E.L. McCallum's *Object Lessons: How to Do Things with Fetishism.* She proposes that the kind of complex arbitration of sexual differences that fetishism offers can be usefully deployed to "enable us to accommodate both desire and knowledge when the two conflict."[12] Since fetishism is "about the negotiation of the boundary of the self, the establishment of identity, of which sexual difference is only one aspect, albeit a fundamental one," it provides useful insights into the ways in which the actresses interpret the characters they portray.[13] Having "real" women embody the female roles meant that audiences could relate to the fact that the actresses were speaking from a female perspective about the ways in which female identities were being constructed.[14] My readings of their performances in the scenarios aim to capture the evolutionary growth of the female characters' agential powers in negotiating their places in the social hierarchy.[15]

While chapters 1 and 2 work with the evidence of the actresses as commodities whose sexual appeal made them vitally important to the success of the commedia dell'arte, they also open up the discourse to consider what kind of artistic contribution the actresses were making to the genre. Chapter 3, "Iconic Prima Donnas," addresses a new facet of the actresses' theatrical impact by examining their popularity in the context of fame studies.[16] The emergence of celebrity culture at this time is closely connected to the rise of market capitalism and its need to sell products by catering to public demand. In pushing back the date to look for evidence of the appearance of celebrities on the late sixteenth-century Italian stage, I acknowledge that the media records are not available in the same abundance,[17] but note that print culture had already made significant changes to the production and reception of theatre.[18] The commedia dell'arte troupes were part of this revolution and were able to flourish by collecting printed materials for their repertoires, hiring themselves out to court patrons, and charging audiences for performances.[19] As the troupes became known throughout Italy, their members acquired celebrity status in the popular imagination, not only by word of mouth but also by the circulation of iconographic and print materials. The actresses achieved celebrity very quickly because they were desirable commodities whose "honest courtesan" training allowed them to impersonate idealized gentlewomen with exceptional skill and grace. In breaking the taboo against females appearing in public spaces, they acquired a certain notoriety that is reflected by the fact that the public called them by their first names, or by the first names of the characters they typically played. As they travelled around the major Italian cities, they became known to mass audiences and revered alongside the outstanding male actors who had first developed the famous masks of Pantalone, Dottore, and the Zanni. The sense of "public intimacy" they created when they appeared on stage – dressed in the beautiful and often revealing robes of a court lady – gave spectators the illusion that they were accessible because of their visibility and close proximity. This "illusion of availability" derived from their "public intimacy" is the first quality that a celebrity must possess, according to Joseph Roach in his study of the rise of celebrity on the eighteenth-century English stage.[20]

As Roach explains, another essential quality of celebrity is "synthetic experience" – the way in which audiences share vicariously in the actors' embodiment of actions and feelings.[21] Noting that theatrical performances provide audiences with a magical consumable product that satisfies our human need to live vicariously, he stresses the new importance that attending the theatre acquired once audience members had the opportunity to pay for the experience.[22] Commedia dell'arte audiences also experienced theatrical performances as paying customers and were possibly more directly implicated in vicariously experiencing the actors' performances, since the improvised nature of the action required them to collaborate in shaping the course of events.[23] Even more than in scripted performances, audience members found themselves closely identified with the actors, who invited them in both direct and indirect ways to support their choices and share their emotional dilemmas.[24]

An examination of the records describing the summer seasons when the first generation of exceptional actresses, Flaminia and Vincenza Armani, competed against each other in Mantua in 1567–68 makes it clear that Roach's criteria for celebrity are already present, as both of these actresses created the illusion of "public intimacy," of "shared experience" with their audiences, and possessed the mysterious "It effect."[25] This ineffable quality is present when celebrities are treated as *role-icons,* a term Roach defines as "preconceptions of abnormally interesting personae" who through the power of mass marketing come to stand in for abstracted qualities.[26] Sociologist Chris Rojek's important study *Celebrity* explains that in a secular society, one that has lost its connection to the sacred, celebrities often become objects of cult worship, inspiring intense "feelings of recognition, awe and wonder."[27] It is possible to relate these concepts to ways in which certain actresses such as Flaminia, Vicenza Armani, Vittoria Piissimi, and Isabella Andreini were regarded. Indeed, the worship accorded to them is not dissimilar to Roland Barthes' tribute to Greta Garbo's ineffable iconic qualities. In discussing her mythic powers to enchant, he observed that "the name given to her, *the Divine,* probably aimed to convey less a superlative state of beauty than the essence of her corporeal person, descended from heaven where all things are formed and finished with the greatest clarity."[28] My reading of Adriano Valerini's funeral oration for Vincenza Armani shows that he thought of her in similar terms.

While celebrity remains elusive, Rojek has offered categories that are helpful in explaining the fame accorded to the early divas as owing to their exceptionality as female artists. He describes three celebrity categories: *ascribed,* which is predetermined by bloodline; *achieved,* which "derives from the perceived accomplishment of the individual in open competition," and *attributed,* which is awarded not necessarily for talent or skill but through some media-generated association with noteworthiness.[29] The commedia dell'arte prided itself on its unique improvisational style; all company members had to display the utmost skill in performing in order to carry the action of the scenario forward. In the case of the *prima* and *seconda donna* this involved displaying their virtuosity on stage by showing how well they could effortlessly perform as trained singers, musicians, dancers, and rhetoricians declaiming neoplatonic discourses. Since they always appeared in pairs, there was a constant basis for comparing and ranking their performances. The famous rivalries that developed between the most celebrated early divas moved the competition to a national scale.

Evidence showing how clearly the actresses showcased this rivalry is included in my close reading of the unique Scala scenario "Il ritratto" (The Portrait, Day 39) which features the clash between Vittoria Piissimi, as the ruling diva, and the newly arrived Isabella Andreini. Offering a glimpse into the ways in which the commedia dell'arte troupes understood the impact their performances had on their audiences, this scenario reveals how the diva was granted the illusion of what Micheal Quinn describes as "absolute presence."[30] Social anthropologist Alfred Gell, in theorizing about the ways in which artists enchant us, proposes that the magical qualities we attribute to them arise from the awe we experience in the face of their transcendent technical mastery – a mastery that eludes our comprehension.[31] Since we are unable to fathom the magical ways in which artists transform the materials they work with, he believes we come to grant them supernatural powers and see both them and their art through a kind of "halo-effect." Our desire for these truly valuable displays of artistic forms stems from the fact that we know they have a transcendent quality,[32] much like Walter Benjamin's description of the "aura" – the singular qualities of the original work of art, highly valued but deceptive and out of reach.[33]

Nowhere does their technical mastery show to greater advantage than in their skill in transcending conventional gender roles, the subject of chapter 4, "Transvestite Heroines."[34] More transgressive than those who played the *prima donna* roles, the actresses who exhibited their skills as male impersonators challenged the sex/gender boundaries that privileged male over female identities. Since female transvestism remained closely associated with the courtesan practice of wearing men's breeches,[35] actresses who appeared on stage dressed as male courtiers evoked a range of desires in their spectators. Having "real" women breaking the social codes that kept them subservient to men proved to be enormously popular, as female transvestism flourished on the stage throughout the centuries to come, despite the increased disapproval of the practice after the Council of Trent.[36] During this period, when young people of both sexes found themselves circulating in the new urban marketplace, transvestism served as a code for sexual ambiguity that extended the erotic possibilities for imagined couplings with same- and opposite-sex partners.[37] When females took over the transvestite heroine roles, originally performed by young aristocratic males in the erudite theatre, they were empowered to represent females as desiring subjects. In this period, as many gender theorists have noted, wearing the clothing of the opposite sex created a strong fetishistic reaction in the audience.[38] Valerie Traub's proposal that female transvestism operates as a "strategic appropriation of the phallus" proves very useful as a means of evaluating the ways in which actresses in the transvestite roles deployed the fetish to negotiate their own sexual identities.[39] In the Scala collection, the most striking examples of female transvestism are found in scenarios that feature Isabella Andreini as Fabrizio, her male persona. Close readings from "Il pellegrino fido amante" (The Faithful Loving Pilgrim, Day 14), "Isabella gelosa" (Isabella's Jealousy, Day 25), and "Li finti servi" (The Disguised Servants, Day 30) in particular showcase her skill as a male impersonator as a sign of her artistic transcendence of gender roles.

Chapter 5, "The Making of a Diva," features Andreini's rise to diva status through the "rhetoric of authenticity" that grows up around her in keeping with Richard Dyer's argument that a star's charisma depends on the public having knowledge that there is an authentic flesh-and-blood person behind the superhuman figure. As part of this rhetoric, it is also possible to discover traces of her personal voice, as she "negotiates the competing and contradictory definitions of her own significance as a celebrity sign."[40] I first look at her "authentic presence" as a *prima donna* who was also a wife and mother, an aspiring *literata* and academician, who attracted a cult of worshippers determined to connect her to Torquato Tasso. I then examine her diva status as manifested through her recognized genius; she was a diva who *achieved* her fame by demonstrating her mastery as both poet and performer in her *Rime,* pastoral *Mirtilla,* and iconic mad performance of *La pazzia* at the Medici wedding gala of 1589. Finally, I consider the legend of her immortality through her celebrity death and her husband's efforts to keep her memory alive by publishing her *Lettere* and *Fragmenti.* As the first great international diva, she leaves us with an invaluable record of a female artist's perspective on the construction of female identities in early modern Italy.

My conclusion reminds the reader of the trajectory that the female performers followed as they moved from sideshow attractions to revered divas and proposes that through understanding how they achieved celebrity status, we can more easily answer the question of what kinds of desire they mobilized in the public. Aware of their dependence on the commercial success of their art form, they knew that their appeal depended on keeping the audiences eager for more. While some cultural sociologists insist that celebrity icons exist independently of the material conditions that produce them, I align myself more with others such as Rojek, who maintains that celebrity culture is inextricably bound up with commodity culture and that "celebrities are commodities in the sense that consumers desire to possess them."[41] I argue that recognizing that commodity fetishism is a part of celebrity culture, rather than being reductive, opens up the opportunity to look for additional ways in which the actresses made their commodification work for them – by revealing the places where their desires and knowledge intersect.[42] Through their creations of unforgettable female characters and their invention of a new mimetic acting style, the Italian actresses revolutionized the early modern Western stage, and in the case of Isabella Andreini, who led the way for her fellow actresses, found the path to eternal fame.

Chapter One

The Early Female Performer as Marketplace Fetish

The phenomenal arrival of female performers on the sixteenth-century commedia dell'arte stage in the 1560s, one hundred years earlier than they were admitted on the English professional stage, is best understood as happening along a continuum that is briefly outlined in this chapter. Records indicate that the commedia dell'arte came into existence as a result of the social and economic upheavals that led to the creation of a marketplace economy at odds with the outmoded church system of charitable relief. We first encounter actors appearing alongside charlatans and mountebanks as they travelled through the northern Italian cities to sell their wares under the disapproving eye of zealous Counter-Reformation church officials. My special interest here is in the records that I quote at length as evidence of both the church's opposition to the theatre in general and, more specifically, the novel presence of women used by the mountebanks to promote sales and enhance the staging of plays.[1] I argue that the displacement of women's bodies on to the selling of goods and theatrical entertainment played to the fetishistic desires of the mass audiences who flocked to the performances. In tracing the carefully articulated series of attacks made by the church, which argued that the presence of the actress was evidence that the theatre was a place of public prostitution, I demonstrate that the church's condemnation serves to acknowledge the dangerous ideological force of its secular rival.

While the term *commedia dell'arte* (theatre of the profession) was first used centuries later in Carlo Goldoni's *Teatro Comico* (1750),[2] it has come to refer retrospectively to "organized professional companies, a few of them famous internationally as well as in Italy, that performed mainly improvised drama beginning in the mid-sixteenth century."[3] However, it would take commedia dell'arte actors almost another century to win legitimacy for their profession because their association with their mountebank origins remained difficult to shake.[4] Generally considered to have come into official existence in 1545 when the first contract among a troupe of players was signed, commedia dell'arte companies were for many years hard to distinguish from other piazza entertainers.[5] Benedetto Croce's perceptive observation that the commedia dell'arte began as an embryonic industry responsive to the demands of the market also references the erotic importance of the actress:

> To the Italians, creators of *commedia dell'arte,* we owe not only its industrial and commercial organization ... but the increase in permanent theatres, the inclusion of women as actresses, the machinery to make scene changes, the formation of theatre arts schools, ... nor would it do to forget the erotic life of the theatre, the figure of the actress, of the singer, the sign of amorous attraction, if it is indeed true that eroticism has its own special circumstances, its own particular story.[6]

More recently, Taviani and Schino as well as Tessari have explored the commedia dell'arte's origins, beginning with the emergence of acting troupes bound by professional contracts.[7] In essence, commedia dell'arte performers existed along a continuum that included the mountebanks, charlatans, buffoons, *zanni,* musicians, and other itinerant performers who peddled their wares across the established trade routes running across northern Italian as well as other European cities.[8] While over time these outstanding companies of actors distinguished themselves professionally, they always remained connected to their lesser counterparts by their need to earn a living.

The dominant presence of mountebanks, beggars, and vagabonds is interpreted by Tessari as proof of the socio-economic upheaval in Italy and the breakdown of the church's medieval system of charitable relief in the face of the burgeoning numbers of vagrant poor.[9] Profound changes were altering the social structure of the relatively prosperous northern Italian cities, which were flooded with displaced agricultural workers and soldiers returning from various wars. As Robert Henke sums it up, "the transition from the predominantly artisan economy of the twelfth through the fifteenth centuries to the emerging manufacturing and merchant economy of the sixteenth and seventeenth centuries caused deep social rifts and a marked increase in unemployment, vagabondage, mendicancy, and banditry."[10] Tessari's insistence that the profile of commedia dell'arte actors would continue to "confront, mirror and blur into" that of the *ciarlatano* (charlatan) and *cerretano* (imposter) throughout their entire history throws light on his belief that they were all part of an important economic and cultural shift that was ushering in a new ideological belief system. He proposes that the love affair that the populace developed with these fascinating purveyors of esoteric learning, secret potions, magical cures, and garish entertainment revealed the loss of faith in traditional religion, in the giving of alms and other forms of charity, in salvation based on good works, and in the mortification of the flesh. Instead, he suggests that in the new secularism heralded by humanism and the breakdown of the hegemonic Catholic Church, the public were looking elsewhere to find meaning in their lives. What the popularity of the mountebanks represents for Tessari is a major shift in what people valued as a source of happiness, as the marketplace and the consumer satisfaction derived from the buying and selling of good and services became the main focus of people's lives.[11] During's *Modern Enchantments: The Cultural Power of Secular Magic* underscores the relevance of Tessari's argument to the historical rise of show business, describing the magical properties of the theatre as important in "providing the terms and content of modern culture's understanding and judgment of itself."[12]

Pleasurable activities in the marketplace were also intricately interwoven with the Carnival season. While it is not clear how Carnival, a specific pre-Lenten calendrical feast in which plays were commonly performed, came to be extended to include the two months between Epiphany and Lent, such a change meant that these itinerant performers could earn a living on the marketplace circuit. The English traveller Fynes Moryson notes that in the 1590s in Italy, "in the tyme of Carnauall all Cittyes vse to haue publike Comedies acted by Cittizens," and goes on to comment in the same passage:

> also not only in Carnauall but all the yeare long, all the Markett places of great Cittyes are full of Montebankes, or Ciarlatanes, who stand vpon tables like stages, and to sell their oyles, waters, and salues, drawe the people about them by musicke and pleasant discourse like Comedies, hauing a woman and a masked foole to acte these partes with them.[13]

If the exact relationship between Carnival celebrations and the emergent forms of popular entertainment remains uncertain, the iconographic evidence of a 1560 woodcut depicting a group of commedia dell'arte actors supporting a float bearing an enormous effigy of Carnival in a triumphant procession suggests that "there was a constant give and take between it [the commedia dell'arte] and the popular sources from which it drew its strength."[14] Over time, as new economic arrangements prevailed, the connections between calendrical festivals and marketplace entertainment became less and less fixed, and street performers, acrobats, rope-walkers, charlatans, mountebanks, and commedia dell'arte troupes could be found on the marketplace circuit throughout the entire year.[15]

Armed with a comprehensive set of rules entitled the *Professio fidei tridentina* drawn up at the Council of Trent (1545–63), the Counter-Reformation church devoted itself to imposing a new orthodoxy on its parishioners. Church officials aimed at a triumphant reclamation of the moral, spiritual, and intellectual lives of its remaining adherents.[16] With every effort devoted to encouraging its membership to be vigilant in avoiding the temptations of illicit earthly pleasures, the church looked disapprovingly at ludic Carnival celebrations as remnants of ancient diabolical rituals. In 1571, one of the most zealous Tridentines, Carlo Borromeo, requested the Spanish papal annunciate to procure a provision for him that would assist him in "removing the serious offences committed against God in Carnival time," and added that not only religious but civil authorities in many places have already "prohibited comedies, jousts, and similar spectacles on feast days under strict penalties not only for those who authorize them, but also for the spectators."[17] In a diocesan address to the people of Milan, the cardinal suggested that their recent suffering of the plague should give them cause to fear what else might happen to them if they continued in their evil Carnival practices:

> Now, remember, Milan, the masquerades, the comedies, the pagan games, the balls, the banquets, the excess of pomp, the intemperate spending, the brawls, the disputes, the murders, the wantonness, the dishonesty, the monstrous insanities and dissoluteness of yours, which precisely in this time especially, we see multiplying and flooding over you.[18]

The additional complication of the extension of the original period of Carnival meant that the public were no longer observing the high holidays prescribed by the liturgical calendar. Carlo Bascapè, Bishop of Novara and a close colleague of Borromeo, made it clear that the extension of Carnival time for the whole period between Epiphany and Lent was a denial of God. Although the medieval church had allowed Carnival to run for the two or so weeks from Septuagesima Sunday (the third before Lent), Bascapè preached the necessity of eliminating Carnival altogether in order to make the entire seventy days before Easter into a period of abstinence, representing the seventy years of the Babylonian Captivity. He condemned Carnival as a return to the pre-salvation period when the Devil had power over the people. In his Septuagesima pastoral (1606), Bascapè chastised his flock for falling into the same kind of sin by indulging in the sensual pleasures of Carnival for such an extended period.[19]

Theatre spectacles in particular came to be singled out as the most pernicious of all Carnival activities because they were symbolic expressions of the World of the Flesh and, hence, in the service of the Devil. In his 1578 letter to Cardinal Paleotti, Archbishop of Bologna, Borromeo emphasized the particularly dangerous threat posed by theatrical representations at Carnival:

> Indeed, I judge them [dramatic performances] to be more dangerous to customs and to souls than those other seedbeds of much evil, the balls, feasts, and such spectacles, because the dishonest and wanton nature of the words, actions, and gestures that are presented in such dramas, being more latent, make a more vivid imprint on men's souls, and it seems to me, that there might be still more damage from them that could result to that city.[20]

In the larger condemnation of theatre as a spectacle contrary to Christian life, accusations of its ancient idolatrous beginnings were revived to condemn current practices as similarly connected to devil worship. Guglielmo Baldesano's "De fuggire li teatri e le vanità de gli spettacoli" (1592) designated the players as "masters of iniquity for the others, and therefore most pernicious to the city and the kingdom, seditious, witches, necromancers, the ruin of property, destroyer of the strictest union that is natural among mortals, that of matrimony." Players were doubly damned because of their scandalous itinerant lifestyle and their presentation of nefarious comedies that brought damnation on spectators, who were influenced by such evil examples. Watching such comedies was idolatrous because it broke the promise that Christians made to God at baptism to renounce Satan and all his pomp.[21]

Despite their efforts to demonize the theatre, the antitheatricalists failed to prove in censorship proceedings that the actors were committing idolatry by worshipping a false god. In their inability to decisively condemn this new theatrical phenomenon and hence to censor its effects, the antitheatricalists' debates reveal the presence of the conditions that Pietz cites as necessary indicators that an object is being fetishized.[22] He begins by examining the etymology of the Portuguese term *"fetisso,"* first used in the sixteenth century by Portuguese traders to explain their somewhat ambiguous and mysterious exchange of goods with Gold Coast African tribes, and proposes that "the emergence of a distinct notion of the fetish marks a breakdown in the adequacy of earlier discourse under quite specific historical conditions" and outlines the fetish as

> recognizable as a discrete thing (a *res*) because of its status as a significant object within the value codes proper to the productive and ideological systems of a given society. This reified, territorialized historical object is also "personalized" in the sense that beyond its status as a significant object it evokes an intensely personal response from individuals. This intense relationship to the individual's experience of his or her own living self through an impassioned response to the fetish object is always incommensurable with (whether in a way that reinforces or undercuts) the social value codes within which the fetish holds the status of a material signifier. It is in these "disavowals" and "perspectives of flight" whose possibility is opened in the clash of this incommensurable difference that the fetish might be identified as the site of both the formation and the revelation of ideology and value-consciousness.[23]

Thus the introduction of some kind of theatrical entertainment in the piazzas during Carnival created in the public a "meaningful fixation ... of a 'historical' object, the enduring material form and force of an unrepeatable event." Next, theatrical performances become "'territorialized' in material space" on trestle stages in the marketplace, where they acquired notoriety as "significant objects within the value codes proper to the productive and ideological systems of a given society." That this "reified, territorialized historical object ... evokes an intensely personal response from individuals" is palpably evident in the impassioned rhetoric of the antitheatricalists and in their commentary on the effects such performances had on audience members. In their "disavowals" of the theatre as a denial of God of the Christian city and their labelling of its actors as "masters of iniquity"[24] whose performances were enticements to commit evil and whose spectators were eternally damned, the clerics reveal "a clash of incommensurable difference" between their orthodox Christian values and those of the new, secular marketplace.

The church's fetishization of the theatre as demonically immoral was an attempt to conceal its awareness that if the theatre was recognized as a legitimate public institution, it might offer the public an alternative cultural reality that no longer prioritized religious salvation. The anti-theatricalists' intense reactions reveal the theatre "as a site of both the formation and the revelation of ideology and value-consciousness,"[25] betraying a profound anxiety regarding the inexplicable ways in which theatrical representations could infiltrate the public imagination. Antonio Seneca, in *Sulla soppressione degli spettacoli Comici* (1597), elaborates on the great need for and great difficulty in censoring contemporary comedies:

> In general the other forms of sin act within the limits of a single part of ours; for example, evil thoughts damage the soul, obscene spectacles the eyes, audacious words the ears, in a way in which if one of these parts falls into error, the others can be free from sin; but in the theatre none of these parts remains immune from offence, because the soul is contaminated by concupiscence, the ears through listening, the eyes by what they see. And all this is so wicked because one can't explain or speak about it without compromising one's modesty. Who could keep his own modesty intact and talk about those imitations of immoral things, those sung and spoken obscenities, those bawdy movements, those filthy gestures?

The "filthy gestures" in question were, as Seneca elaborates, connected to teaching the public ways to destroy the fabric of Christian society and the sacrament of holy matrimony,

> since all the plots of similar representations turn on love affairs, engagements and marriages, on the art of love and its remedies. Characters playing the lovers come on stage, speak of lecherous things, and frequently mention unnameable body parts, and most shameful to say, prescribe love potions which can remake virginity and eliminate the impediment for taking a wife.[26]

So too, Domenico Gori's *Trattato contro alle commedie lascive* (1604) reveals his obsessive interest in the sexually explicit scenes found in contemporary comedies:

> We certainly read in Plautus and Terence many of these comedies that are recited in these times, but in which of them have we ever heard (granted that their immodesty may seem too much for us) that on a stage a man and a woman might present themselves wrapped around in a sheet? Who dared among the ancients to have Europa appear completely naked? When was it ever permitted in ancient time that a woman might enter the stage and under her garments conceal a man? And yet all these indignities have been seen in past years in the theatres in Florence. What baseness did the ancients speak that these don't say? What acts so obscene that the ancients could ever represent that have not been surpassed by those of last year committed at the balls that followed immediately after they were performed in the comedies?[27]

As the above quotes indicate, the antitheatricalists reveal an obsessive fascination with the new form of commercial theatre and, through their endless repetition of the same charges, an anxious inability to "disavow" its existence. In their ambivalence the antitheatricalists reveal their fear of the power of this increasingly mimetic form of theatrical representation.[28] The extremity of their claims about the evils of these performances exposes their attempt to undermine the secular stage by reiterating the arguments against its fantastical "sinful" properties in order to keep it demonized in the minds of the faithful. Inevitably, the presence of female performers proved an irresistible target, because the church would continue to insist that women should not have access to the public sphere. In keeping with the ancient prohibitions that had limited the public appearance of women, Spanish Jesuit Juan de Pineda reiterates, "Saint Paul did not want women to speak publicly because, as Saint Anselmo said, it would provoke those who heard them to feel unlawful desire, and even worse than looking at [women], would be looking at and hearing them at the same time."[29]

It is therefore highly significant that the church's inability to prohibit this new form of commercial theatre extended to their failure to exclude women from joining it. Pietro Maria Cecchini's remark in 1618 establishes the traditional date for the entry of women onto the public stage as 1560, and also makes it clear that a great change had occurred in their replacement of boy actors: "it is not yet fifty years since women have appeared generally on the stage; since then their presence has become a virtual necessity in almost every instance of any importance; and even if young men could take their place, the conclusion has been reached that women are much better."[30] It seems logical that this phenomenal change likely occurred as a result of the severe economic and social upheavals that left many women without other means to earn a livelihood. The great Jesuit critic Giovan Domenico Ottonelli's grudging observation supports this interpretation:

> Actresses, except for the bench or the stage, are normally limited to the toil of the needle and the distaff, and endure a life of suffering, earning their bread by daily sweat and with great difficulty. But when they join the companies they have a better and safer situation; they are honoured and cherished; and they can claim the esteemed title of Signora.[31]

If the need to earn a living drove women to the stage, then a connection with prostitution seems likely, all the more so because unmarried women had little public status. However, because of the marginal itinerant lifestyle, even actresses who were married (often to company members) were suspect, since their first obligation was to bring in money. The first record in Italy of a theatrical contract naming a woman, Donna Lucrezia of Siena, signed in Rome in 1564, enlisted her services for the upcoming carnival to perform plays in a company of six men.[32] Ferdinando Taviani and Mirella Schino cite details from this contract to support their claim that actresses probably arrived in the profession from the class of honest courtesans (*cortegiane oneste*), who were forced out of Rome after the Council of Trent. They suggest that Lucrezia's designation of *domina,* the fact that the contract was signed at her house in the campo Marzio, and her lack of a surname in the style of the great courtesans, signal her probable occupation.[33]

That actresses had little choice in signing contracts tailored to the financial needs of their employers can be deduced from a document that precedes that of Donna Lucrezia by two decades. A contract signed at Bourges in 1545 between Marie Ferré, the wife of a street entertainer, and Antoine del'Esperonnière's troupe offers proof of a well-defined repertoire. Ferré was to perform ancient Roman comedies, other historical dramas, morality plays, farces, and acrobatic tricks in a manner pleasing to the public, in exchange for board and lodging and twelve francs a year. Any gifts from admirers were to be split with del' Esperonnière's wife.[34] The final clause of the contract clarifies that Ferré's value as a performer binds her to her employer rather than her husband, since it seems that extra entertainment will be required to bring in the "gifts" that she is to share with his wife.[35]

The 1545 contract may point to a much earlier but untrained female presence on the travelling circuit of acrobatics, rope-walkers, musicians, and players according to Winifred Smith.[36] Another source, Antonio

Grazzini's 1552 carnival song "Canto di Zanni e di Magnifichi," invites the public to attend a travelling mountebank show with "other notable players/Lovers, Ladies, Soldiers and Hermits/Remain on guard at the hall." Although it is impossible to tell if there were women in the "ladies" roles, there is no doubt that a strong pitch was being made to female audience members, who were advised to invite the players into their homes to compensate for not being able to see them in the *stanze*.[37] When the friar Tommaso Garzoni wrote his scathing commentaries on the scurrilous practices of the lower sort of strolling players in *La piazza universale di tutte le professioni del mondo, e nobili ed ignobili* (1585), he derided a newer marketing device, the outlandish sight of a female transvestite leading the parade:

> When these enter a city, immediately a drum makes it known that the gentlemen players have arrived. The Signora, dressed as a man and with sword in hand, advances to survey the field, inviting the public to a comedy or a tragedy of a pastoral in a palace or at the Pilgrim Inn, to which the mob, by nature eager for novelties and curiosities, immediately rushes to get seats and, paying its entrance money, enters the hall that has been prepared.[38]

Garzoni also paints an unforgettable portrayal of a vast assortment of mountebanks, charlatans, *ciurmatori* (swindlers), and buffoons gathered in St Mark's Square in Venice, offering every imaginable sideshow act as they compete for the fickle crowds. The brief moment in which the Tuscan appears with his "tumbling whore" captures the bizarreness of her act and her irresistible sexual appeal.

> Shortly afterwards the Tuscan burst forth through the curtains and mounts the platform with his whore ... The crowd closes around him, transfixed on the spot, all eyes and ears. And behold, in a stroke, he begins some ridiculous story in the Florentine tongue, during which the girl draws her circle on the platform, splays out her arms and legs to pick up the ring outside the circle, and then removing a coin from two crossed swords while sprawled out backwards, whetted a strange desire in the crowd with her lascivious grace.[39]

This same "lascivious grace" may explain why a Signora Angela was commended by the ducal secretary Luigi Rogna as "the one who leaps so well" during the summer of 1567 when she performed with Flaminia and Pantalone's company in Mantua.[40] The popularity of acrobatic female performers who could both sing and dance is evidenced by the example of a certain *cantimbanca* (singer), La Vettoria, who, "dressed like a trim and neat boy, packs in large crowds with her dangerous leaps, her divine dancing, her sweet singing, and her beautiful gaze."[41] Both of the notices that describe her daily performances in Florence mention that she had to be escorted home every night by four policemen to avoid being crushed by the crowds who tried to follow her home, and also protected from the "dirty old men who keep gazing at her with their mouths open because they want to play games with her and have a taste themselves."[42]

Ottonelli, in his great compendium of anecdotes documenting performances throughout the first half of the seventeenth century, discusses the irresistible ability of the *saltatrice* (female acrobats) to enhance a performance, whether on the bench or stage. As he writes of several famous incidents involving female transvestite rope-walkers and acrobats, his attention to the details of their movements captures as it condemns the mysterious "lascivious grace" identified by Garzoni:

> What an unseemly sight it offers to the eyes of the viewers, when these little females, to leap more quickly and make many marvellously beautiful turns, appear on the bench or stage dressed in men's clothing, in a lewd farce; and arching, extending and vibrating their bodies with filthy and extravagant gestures and postures, give rise to a thousand libidinous thoughts in the minds of the weak, and show, by thus deforming their own bodies, the far greater deformity of their souls.[43]

Female performers brought a wide range of skills to the stage, and although the great actresses would try to distance themselves from their acrobatic *saltimbanche* and musical *cantimbanche* counterparts, they too were expected to possess great physical as well as vocal agility, indicating that they must be viewed along the same continuum as the male actors. This point is buttressed by the research of Katritzky, who answers her own question "Was *Commedia dell'Arte* performed by mountebanks?" in the positive by citing iconographic evidence that shows the extensive theatrical activities of the mountebanks.[44] Her evidence for the close relationship between mountebanks and actors, based on numerous depictions recorded in *alba amicorum* (pocket-sized volumes collected by travelling German students), also shows that the *cantimbanca* was a regular feature on the mountebank stage. Katritzky follows the German traveller Thomas Platter's journal entries describing his reactions to performances offered at Avignon over several weeks in winter 1598 by a certain mountebank Zanni Bragetta and six companions.[45] She concludes that "in the earliest pictures, as in Platter's description of Bragetta, Zanni himself is the salesman, with a male or female violin-playing companion." After 1580, she notes, Zanni is accompanied by the salesman and often also by a woman, who is usually depicted in an elegant gown and high-necked ruff, often playing an instrument and typically flirting suggestively with Zanni. In figures 1.1 to 1.3 we can see the female musician becomes progressively more involved in the action.

In fact, Platter's description of Zanni Bragetta's troupe of five men and two women, who appear "all costumed and neatly masked,"[46] attests to their highly accomplished performances in full-length commedia dell'arte style comedies and pastorals, augmented with music, singing, dancing, mime, and acrobatics as part of their routine. During a typical performance

> they set up a long table in the market place ... and placed a large locked chest next to them on the table. And when they had played an amusing comedy on that same table ... then Zanni, who was their leader, unlocked the chest, and one of his companions, who stood next to him in the costume of a medical doctor, asked him what sort of wares he had in there.[47]

As Katritzky outlines it, Platter's description relates how the Zanni, with the help of all the costumed actors, pitches the miraculous qualities of a precious salve that he eventually agrees to sell at an incredibly reduced price. The buyers then throw their handkerchiefs with coins knotted inside at the actors.[48] Figure 1.4 provides an example of the throwing of the handkerchiefs.

As they return the handkerchiefs to audience members with the little tin of salve inside, Platter cynically notes, the female mountebanks also take the opportunity to supplement their earnings:

> They took out the steuben and knotted the little tin into it, throwing everyone back their own handkerchief again, and sometimes, when the women thought it appropriate, they added a little note to the tin, detailing where they could be met, and at what hour, and thus many such practices are combined on the side.[49]

Ottonelli is even more to the point in claiming that the woman is par-

Figure 1.1. Two mountebanks on a trestle stage. From Sigmundus Ortelius, *Album amicorum*, 20 March 1574. © The British Library Board, MS. Eg.1191, fol. 18r. All Rights Reserved 26/09/2013.

Figure 1.2. Three mountebanks on a trestle stage. From M.A. Pribil, *Album amicorum*, 1587–94. © Kupferstichkabinett. Staatliche Museen zu Berlin, 79 A 3, fol. 403v.

Figure 1.3. *Ceretani, o cantimbanchi*. From a sketchbook of Italian costumes, ca. 1580–1609. © Kupferstichkabinett. Staatliche Museen zu Berlin, 79 C 28, fol. 21r.

Figure 1.4. Three mountebanks and a monkey on a trestle stage surrounded by seven spectators. From Erhard Grünthaler, *Album amicorum*, 1591–1612. Reproduced by permission from ÖNB/Wien, Cod. ser. n. 13.244, fols. 177v–178r.

ticularly good for "sporte." Here he answers his own query, "In what way does the common actress help the earnings of the actors or charlatans?":

> 1. Because some who would not [otherwise] buy the charlatan's nostrum [literally, secret], do so thanks to the woman. And to what end? In order to throw a handkerchief at her with money in it – throwing it with the intention of hitting her face or breast, and then to receive it back later from her hands with a thousand crude and improper thoughts, indifferent to the quality of the secret [itself], whether it be good or bad.[50]

If, as already noted, the commercial theatre from mountebanks to professional troupes owed its unprecedented success to the creation of a nascent mass market through sensational packaging of its goods and services, its secret weapon proved to be the addition of female performers. While my treatment of the fetish has concentrated thus far on the church's attempt to maintain its cultural dominance by accusing the theatre of immoral representations of illicit sexual activities, church condemnation also extended to the commercial practices that enabled the theatre to survive and that cut into the church's ability to tithe. Thus, Ottonelli's detailing of how the woman on the trestle stage is used to sell the charlatan's "secret" reveals the symbolic displacement of the value of the product onto an embodied self.[51] In this instance, we are witnessing the exact conditions that produce the commodity fetish. In "Fetishism and Materialism," Pietz discusses Marx's explanation of "the commodity-form ... as nothing but the determined social relations between humans themselves which assumes here, for them, the phantasmagoric form of a relation between things."[52] He explains:

> When a given type of useful thing comes to function as a general-equivalent exchange object in trade activities, it comes to be recognized as embodying a new quality: that of a general form, the very medium of exchange (money). This historically emerging general form expresses, in its being as a material *object*, the exchange *relation* that produced it: it *is this* relation realized as a sensuous object.[53]

An excellent example of early consumer capitalism at work, the "secret" potion has been made so irresistible to audience members that they are willing to exchange coin for it, according it an abstract value that mystifies its real properties and labour costs. However, in this case those for whom the sales pitch has not been sufficiently alluring have an additional opportunity to directly experience the secret potion's qualities "as a sensuous object" by throwing their coins at the face and breasts of the woman assisting in the sale, since this physical action may, as Ottonelli notes, give them an even greater sexual thrill than that promised by the "secret" itself.[54] And since the mountebank's assistants, as Platter comments, often included in the returned handkerchief a note offering themselves in addition to the potion, they also enter into the symbolic exchange relationship. As Pietz writes:

> Money's reversibility (its ability to be the thing exchanged away or the thing exchanged for) allows the differentiation of the act of exchange into two separate acts: buying a thing for money and selling a thing for money. This initiates a real process of deferral-distanciation through differentiation (as opposed to a textual *difference)* in which the spatial and temporal separation of the moments of exchange generate the logistical (financial) instruments enabling a modern economy ... The magical moment of fetish formation in this process is the transition of the general form into a universal form, its modal shift from existence and possibility to necessity – the mysterious transubstantiation of common social practices into custom or law sanctioned by the community as a whole.[55]

The woman on the trestle, whose sexual desirability and commercial exchangeability are conflated, thus participates in "this magical moment of fetish formation" when she becomes a universalized object of desire for her audiences. Ottonelli continues to build his case by pointing out that she may also sell the products directly to increase sales:

> 2. The woman earns money on the trestle because sometimes she acts as a saleswoman, offering certain fine commodities, whether perfume, or soap, or lozenges or such similar things, which are pretty and appealing; and there is no danger of her not getting rid of them quickly and successfully, for many vain and lascivious men rush to play the part of customer.[56]

In this instance, she is using her exchangeability with the products to stand in for them both spatially and temporally, trading on her universal desirability to carry out the exchange with her male customers.

Finally, in Ottonelli's third instance, the woman on the trestle becomes interchangeable with her performability:

> 3. The woman earns money on the trestle too because she pleases by singing and playing an instrument; moreover she often entertains the crowd with various physical and captivating games, after which a cup is circulated among the spectators to solicit a tip for the lady; nor are many slow to give it. Further, as Beltrame noted, because beautiful actresses are often praised, flattered, and occasionally courted by people of rank, and are virtually raped with presents, great monetary gain undoubtedly accrues to many of them.[57]

The actress on the trestle and the stage exchanges her artistry as a musician, singer, dancer, acrobat, raconteur, mime, and rhetorician for money. On the trestle, this may involve the direct exchange of paying money for the show after experiencing the performance. On the stage, as the gifted actresses established themselves, they became the focus of an ongoing controversy as the church continued to insist that their presence was only a device to sell tickets with the promise of some kind of exchange of sexual favours.

The conflicted status of the actress would became one of the dominant issues that the emergent group of theatre apologists debated with their religious opponents as they struggled in vain for legitimacy over the course of the seventeenth century. The great challenge that such outstanding actor/authors as Pier Maria Cecchini, G.B. Andreini, and Nicolò Barbieri faced in their treatises was to defend their new profession by claiming its separation from its mountebank-buffoon origins, and to prove that the commedia dell'arte was not about cheap thrills and dirty jokes. Barbieri, who admitted to training with a mountebank,[58] insisted that the comedy of the trained actors was "tasteful and not clownish, instructive and not excessive, witty and not destructive."[59] As the argument went, according to G.B. Andreini, "comedy is none other than a kind of political and economic theatre, invented first by philosophers and then perfected by Aristotle, to purge vice and instil virtue; now, if comedy is such, who are those who represent it? *Virtuosi*."[60] Following up on Andreini's *La ferza* (1625), Barbieri's *La supplica* (1634) took on the systematic development of this argument to prove that the new city comedy devised by the commedia dell'arte was a legitimate and morally efficacious art form and that its skilled practitioners were, by association, "virtuous" in both senses of the word. But the exhaustive counterdiscourses that appeared throughout the seventeenth century through Ottonelli's encyclopaedic commentaries and rebuttals directed at Barbieri and other apologists make it clear that the church refused to concede the "virtuous" argument because of the embodied female presence of the actress.

In reading through Barbieri's repeated attempts to defend the actresses and the rebuttals that Ottonelli would make against them some years later, we can discern the clash of incommensurable values. In three consecutive chapters Barbieri takes on the accusation that actresses are employed only because of their sexual attractiveness.[61] In a later chapter entitled "Is it more natural to have females play the young unmarried women's roles than to have boy actors cross-dress?" he defends their superiority by claiming they are more natural and less affected than the boy actors. He goes on to dispute the church's admonition to "flee the stage for fear that the actresses don't break down one's virtue" by noting how ridiculous it is to have to flee from women in general since they make up half the population of the world."[62]

On the other side of the debate, the antitheatricalists continued to urge spectators to do just that – flee in order to save their souls. Best summed up in Ottonelli's great compendium in the latter half of the seventeenth century, the charges against the actresses were the ultimate impediment to granting professional legitimacy to the commedia dell'arte. Taking on Barbieri's arguments point by point, Ottonelli denied that actresses were necessary, stating that male actors "have no need to use women to perform comedies to give pleasure to the audience."[63] Ultimately, the seriousness of the charge stemmed from their inherent evil as daughters of Eve:

> But of all the characters, the woman on the platform or stage, has the advantage of attraction, wherein I believe that the introduction of women into the theatre to have been an invention and suggestion of the devil ... The face of the actress is an invitation to dishonesty ... Aristotle has written that women have two pupils in their eyes, in which they conserve a very powerful poison. And I note that even one glance is sometimes enough to steal the heart and affections of a spectator.[64]

More telling perhaps was the accusation that actresses were worse than prostitutes. Here are the damning comparisons he makes within his inquiry, "If prostitutes are legal, couldn't we also accept the commercial actresses?":

> Prostitutes are permitted to remove the occasion for adulteries and graver sins; as Saint Thomas teaches ... the Church will tolerate the sin of going to a prostitute to avoid a greater sin.[65]

> Now I tell you that these indecent actresses are worse and more insolent [than prostitutes, who at least operate in private], who while in the presence of large crowds of spectators commit the sin of representing carnal embraces, lustful fondling, dishonest kisses and disgraceful fornications ... Thus I conclude that the actors, most if not all of them, use licentious amorous discourse to reinforce the sensual impact on the spectators, or else to attract the attention of some patron in the hope of earning a lot of money.[66]

Ottonelli's universal and unwavering condemnation of the actress (and by extension of the professional theatre) was strengthened by the supposition that the offstage lives of the troupes were full of irregularities because of the need for the men and women to perform and travel together. Hence, the offstage lives of the actresses were considered to be simply extensions of their performances onstage.[67] Here the Spanish Jesuit Pedro Hurtado de Mendoza spells out how what is seen onstage cannot be divorced from what happens offstage:

> On stage, the theatrical work turns on telling the love stories of the characters, and these so-called love relationships between men and women are red hot darts; likewise in the theatre, actors embrace, squeeze hands, kiss and touch each other, set the time and place for a secret meeting. Why should they not do for real in a bedroom what they do for a joke on the stage?

In his estimation, their offstage lives cancelled out any claims the commercial theatre might have to legitimacy: "the women are always, or nearly always shameless. The actors cohabit freely, without the women being segregated in separate bedrooms; thus the men frequently watch them getting dressed, undressing, combing their hair; and on occasion when they are in bed, or when half-naked; and they are always trading dirty jokes among themselves." As he continues, this sexually permissive offstage lifestyle was so inextricably bound up with the onstage performances that the two mirror each other:

> The husbands are cowardly so that the wives don't respect them and the lovers don't fear them. The women are often prostitutes plying their trade. Often players find themselves on stage together where a man undresses and dresses a woman in order to make a quick change so that she can play another role. What more can I say? A young man laces up a woman's shoes and ties up her high stockings with silk ribbons, not only on the stage, but also near a bed.[68]

Hurtado de Mondoza cites a lurid anecdote reported to him by a fellow cleric who claimed to have heard it from a member of an acting troupe staying at the same inn:

> On one occasion a friend of mine, a priest, found himself in an inn, and a company of players happened to arrive at the same place. When the priest attempted to admonish one of them, and to persuade him to give up the life, he heard from him of the many sins they all, both married and single, were committing. The astonished priest asked him how it could be that the married men were not satisfied with their own wives, and in reply was told, 'Good father, the bridle is changed every second night.' He was alluding to a common mistake made by those who travel packs of mules, who often put the bridle of one mare on another by accident. Thus, the witty actor implied that in their community his companions frequently made use of each other's wives.[69]

While the commedia dell'arte gradually acquired greater status during the seventeenth century, such damning commentaries continued to taint its reputation. If Ottonelli eventually offered reluctant admiration for the exemplary Christian lives of Barbieri, Cecchini, G.B. Andreini, and a few others, he continued to advocate for strict moral control over both the subject matter and the performer. Actresses, irreducibly female, remained excluded in Ottonelli's Christian reformed theatre; even if the actress had a spotless reputation, Ottonelli insisted that spectators would not be able to distinguish between her and the roles she played. In the end, Ottonelli's desire to eliminate the visual threat presented by the actresses found expression in his grudging admission that actresses, though they should never appear on stage, might be allowed to speak from the wings if absolutely necessary.[70]

If actresses remained a contested site for the antitheatricalists who demonized them, they also came to be defended not only by fellow company members but also by an adoring public. Their alluring qualities were acknowledged by even the most severe critics, such as Hurtado de Mendoza: "they are often extraordinarily beautiful, elegant in their bearing and dress, well-spoken, spirited, talented dancers and singers, experts in the art of recitation,"[71] and these qualities led to their corresponding divinization in the treatises of their supporters and in their enormous fan base. As Isabella Andreini's equally famous actor-author son wrote:

> If the commedia is full of marvel and if admirability is a precept of this so

> rare dramatic poem, why should we deprive it of the greater marvel that it is to hear the astonishing wonder-working speaking woman in the theatre? ... Don't you see that [in removing women from the stage] you take from us the verisimilar, the soul and heart of this poem, and every grace, and every affect, hindering the theatre with this defect?[72]

Andreini's plea was answered in that it proved impossible to eradicate the actress from the stage. Present as a "divinized emblem," produced by "a new purposive desire,"[73] the actress was also positioned to seek ways in which the desire expressed for her as a sexual and cultural commodity could be actively reciprocated and reclaimed by her, both in her onstage performances and in her offstage existence. In chapter 3 I consider the actress as Andreini saw her, as divinized emblem. In the next chapter I follow the trajectory set up in this one of looking at female performers as a device to bring customers to the theatre for pornographic titillation.

Chapter Two

Pornographic Bawds, Courtesans, and Maidservants

The commedia dell'arte provides an early modern theatrical example of the fetishizing of the female body as a scopic commodity. This marketing device, usually regarded as occurring as a result of the mass production of consumer goods in the late-nineteenth century, is present here in nascent form as part of the creation of commercial theatre.[1] By about the 1630s, actresses had become such standardized items that the predominantly male audiences would boycott performances without them.[2] According to Ottonelli, even "ugly" actresses appeared to be beautiful on the stage because of the makeup and the roles they were playing.[3] In the previous chapter I noted the moment during the point of sale when the spectators throw handkerchiefs containing money at the bodies of the woman on the trestle or stage. Jon Stratton locates the emergence of "active commodity fetishism" when the point of sale occurs.[4] By displaying her charms to the public, the woman on the stage becomes a spectacularized object whose attractiveness and talent make her desirable to all. Her body, directly associated with the "secret" product that promised increased sexual prowess and pleasure, becomes the site that also sells theatrical entertainment.

The widespread practice of prostitution in the large Italian centres had already established a market for the commodification of women's bodies, and accelerated their spectacularization on the public stage. Prostitution was so prevalent by the early sixteenth century that the Venetian diarist Marino Sanuto wrote that there were 11,654 prostitutes in a city of 100,000.[5] The English traveller Thomas Coryate commented that, during his visit to Venice in 1608, "the number of these Venetian Cortezans it is very great. For it is thought there are of them in the whole City and other adjacent places, as Murano, Malomocco, &c., at the least twenty thousand, where of many are esteemed so loose, that they are said to open their quivers to every arrow."[6] While these numbers may well have been exaggerated, there is no doubt of the "overwhelming presence and demand for female prostitutes, not to mention the more refined *cortigiana onesta*" in Venice and other major urban centres.[7] Fynes Moryson confirms the fetishistic fervour that had spread to Venetian "men of all sortes," who were driven

> with fierce affections to forbidden lusts, and to those most which are forbidden, most kept from them, and with greatest cost and danger to be obtained. And because they are barred not only the speech and conversation but the least sight of their love (all which are allowed to men of other nations) they are carried rather with a blynde rage of passion ... to adore them as Images, rather than love them as women.[8]

If widespread prostitution had accustomed male spectators to view the female body as an image for visual consumption, the commedia dell'arte enhanced that demand by offering glimpses of naked female bodies and simulated sexual acts on stage. Although "pornography" refers "both to a historically specific genre of writing and to a range of generically specific visual representations" that leads Ian Moulton to avoid the term in his study of sixteenth-century erotic writing, I propose that the mass marketing techniques of the commedia dell'arte justify treating the latter as an prototypical exception.[9] My definition of pornography "as the visual (and sometimes aural) representation of living, moving bodies engaged in explicit, usually unfaked, sexual acts with a primary intent of arousing viewers" is borrowed from Linda Williams, and also incorporates Beverley Brown's addendum that pornography reveals current regimes of sexual relationships as "a coincidence of sexual phantasy, genre and culture in an erotic organization of visibility."[10] Although it is very difficult to say how far the implied sexual acts, which were frequently referred to, went in actual performance, the accompanying discourses indicate their importance as stage business or *lazzi*. As Williams notes, "the important point is that fetishization of the woman provokes a disturbance in the text – whether ... to create a narrative or ... to retard it,"[11] much as a *lazzo* could do.

Over time, as noted in chapter 1, women extended their stage repertoire and became full-fledged members of the companies, building their acrobatic and other street-entertainment skills into the fixed female character type roles they performed.[12] As such, actresses circulated as alluring objects inviting male spectators to imagine themselves in a special relationship with them. Since it was important to get each spectator sufficiently involved in the transaction to buy the product and/or pay the price of admission to the show when it was offered in a private stanza, part of the sales technique was to pitch the product as having irresistible appeal. The following prologue, written by Domenico Bruni, for "La fantesca grassa" (The Fat Maid), provides an example of the pornographic techniques the actress employs as she introduces the play and sells herself, seducing the audience with suggestive gestures contrasting the pleasures of having sex with her rather than a thin *innamorata*:

> Che cosa è più bello in una donna che due guancie grassotte, duo fianchi rilevati, due bracciotte rotonde, due coscia carnose e l'altre parti grosse e grasse che formino una donna di carne da godere e non una figure d'ossa da sprezzare? Sogliono per vezzo gl'innamorati dire alle amate loro: "Carne mia!." La carne è temperata col grasso umido e non con l'osso secco ... Ma se avesse dormito con una di queste grasse che sono tutto buttiro e pasta di marzapane, vaghe all'occhio, delicate al tatto, delizie del senso e nettare d'amore, voglian noi dire che'egli avesse fatto un simil voto e lamentatosi per simili venture? Ma che, in buona fé, no che non l'averebbe fatto.[13]

> What thing is more beautiful in a woman than two plump cheeks, two curvy hips, two big round arms, two fleshy thighs and the other big and abundant parts that form a woman of meat to enjoy and not a figure of bones to disdain? It is a common practice for lovers to say to their beloveds: "My flesh!" Flesh is tempered with wet grease and not with dry bone ... But if he had perchance slept with one of these fatties who are all buttery and marzipan paste, delightful to look at, delicate to touch, delicious to feel and nectar to love, would they want to tell us that he had made a similar vow and complained of the same ill luck? Say what, in good faith, he would never do it.

Similarly, in a prologue written for "La ruffiana" (The Procuress) the protagonist defends her profession to male spectators, whom she invites to relieve their lust, by playing directly to their fantasies and the ease with which she can satisfy them:

> Avete voi, cari Signori, alle volte veduto per la città un giovanotto con gli occhi incavati, lividi e lacrimosi, pallido nella faccia, languido ne' movi-

> menti, fermarsi ad ogni passo, stringer le mani, battere i piedi, mirare il cielo, rodere i guanti, stracciare il fazzoletto, essalare dal petto confusamente sospiri e lamenti, essere in istato di cadere in braccio alla morte? Ah, che se un'accorta ruffiana se gli accosta, conossendo che il male è mal d'amore, lo conforta, li promette, lo affida, lo assicura e lo aiuta in maniera tale che lo vedete riasquistare i colouri, ravivarsi il moto, invigorirsi le membra, rallegrarsi gli spiriti e rinassere ad ogni delizia.
>
> ... Sopra la mia porta, a lettere maisucole, vederete scritto: Rufiana, le cui lettere significano: R ricetta, U vera, F facile, I in condure, A a fine, N negozii, A amorosi. Però chi ha bisogno di questa ricetta vera, facile in condurre a fine negozii amorosi, non lassi me per un'ultra; ché, raccomandandomi alla grazia vostra come a protettore di ruffiani, mi inchino. Addio.[14]

> Have you, gentlemen, sometimes seen in the city a young man with sunken eyes, wan and tearful, pale of face, dragging himself, hesitating with every step, wringing his hands, stamping his feet, staring at the sky, gnawing at his cheeks, tearing his handkerchief, exhaling muddled sighs and groans, as if he were about to fall into the arms of death? And say a cunning ruffiana draws near him, knowing that he is sick from lust, comforts him, gives him hope, confides in him, reassures and aids him in such a way that you see him get his colour back, start moving, shake a leg, cheer up, and reawaken to every pleasure.
>
> ... Over my door in capital letters you will see written: Rufiana, of which the letters mean: R recipe, U sure, F certain, I to bring, A to a successful conclusion, N affairs A amorous. Therefore, who has need of this sure recipe, certain to bring amorous affairs to a successful conclusion, don't abandon me for another. And so, entrusting myself to your mercy as a protector of procuresses, I bow. Farewell.

By the end of her invitation to watch the play, she has turned the stage into an imaginary brothel, a place where fictional stage representations will hold up a mirror to contemporary Italian city life. While there is no simple explanation of how *buffoni*-style marketplace entertainers merged with professional actors and actresses to form companies, it is thought that it happened in answer to public demand for access to the new city comedy that had been developed in the academies and courts.[15] This new vernacular scripted comedy, which incorporated elements from popular entertainment into its classical adaptations, appealed because of the "directness and vitality" with which it treated "the local and the seamy" facets of "immediate life" in its portrayal of contemporary Italian society.[16] When the commedia dell'arte developed its repertoire of improvised comedies, it did not take long before it acquired a mass, widespread audience because of its ability to adapt itself to the demands of the public.[17]

Louise George Clubb has argued that, rather than seeing the commedia dell'arte as the antithesis of regular theatre, it should be recognized as "an alternative style of participation in the accretive repertory begun in *commedia erudita.*" She notes that "by the late sixteenth century the great theatrical enterprise belonged not only to a primarily private and festival drama but to Italian commercial show business and, more or less, to all the players and playwrights of Europe."[18] In her foundational work on the development of Italian Renaissance comedy, Clubb demonstrates that it emerged out of an ongoing process of experimentation whereby various compositional units, which she names "theatregrams," were endlessly combined, permutated, and contaminated to produce new generic forms. One of the most striking new theatregrams she identified was the *giovane innamorata*, the young marriageable female, negligible in Plautus and Terence, who becomes a staple figure in the cinquecento genre. "The figure of the woman desired and desiring" who had to be pursued and led to the marriage bed appeared in the new urban comedy of Bibbiena, Ariosto, Machiavelli, and Aretino as an object of desire/merchandise to be exchanged. The importance accorded to the romantic heroine reflects the new emphasis on the institution of marriage as the foundational organization of the new bourgeois state. When the commedia dell'arte developed its particular version of the romantic comedy, it featured two *innamorate*,[19] the *prima* and *seconda donna*, who as daughters of their respective households are vigorously pursued as marriage objects. The other female role, and the focus of this chapter, was the servant, bawd, or nurse, who, Clubb notes, also increased in importance as the "confidant/go-between of the *innamorata*"[20] who helps carry out the intrigue. It is she, I argue, who serves most directly as an embodied site of the sexual desire, functioning not only as a panderer but also as an available sex object who circulates among all the male characters. However, the fact that male actors continued to play the maidservant role for some time suggests that a male actor in female clothing could elicit sexual desire for a female character.[21] In addition, "her" body also provides the site where male fears of castration are symbolically realized through the constant threat of cuckoldry.

Typically, a commedia dell'arte scenario features a standardized plot line in which fixed character types, based on caricatures of the new social types emerging in the urban centres, act out their fears and fantasies of sexual pleasure and social advancement. The two households portrayed on stage, belonging to the old men, Pantalone, the nouveau-riche Venetian *magnifico*, and Gratiano, the Bolognese doctor/lawyer, contain their sons, daughters, and servants, who actively intrigue against these patriarchal figures in order to achieve the marriage arrangements of their choice. The main stage action is thus taken up with the competitive pursuit among the men for the sexual favours of the *innamorata* through her pandering maidservant. This display of women's bodies and the enactment of sexual activities on the stage reflects the "new preoccupation with women's bodies and with sex generally" that Stratton describes as occurring in the sixteenth century, along with the rise of the bourgeois family. As the central objects of desire, the female characters reinforce the new emphasis on "the genital sexualizing of desire, and its enhancement, especially in men" that Stratton suggests Freud is describing in his account of the formation of the Oedipal complex.[22] In the fantasy world of the scenarios, male spectators from every class are interpellated into sharing both the thrill of vicariously participating in the pursuit of the elusive female and the corresponding anxiety of being symbolically castrated by being cuckolded. If Freud's analysis offers a description of the individual male's sexualization in the new nuclear family, Jacques Lacan's rewriting of Freud's castration complex has broader cultural valence.[23] Here the crucial moment when the (male) child recognizes that his desires can never be satisfied marks his entry into a symbolic world that can only be accessed through the language of lack.[24] Freud's emphasis on the penis is replaced by a focus on the phallus, a mythic signifier, which marks the formation of society at the juncture of logos and desire. Since the phallus remains in permanent circulation, desire for it forever leads men to seek it through the acquisition of the woman as "Other." Women, in this scenario, according to Lacan, "become" the phallus.[25]

Becoming phallic fetishes (as Luce Irigaray notes, in her classic essay "Women on the Market," written as a feminist commentary on Lacanian theory) involves more for woman than their sexualization in the Oedipal family. Irigaray posits that "women's bodies – through their use, consumption, and circulation – provide the condition for making social life and culture possible, and as such, the production of women, signs, and commodities is always referred back to men." Further, she observes that "when women are exchanged, the woman's body must be treated as an *abstraction*. The exchange operation cannot take place in terms of some intrinsic, immanent value of the commodity. It can only come about when two objects – two women – are in relation of equality with a third term that is neither the one nor the other." The values that are assigned to women thus come from their exchangeability as property. In this economy, "sexual pleasure" corresponds to its abstract form, the acquisition of the wealth that exchanging women can bring, with the highest prize being the dowried virgin and the lowest the "used-up" prostitute. Thus, Irigarary captures the analogy between Marx's fetishization of the commodity and the Freudian/Lacanian sexual fetishization of women, whom she describes as *"fetish-objects,* inasmuch as, in exchange, they are the manifestation of the circulation of a power of the Phallus, establishing relationships of men with each other."[26]

The commedia dell'arte's ability to sell its product – the romantic comedy – can be attributed to the mirror it held up to the circulation of phallic desire in early modern Italian society. In a typical scenario, directed towards male spectators, the female roles of *innamorata* and maidservant feed voyeuristic desires/anxieties by appearing to embody the phallus through metonymic and metaphorical significations.[27] Once women on the stage were regarded as performers, they were no longer equivalent to prostitutes or courtesans who sold their bodies directly. Rather, as metonymic substitutes, the actresses acquire the status of fetishes whose sexual availability is contingent and ambiguous. In their stage roles, they also operate both metonymically and metaphorically as stand-ins for the new social stereotypes of bawdy maidservant and refined gentlewoman and as emblematic symbols of the relational exchange value these roles carry in the marriage market. The maidservant's lesser exchange value is marked by the comparative ease with which her body can be used and circulated among the male characters.[28] Just as the fetish represents the threat to identity through "lack," the maidservant's inferior status will keep her from making a marriage above her class.[29] Below I illustrate these points by providing examples of courtesans and maidservants caught up in situations where their promiscuity drives much of the action and provides the comic relief of making cuckolds of several of their pursuers.

The First Recorded Commedia dell'Arte Performance: Munich 1568

An excellent early example of the fantastical depiction of female characters as sites of circulating sexual desire can be found in the account of the improvised Italian comedy performed as part of the lavish wedding festivities in Munich of Duke Wilhelm of Bavaria and Renée of Lorraine on 8 March 1568. Acknowledged as the first extant account of entertainment in the style of commedia dell'arte, it gives us a privileged glimpse into the preparations, performance, and audience reception from the perspective of one of the key participants, court musician Massimo Troiano da Napoli. Evident in this account is the immense delight that the court took in watching the iconic antics of the Venetian *magnifico* Pantalone and his sidekick Zanni in their pursuit of the courtesan Camilla in the absence of her nobleman patron Polidoro. Although Camilla is more than a maid, her courtesan status, while making her highly desirable, also signals her status as sexually compromised goods.

Troiano gives an account of an event performed by an all-male amateur cast comprised of various noblemen from the Bavarian court and a number of professional musicians, in the form of a dialogue between two fictitious courtiers, Fortunio and Marino. Through their exchange, Troiano is able to highlight the central role that he and his choir leader Orlando de Lasso played in creating the improvisation and playing several of the roles. According to Fortunio,

> la sera dopo cena si fece una Comedia all'improviso alla Italiana, in presenza di tutte le Serenissime Dame, che quantunque le più che vi erano, non intendevano lo che si dicevano, pure fece tanto bene e con tanta gratia: il Magnifico Venetiano, Messer Orlando di Lasso, col suo Zanne, che smascellare della risa a tutti fece.[30]

> This evening a comedy was performed in the Italian manner *all'improvviso,* in the presence of all the most illustrious ladies, and notwithstanding that most who attended did not understand what was said, so accomplished and so delightful was the Venetian Magnifico, Messer Orlando di Lasso, together with his Zanni, that their jaws ached with laughter at all the antics. (49)

Troiano also makes it clear that he and Orlando invented the plot and composed the dialogue at the direct behest of Duke Wilhelm himself. Such information reveals the collusion on the part of the court artists to showcase the kind of entertainment that reflected the court's interest in the new commercial theatre. Much of the pleasure experienced by the noble audience seems to have derived from watching an entertainment that projects the excessive indulgence in feasting, fighting, and fornicating onto the comic character types Pantalone and Zanni, who caricature the nouveau-riche Venetian merchant and the new class of domestic servant. While Troiano's versatile transitions in playing three different roles (from rustic peasant to the nobleman Polidoro to the Spanish Capitano) indicate his significant contribution, he focuses his account on Orlando de Lasso's brilliant portrayal of Pantalone. Their intermingling with the noble amateur players who took the remaining parts sets up an interesting dynamic that celebrates male camaraderie, as they all participate in the attempt to gain sexual favours from the upscale courtesan Camilla, the property of the aristocrat Polidoro. Camilla was performed by the Marchese di Malaspina, a guest, whose transvestite disguise complicates the way in which Camilla's role would have been received by the mixed audience.[31]

As the phallic fetish, Camilla remains at the centre of the circulating desire that drives the actions of all the male characters from the moment Polidoro takes his leave of her. First, Pantalone appears playing a lute and sighing and moaning for love, in a signature piece played by Orlando so successfully that "et insino che Pantalone stette in scena, altro che smascellamenti, di ridere, non si udiva"(80) (as for as long as Pantalone is onstage nothing is heard but uncontrollable laughter) (50). After Pantalone performs another extended buffoonish routine with Zanni, their attention turns to wooing Camilla. When Pantalone sends Zanni over to Camilla's house with some chickens to speak on his behalf, Zanni promises to intercede for him, but does the opposite. Ever capricious, Camilla, as Fortunio editorializes, does the deed with Zanni instead: "Il Zanne tutto pauroso a casa di Camilla se ne andò; Camilla lei si innamora di Zanne, e lo fece entrare in casa; (e questo non è di Meraviglia, che spesse volte le donne lassano il buono, & al peggior s'appligliano)" (81). (Zanni, all fearful, goes to Camilla's house. Camilla falls in love with Zanni [and this is not so odd, for women often leave what is good for something worse] and allows him into the house) (50). In the second act, Camilla tricks another suitor, Capitano, when he begs to come in: "con losenghevole parole li cava da mano una collana d'oro, e li promette per la sera" (81) (with flattering words extracts a necklace from him and makes an assignation for that evening (51). Meanwhile, Zanni deceives Pantalone into believing that he can have Camilla only if he turns up at her house impersonating Zanni. When both Pantalone and Zanni are visiting her wearing each other's clothes, Polidoro comes home, and pandemonium ensues as Camilla is caught with a house full of men. Ultimately, Polidoro "discendo alla Camilla, che si dovesse risolvere di maritarsi, che lui per alcuni degno rispetto, piu tener non la vuole; dopo il molto dir di no se resolve, di far quello che Polidoro, li comandava: e così fu d'accordo, di torre il Zanne per suo legitimo Sposo" (82) (tells Camilla that she must make up her mind to marry because, for a very good reason he no longer wants to maintain her. After much protest she decides to do what Polidoro commands, and so agrees to take Zanni as her lawful husband) (51).

After more skirmishes between Pantalone and Zanni, the play ends with Camilla being given to Zanni in marriage, followed by a marriage dance in the Italian style. As a fitting ending to a court entertainment, Camilla's courtesan status and sexual promiscuity is handled by marrying her off to a servant. Rather than reducing Polidoro to the shameful status of cuckold, this comedy works as an aristocratic fantasy, perhaps signifying a symbolic end to the youthful dalliances of Duke Wilhelm himself.

The importance of this first record of the commedia dell'arte has been greatly enhanced by the life-size frescoes painted sequentially on the thirty walls of the spiral staircase named the Narrentreppe (Fools' Staircase) located in the Castle Trausnitz at Landshut. While it has been tempting to match these to Troiano's account, the fact that they were finished in 1579, when Wilhelm moved from Landshut to Munich to succeed his father Duke Albrecht, makes it unlikely that they are directly connected to the performance.[32] However, Katritzky's suggestion that these depictions of Pantalone and Zanni feasting, brawling, and chasing after prostitutes and courtesans record Wilhem's past indulgences makes them even more significant as proof of the sexual licence he may have enjoyed. Of the many scenes where female characters are being led to and from sexual encounters, two are of particular interest here. In the first, shown in figure 2.1, we see Pantalone leaving the courtesan's house as she leans into a farewell that suggests the intimacy of their encounter. In the second, shown in figure 2.2, a naked maid-courtesan appears wrapped in a sheet, leaning out of her window to pour a chamber pot full of urine over the exiting Pantalone and Zanni.

The golden shower *lazzo* is repeated in "Le disgrazie di Flavio" (Flavio's Disgrace, Day 35) of Flaminio Scala's *Il teatro delle favole rappresentative* when the maid Franceschina "gli versa l'orinale del piscio addosso" (empties a urinal full of piss) on Flavio and Pantalone, who are quarreling under her window (act 2, 360).[33] Although we cannot confirm that actresses playing Franceschina performed semi-naked,

Figure 2.1. Pantalone leaves the house of the courtesan. Fresco from Landshut, Burg Trausnitz, Narrentreppe, R. 2, 1575–79. Reproduced by permission from Bayerische Verwaltung der staatlichen Schlösser, Gärten und Seen, DE000052.

Figure 2.2. Pantalone, followed by Zanni, prepares to challenge Capitano. Fresco from Landshut, Burg Trausnitz, Narrentreppe, 1575–79. Reproduced by permission from Bayerische Verwaltung der staatlichen Schlösser, Gärten und Seen, DE000053.

she is the character most associated with the display of bare flesh. In figure 2.3 the artist Brambilla depicts a *zanni* grabbing the breast of the kneeling kitchen maid, and in figure 2.4 a bare-breasted Franceschina dances at her wedding ball.

Maidservants in Scala's "The Jealous Old Man, Day 6"; "Lucky Isabella, Day 3"; "Isabella's Tricks, Day 4"

Further evidence of the maidservant's sexualized role is visible in a sampling of three Scala scenarios: "The Jealous Old Man, Day 6," "Lucky Isabella, Day 3," and "Isabella's Tricks, Day 4." I include these three because they represent the maidservant as the knowing pawn who plays her role in setting up the cuckholding plot so central to the commedia dell'arte's satiric exposure of the sexual politics of the new merchant class. To highlight the part she plays in creating pleasure for the spectator in the cuckolding scenario, I offer a reading of the scenarios that employs Freud's analysis of how this smutty joke works. In *Jokes and Their Relation to the Unconscious,* Freud describes "tendentious jokes [as having] sources of pleasure at their disposal to which innocent jokes have no access."[34] These pleasures are found in *hostile* jokes that serve the purpose of discharging aggressive, satiric, or defensive behaviour, and in *obscene* jokes that are about exposure. In this category, he makes a number of useful observations describing "smut" as "the intentional bringing into prominence of sexual facts and relations by speech ... [It is] originally directed toward women and may be equated with attempts at seduction."[35] Such sex talk is about the desire to see the organs of the sexually different person, and if, as will often happen in the case of women of "higher social levels," the response is denied, "the sexually exciting speech becomes an aim in itself in the shape of smut." The sexual aggressiveness blocked by this resistance "becomes positively hostile and cruel, and it thus summons to its help against the obstacle that sadistic component of the sexual instinct."[36] No longer directed at the woman who has refused the seduction, the sexual joking will be saved by the men until they are "alone together" to enjoy it. The tendentious joke calls for three people: the one who makes it, the second who is "taken as the object of the hostile or sexual aggressiveness, and a third in whom the joke's aim of producing pleasure is fulfilled ... Through the first person's smutty speech the woman is exposed before the third, who, as listener, has now been bribed by the effortless satisfaction of his own libido."[37]

Figure 2.3. *Cucina per il pasto di Zan Trippu* (*Preparing the Feast for Zan Trippu's Wedding*). Anonymous print from Ambrogio Brambilla, 1583. Reproduced by permission from Biblioteca Teatrale S.I.A.E. – Roma.

Figure 2.4. *Il bellissimo ballo di Zan Trippu* (*The Beautiful Wedding Dance of Zan Trippu*). Anonymous print from Ambrogio Brambilla, 1583. Reproduced by permission from Ashmolean Museum, University of Oxford, WA1863.5840.

Freud's diachronic analysis of the origin of "smut" offers a useful blueprint to understand the many ways that smutty jokes unfold in a commedia dell' arte scenario. The richness of their range and scope demonstrates the kinds of metaphoric allusions and metonymic displacements such jokes draw upon to prolong the suspense and intensify the sexual thrill.[38] Above all, his theory illuminates the operation of the cuckold joke, which belongs in the category of the tendentious joke in that it is aggressive or hostile in its expression of male competition, cynical in its attitude towards marital fidelity, and obscene in its aim of exposure. It is told paradigmatically by a man, speaking to a male audience; the hostility intended to expose the woman is frequently displaced onto the cuckolded husband, who becomes the butt of the joke, in this case providing vicarious pleasure to the male spectators.[39] In the three examples I consider here, the maidservant serves as the conduit for the implementation of the cuckolding joke that drives so many commedia dell'arte plots.

The exquisite Boccaccian cuckolding tale entitled "Il vecchio geloso" (The Jealous Old Man, Day 6) involves a brilliant trick that is played upon the husband, Pantalone, when he visits a country villa outside of Venice with his beautiful young wife, Isabella.[40] The plan is set up by Orazio, who opens the play by telling Flavio about his plans to have sex with Isabella on this occasion, and we as audience share in the privileged information from the outset. Here the maidservant figure, Pasquella, the wife of the gardener, Burattino, plays the bawd by offering her eager support to Orazio, agreeing to conceal him in a room in her cottage and to bring Isabella to him. As a bountiful housekeeper who sets out the tables and chairs and brings out the bread and wine, the Pasquella character signifies the fantasy of female sexual plentitude while at the same time identifying herself as duplicitious in agreeing to support Orazio's cuckolding of Pantalone. Her association with bodily functions becomes a pivotal trope in the cuckolding trick, as the pretext for taking Isabella into her house is her need to urinate. This part of the joke is invoked repeatedly, as each member of the party comes one by one to ask if they too may go inside to answer a call of nature. Since Pantalone's extreme jealousy has led him to stand guard over Pasquella's door in order to prevent anyone from joining Isabella, he unwittingly serves as her pimp, telling each of them, "Di grazia, non andate a disturbar mia moglie, la quale fa un servizio" (Please, don't disturb my wife, she's relieving herself) (act 2, 81). When she finally emerges some time later, bathed in sweat, the spectators' pleasure in sharing in the punning deception of answering one call of nature with another is increased by the image of Pantalone tenderly wiping her face with his handkerchief and assuring her that "quando gli vengono quelle voluntà, che se le cavi e non patisca" (when you have needs, it's best to satisfy them) (act 2, 81).

Although we are left in no doubt about the intense sex that Orazio and Isabella have in Pasquella's room, since Burattino later requests that Orazio pay for a new bed to replace the one they have broken, the smutty part of the joke is by no means over. In the final act, the duping of another old man, Graziano, repeats certain features of the Orazio-Isabella assignation, except this time the action is displaced onto an unwitting Pasquella, who is tricked into entering the bedroom where Graziano was expecting Flaminia. In this iteration there is even less left to the spectator's imagination, as Pasquella comes running onstage, fighting her way out of Graziano's embrace and announcing that he has raped her. Pasquella's exposure and Burattino's subsequent public shame as a cuckold are used to set up Burattino's unforgettable retelling of the events of act 1 to an unsuspecting Pantalone. When Pantalone realizes that this is his story, and that he now wears the horns, the cuckolding joke comes full circle at his expense, doubling the spectators' pleasure.

In "La fortunata Isabella" (Lucky Isabella, Day 3), the maidservant Franceschina, the wife of the innkeeper Pedrolino, is featured as the insatiable sexual partner of the patriarch Graziano. Introduced at the top of act 1, Franceschina becomes a topic of conversation between the sons and Pantalone, who is also preoccupied with her. When Graziano arrives on the scene bragging that he is on his way to have sex with Franceschina, he turns a deaf ear to his sons' pleas to help them find wives, and instead laughs with them about his successful conquest, insisting "che vuol far a suo modo, mentre che vive" (that as long as he lives, he's going to do what he wants) (act 1, 45). When the bountiful Franceschina makes her entrance, "con un cesto in capo carico di robbe" (carrying a basket loaded with goods on her head) (act 1, 45), the spectator is invited to view her as fair game and take pleasure in hearing her propositioned by all the men around her. Confident of her sexual appeal, she first rebuffs Pantalone, telling him "che l'amore ne i vecchi si chiama dolore" (love in old men is called pain) (act 1, 45). Next, Isabella's servant Burrattino asks Pedrolino if he can have sex with her, followed by Arlecchino, who fondles her and is then beaten by his master Capitano. On each of these occasions, Pedrolino breaks up the encounter and defends Franceschina as his alone.

Unaware that he is already the butt of the cuckold joke, Pedrolino doubles the spectators' suspenseful pleasure by setting up the cruel bed trick intended to make it appear as if Graziano is having sex with the mysterious female traveller whom he has offered to take into his house. At this juncture the many plot strands are woven together, and the unknown traveller, who is really the *innamorata,* Isabella, masquerading as a servant, is enticed into Graziano's house by Pedrolino with the ruse that Graziano's son Orazio, with whom she has fallen in love, will find her there. Instead Pedrolino circulates the rumour that Graziano has had sex with her. Unknown to him, Franceschina hears this news, and seeks out Graziano, jealously demanding more sex with him as well (act 3, 51).

The suspense has now been built to the point where the joke can be turned back on Pedrolino who, operating under the illusion that he is masterminding the sexual intrigue, hides to eavesdrop on Orazio's angry querying of his father Graziano's actions. Graziano, fresh from having sex with Franceschina, thinks that Orazio is talking about her and not his houseguest Isabella. Their prolonged dialogue, wherein Graziano describes to the horrified Orazio all the seamy details that Orazio believes refer to Isabella, delights Pedrolino, who laughs uproariously from the sidelines. Finally, when the devastated Orazio asks his father how he could have hurt him so much by stealing his wife-to-be, the astonished Graziano clarifies the identity of his sexual partner: "che ella ha marito, et infine li dice aver goduta Franceschina, moglie di Pedrolino, e non Isabella" (that she has a husband, and at last tells him that he has been having sex with Franceschina, the wife of Pedrolino, and not Isabella) (act 3, 51–2). This revelation refocuses the listening pleasure onto Orazio, who now goes into the house to claim Isabella, accompanied by his unrepentant father, who once again insists that he wants to have more sex with Franceschina. The final scene, where the others persuade Pedrolino that he is such an alcoholic that he has misunderstood what Graziano said, concludes the joke at his expense and gives the spectators the last laugh.

In "Le burle d'Isabella" (Isabella's Tricks, Day 4), Franceschina plays the role of the maidservant who has been seduced by her master Pantalone and then passed off to the innkeeper Burratino. To sweeten the deal, as he regales Pedrolino with the details, Pantalone explains that "dopo l'aver avuta la verginità di Franceschina, sua serva, la maritò in Burattino, con dote di cinquecento scudi, e d'averli fatta una promessione rogata: al primo maschio che ella farà, li dona (in vita sua di lui) mille ducati" (after he took his servant Franceschina's virginity, he married her off to Burattino with a dowry of five hundred *scudi* and a promissory note that he would give their first son, born in his lifetime, a thousand ducats) (act 1, 56). When Franceschina and Burattino come on the scene immediately after, they are fighting over Burattino's failure to impregnate her – a task that she thinks he is unable to complete.

As Burattino rushes about taking urine samples to the doctor, Pedrolino prepares a master plan that, in its cuckolding of Burattino, aims to titillate the spectator by its blatantly obvious trickery. Disguising himself as a foreigner, Pedrolino begs alms from Burattino on the grounds that he has been banished from his homeland because of his ability to impregnate women. Burattino next calls Franceschina, who willingly consents to make use of Pedrolino's services before he has to leave, and takes him inside with Burattino's blessing. For the last half of act 3, Pedrolino and Franceschina's sexual activity is juxtaposed with the double bed trick that Isabella masterminds to get Capitano Spavento into her bed and Flaminia into bed with Flavio. While the scenario ends with Franceschina and Pedrolino denying they have had sex, the evidence is there for the spectators to judge.

Although Pasquella protests when she is raped in "The Jealous Old Husband," she along with the Franceschinas in "Lucky Isabella," and "Isabella's Tricks" play with their sexual knowledge in whatever ways they can turn it to their advantage. At the same time as they perform their sexual identities with a certain duplicity, they reveal to the spectator their awareness of their sexualized status within the new patriarchal household. In the next example of "Francisquina," as she is called in the *Recueil Fossard*, her role is fleshed out with dialogue and gestures to offer a more complex response to the economic realities of her position as a circulating sexual object.

Francisquina in the *Recueil Fossard*

The *Recueil Fossard*, the best-known collection of woodcuts and engravings depicting the early commedia dell'arte, is especially valuable for our purposes for its representation of a sequence of images capturing the role of the maidservant Francisquina.[41] A recent article by Matthew Buckley stresses how vitally important the *Recueil Fossard* is as not only "a record of commedia performance but ... a set of images that seems to have been designed to convey an understanding of commedia's techniques and method."[42] Above all, he is struck by the way the images reveal the commedia's emphasis on "the body's exoteric figurality, its grotesque, quotidian, silent claim to determine meaning."[43] Such is the case with the depiction of Francisquina, who appears as a key figure in what is likely to have been a pictorial record of an actual performance by members of the Italian troupe I Confidenti, who performed in Paris during the 1580s.[44] Strong archival evidence supports Fernando Mastropasqua's sequencing "of eighteen of the woodcuts, arranged into three groups of six, each group representing one act of a three act play" as being basically correct in their selection.[45] In the composite shown in figure 2.5, Katritzky's refinements to his model support a reading that highlights Francisquina's importance to the dramatic narrative, especially in act 3.[46]

Taken together, these three rows can be read as representing six scenes from succeeding acts of a three-act play. In order to follow my reading of the sequences I am highlighting, it is necessary to study the composite closely, to find Harlequin and Francisquina making love in what would be act 1, scene 5 in the fifth woodcut in the first row (fig. 2.6). Katritzky's logic, which I am following here, creates this order on the basis that it works in sequence with act 1, scene 3, where Pantalone is spying on Harlequin and Zany and complaining about their eating him out of house and home, and with act 1, scene 4, where Harlequin and Zany compete for Francisquina as both of them set up the sex scene in act 1, scene 5. The other substitution Katritzky makes is to move the scene depicting the prostrate figure of the love-stricken Harlequin over to the first scene in the third row, or act 3, scene 1.[47] This new sequence for the five scenes in act 3 is supported by Katritzky's discovery of four subsets of engravings that feature all five woodcuts consecutively, in one continuous block.[48] What makes these souvenir copies especially interesting is the evidence they provide of the central interest that this classic cuckolding sequence had acquired in the popular imagination. Their existence confirms that the narrative sequence whereby Francisquina progresses from being Pantalone's whore, and Harlequin's wife, to Leandro's coy temptress draws attention to her growing self-awareness, and makes her a character of interest to the reader-spectator.[49]

My socio-semiotic reading of the six woodcuts in which Francesquina's narrative is told – act 1, scene 5 and then the sequence in act 3, scenes 1 to 5 – interprets her as a site of sexual desire whose servant body becomes fetishized through a chain of signifiers that play with the mystification of her use and exchange-values, as she oscillates between her roles as waged servant, usable sex object, and marriageable love commodity.[50] Looking at the pictorial frames from outside the stage

Figure 2.5. Composite by M.A. Katritzky of 18 *Recueil Fossard* woodcuts. Reconstruction of a three-act commedia dell'arte performance. Reproduced by permission from Katritzky, "*Recueil Fossard*" and "A Renaissance Commedia dell'Arte Performance"; Nationalmuseum, Stockholm.

curtains, the reader-spectator is put in the privileged position of having information that is unavailable to the characters, who remain caught in the power dynamics that the scenario exposes. Much of the pleasure comes from the reader-spectator's engagement with the instabilities of the signs as the servants overturn their master's authority. Through the contradictions presented in the images, the reader-spectator can watch the ambiguous operations of the fetish at work, and enjoy the pleasures of interpreting the incongruities that arise from the clash of realities as the servants expose their status as usable commodities very much aware of the power dynamics working against them. Thus, if we study act 1, scene 5 (fig. 2.6), we see Pantalon, continuing his spying from an earlier scene, experiencing the shock of witnessing his servants exploiting their positions.[51]

The focus is on the sex act, as Harlequin (who appears to be referencing some rule book about making love) attempts to bring Francisquina to orgasm. His dialogue suggests that he is trying to perform sex "the way love teaches it," and as such is parodying the refined techniques of courtly love. Francesquina reminds him of this higher symbolic value by naming it as a pleasure so costly in terms of her life and honour that it must be kept secret. It is also clear that she knows all about orgasm and is enjoying herself as much as possible – given Harlequin's ineptitude. As such, she draws attention to her "turf" as a fetish object, and gestures to her wish to keep her potential exchange-value intact by not telling anyone what she is doing. Pantalon, on the other hand, channels our voyeuristic pleasure from his hidden vantage point, because at this point in the action his secret fetish use-object is pleasuring someone else, who also works for him. It is against this scene that the Francesquina narrative that resumes in act 3 needs to be read, as it sets up the contradictory realities of marrying her off to Harlequin after Pantalon has "used" her up.

If we now go to the first picture in the last row, act 3, scene 1 (fig. 2.7), we see the prostrate Harlequin with his left hand raised in a gesture that refers to his earlier attempt to satisfy Francisquina.

The first speaker, Francatripa, invites us, the readers-spectators, as fellow lovers, to observe the terrible effects of unrequited love on Harlequin, but undercuts the chivalry by telling us that the real reason Harlequin is dying is not because his love is out of his reach, but "for failing to provide a good fuck." The reversed position of Harlequin, now almost flat on the floor, recalls the earlier sex scene but removes the suggestion of exalted romantic love from the act. Sex, like the food

Figure 2.6. Scene from *Recueil Fossard* with Pantalon watching Harlequin and Francisquina (act 1, scene 5). Photo © Nationalmuseum, Stockholm.

PANTALON
Je suis des-honnoré, ce ruffian pipereau,
M'ayãt disné par Coeur, encores me tourméte,
Et fait de ma maison un clapier & bordeau,
Avec cest putain que j'ay prise à servante.

HARLEQUIN
Lever le cotillion, & la chemise aussi,
Sa Dame renverser comme l'amour l'apreuve,
Et couler sur la motte après sa main ainsi,
Francisquine mon Coeur, en ce point con se treuve.

FRANCISQUINA
Ma vie & mon honneur entre vos mains je mets,
Harlequin mon amy, prenez la jouyssance,
Que tant vous desirez, mais faictes que jamais,
Home aucú quell qui soit, n'en aye cognoissance.

SIR PANTALON
I am dishonoured, this ruffian cheater,
Having eaten me out of house and home, he still torments me
And is turning my house into a whorehouse,
With this slut who I took as servant.

HARLEQUIN
To lift skirt and chemise as well,
To throw one's Lady on her back the way love teaches it,
And then to slip one's hand into the turf like this,
Francisquina, my love, here where your sex is.

FRANCESQUINA
I place my life and my honour in your hands,
Harlequin, my friend, take as much pleasure
As you wish. But make sure that
No one at all may ever know about it.

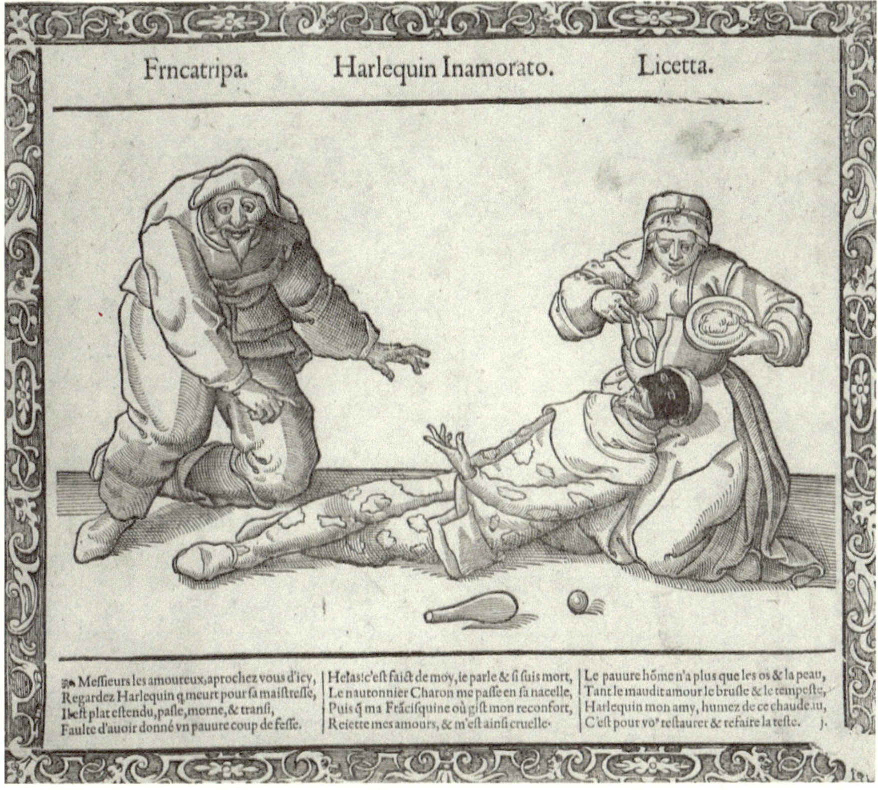

Figure 2.7. Scene from *Recueil Fossard* with Francatripa, Harlequin *Inamorato*, and Licetta (act 3, scene 1). Photo © Nationalmuseum, Stockholm.

FRANCATRIPA
Messieurs les amoureux, aprochez vous d'icy,
Regardez Harlequien q meurt pour sa maitresse,
Il est plat estendu, pafle, morne, & tranfi,
Faulte d'avoir donné un pauvre coup de fesse.

HARLEQUIN INAMORATO
Helas! C'est faict de moy, je parle & si suis mort,
Le nautonnier Charon me passé en sa nacelle,
Puis q̃ ma Francisquine où gist mon reconfort,
Reiette mes amours, & n'est ainsi cruelle.

LICETTA
Le pauvre hõme n'a plus que les os & la peau,
Tant le maudit amour le brusle & le tempeste,
Harlequin mon amy, humez de ce chaudeau,
C'est pur vo'restaurer & refaire la teste.

FRANCATRIPA
Sir Lovers, come closer,
Look at Harlequin who is dying for his mistress,
He is stretched out flat, pale, glum and numb,
For failing to provide a good fuck.

HARLEQUIN ENAMOURED
Helas! I am finished, say I and lie dead,
The captain Charon has taken me in his barque,
Because my Francisquine in whom my comfort lies,
Rejects my advances and is so cruel to me.

LICETTA
The poor man is only skin and bones,
Burnt and ravaged by this wretched love,
Harlequin, my friend, moisten your lips with this broth,
It will restore you and help you regain your wits.

Figure 2.8. Scene from *Recueil Fossard* with Pantalon marrying Harlequin and Francisquina (act 3, scene 2). Photo © Nationalmuseum, Stockholm.

HARLEQUIN
Puis, seigneur Pantalon, qu'il vo' plaist me dõner
La belle Francisquine en loyal marriage,
Je vous promets la foy de ne l'abandonner,
Tãt qu'au cul me tiendra ceste amoureuse rage.

SEGNOR PANTALON
Mettez es mains ensemble, & puis vo'jurerez,
Que serez à jamais l'un à l'autre fidelles:
Pour vostre advancement, de ma part vous aurez
Six curedês de rente, un pot, & deux escuelles.

FRANCESQUINA
Monseur j' ê suis d'accord, puis qu'il vo' plaist ainsi,
Ce sera pour couvrir la faulte que j'ay faite:
Harlequein est bon drolle, & homme sans soucy,
Je le veux pour espoux, autre je ne souhaite.

HARLEQUIN
Well, Segnor Pantalon, I ask for
the beautiful Francisquine's hand in loyal marriage,
I promise you not to abandon her,
As long as this raging love keeps grabbing me by the balls.

SIR PANTALON
Join your hands together, and swear
That you will forever be loyal to one another:
To set you up, you will receive from me
Six toothpicks as allowance, a pot and two ladles.

FRANCISQUINA
Sir, I agree, since it pleases you,
This will undo the mistake I made,
Harlequin is a jovial fellow and a carefree man,
I want him for a husband, nothing more I wsh.

and drink offered him by Licetta, is a basic human need – as all the servants know.

Thus the next scene (act 3, scene 2; fig. 2.8) has the power to surprise when Pantalon offers Francisquina to Harlequin. In scene 2, the positioning of the three figures, with Pantalon forcing their hands together, superimposes exchange-value onto Francisquina as Harlequin's bride. Once again Harlequin's left, and hence dubious, hand reaches over Pantalon's sword while Francisquina's appears to almost touch Pantalon's giant codpiece as he makes them swear to the bourgeois values to "forever be loyal." Given that Harlequin promises his love and loyalty only while "his balls are hot," and that she is obviously extremely pregnant, her exchange-value is seriously compromised. At the same time, her bland acquiescence makes it very clear how complicit she is in accepting the trade-off.

The following scene (act 3, scene 3; fig. 2.9) represents the perfect cuckolding joke carried to such extremes that any kind of magic thinking that commodities can be fairly exchanged is cancelled out by the proliferation of eight little bastard Harlequins, phallic sons of Pantalon.

Harlequin has been stuck with the task of supporting Pantalon's offspring without any recognition on his part. Pantalon responds by calling Harlequin "a poor cuckold," and shows no mercy when he mentions that Harlequin chose to marry Francisquina even though she was already pregnant. The larger social implications of such an abuse of power by the master of the household make the joke exceptionally cruel for Harlequin.

Francisquina's oscillating value as the desired sexual object and disposable whore is reintroduced in the next scene (act 3, scene 4; fig. 2.10), since she now has the protection of being a married woman. Here a thinner, better-dressed Francisquina embraces Pantalon, who leans towards her with his giant erect phallus and leg thrust over hers. No longer calling Pantalon "Monsieur," as she did when she agreed to marry Harlequin, he is now "dear friend, Pantalon." Crouching behind them with his dagger in one hand and hat in the other, Harlequin recognizes her as "the used-up slut." With her gaze directed partly towards the viewer or Harlequin rather than Pantalon, Francisquina tells us that she knows exactly what is going on and how to work it to her own ends.

In the fifth and last scene that refers to Francisquina's storyline (act 3, scene 5; fig. 2.11), she is the final figure to appear and has acquired a certain respectability as she stands with her arms demurely folded under her neatly belted, long apron. At the left, Harlequin with his dagger

Figure 2.9. Scene from *Recueil Fossard* with Harlequin and children visiting Pantalon (act 3, scene 3). Photo © Nationalmuseum, Stockholm.

HARLEQUIN
Desloyal Pantalon, je me doy bien fascher,
Tu m'as faict espouser une paillarde infame,
Elle vient maintenant d'une fille accoucher,
Et il n'y-a qu'un mois que je l'ay prise à femme.

J'en créue despit, Ce pendãt (malheureux)
Huit enfans, tous à toy, je t'a porte & ameine,
A fin de les nourrir en ce temps rigoureux:
Le pere doit ayder à ses enfans en peine.

MESSERRE PANTALON
A Dieu pauvre génin, tu te romps le cerveau,
Je n'ay eu en ma vie ta femme affaire:
Si tu as voulu prendre & la vache & la veau,
Nourry les si tu veux, je n'y sçaurois que faire.

HARLEQUIN
Disloyal Pantalon, I must be very angry with you.
You made me wed an infamous whore,
She just gave birth to a girl.
And I only wed her one month ago.

I am dying of rage: here are
Eight (wretched) children, all yours, who I bring to you,
So that you can feed them in these hard times:
The father must help his children when theyre in dire straits.

SIR PANTALON
My God, poor cuckold, you are hurting your brain,
I have never had any business with your wife:
You wanted both cow and calf,
feed them if you like, I have nothing to do with this.

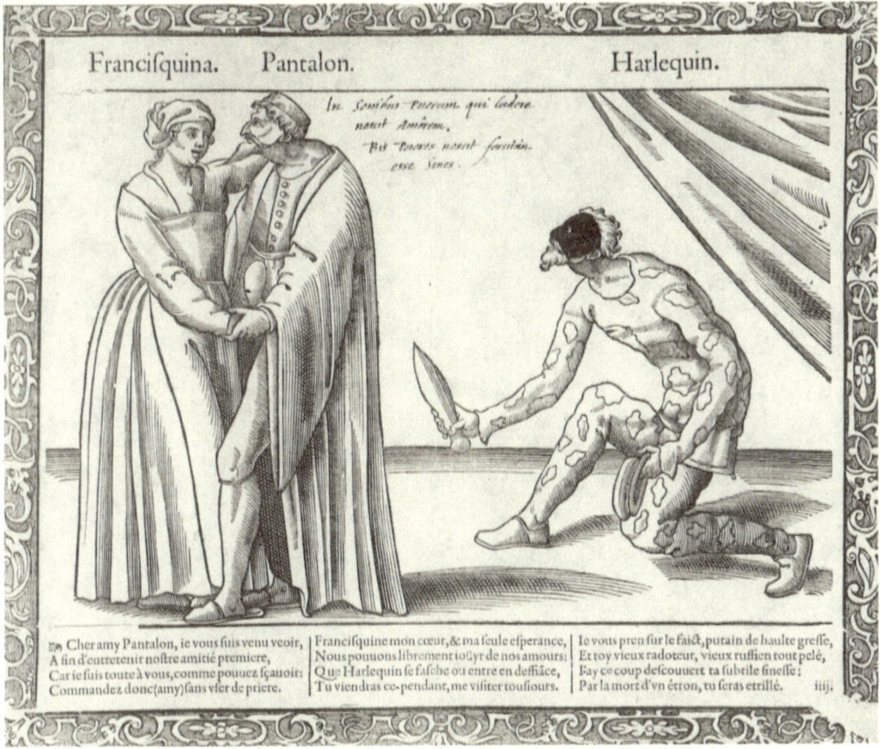

Figure 2.10. Scene from *Recueil Fossard* with Francisquina and Pantalon reuniting, with Harlequin watching (act 3, scene 4). Photo © Nationalmuseum, Stockholm.

FRANCISQUINA
Cher amy Pantalon, je vous suis venu veoir
A fin d'entretenir nostre amitié premiere,
Car je suis toute à vous, comme pouuez sçauoir
Commandez donc (amy)sans vser de priere.

PANTALON
Francisquine mon coeur, & ma seule esperance,
Nous pouuons librement joüyr de nos amours:
Que Harlequin se fasche ou entre en deffiãce,
Tu viendras ce-pendant, me visiter tousiours.

HARLEQUIN
Je vous pren sur le faict, putain de haulte greffe
Et toy vieux radoteur, vieux ruffien tout pelé,
J'ay ce coup descouuert ta subtile finesse:
Par la mort d'un étron, tu sera etrillé.

FRANCISQUINA
My dear friend, Pantalon, I came to see you,
in order to continue our initial friendship,
because I am all yours, as you know:
Command then, friend, without begging.

PANTALON
Francisquine, my love and only hope,
We can enjoy our love without constraint:
Whether Harlequin gets angry or jealous,
You will always visit me nonetheless.

HARLEQUIN
I will catch you in flagrant delicti, you used-up slut,
And you, old driveller, old bald ruffian,
I discovered your subtle shrewdness:
I swear on the death of shit, you will be whipped.

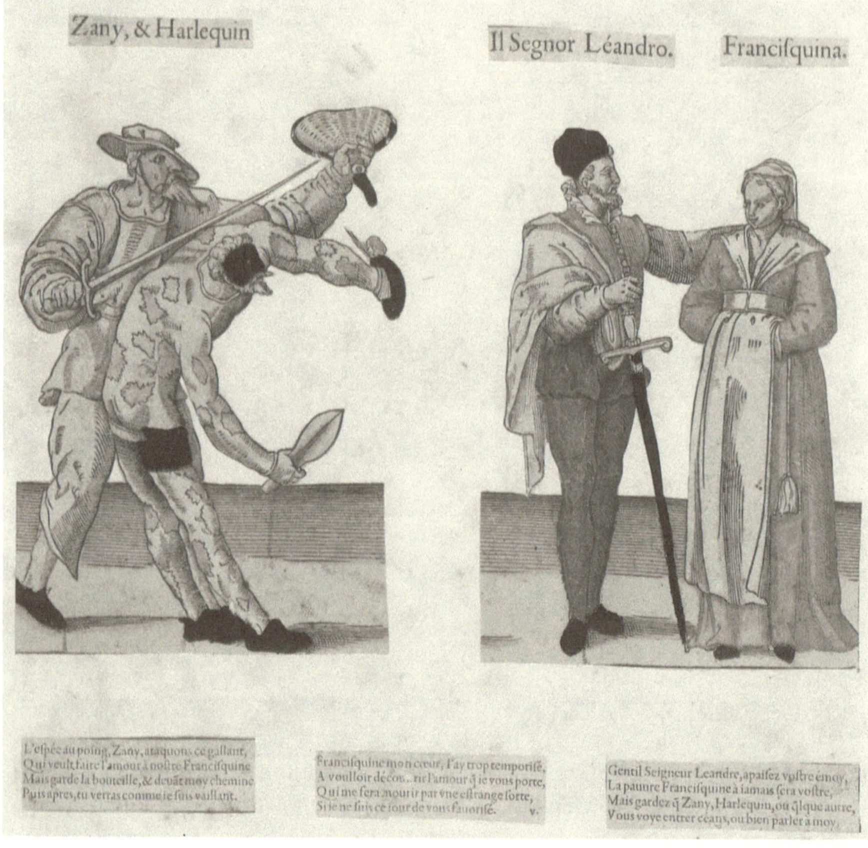

Figure 2.11. Scene from *Recueil Fossard* with Zany and Harlequin watching Leandro and Francisquina (act 3, scene 5). Photo © Nationalmuseum, Stockholm.

HARLEQUIN
L'espee au poĩg. Zany, attaquons ce galant.
Qui veut fair l'amour a nostre Francisquine.
Mais garde la bouteille, et de m'ai moy chemine.
Puis après, tu verras come je suis vaillant.

LEANDRO
Francesquine, mon coeur, j'ai trop temporisé
A vouloir découvrir l'amour que je vous porte,
Qui me fera mourir d'une étrange façon
Si je ne suis ce jour de vous favorisé.

FRANCISQUINA
Gentil Seigneur Leandro, appaisez vostre esmoy,
La pauvre Francesquine a jamais sera vostre.
Mais gardez ã zany, Harlequin ou
quelque autre.Vous voye entre ceãs, ou bien parler a moy.

HARLEQUIN
The spear raised, Zany, let us attack this gallant
Who wants to make love to our Francisquine,
But keep the bottle in your hand when you walk in front
Then you will see how brave I am.

LEANDRO
Francisquina, my dear, I waited too long,
To discover my love for you,
Which will kill me in a strange way,
If, on this day, I did you a service.

FRANCISQUINA
Noble Sir Leandro, control yourself,
Poor Francisquina will never be yours.
But beware of Zany, Harlequin or any other
Who you see come here or talk amicably with me.

and hat and Zany with a rapier and a bottle are poised, uttering their cowardly plans to attack Leandro, who stands with one arm stretched around Francisquina.

Dressed in doublet and hose, ruff and cape, the gentleman lover leans on his unsheathed rapier, as he propositions her with the standard courtly phrases, nonetheless insisting that she give in to him by telling her he plans "to die" having sex with her. Calling herself "poor Francisquina," she protests that he has no right to enter into her space, or even to address her, and that he'd better watch out for Zany and Harlequin. But her "no" is by no means final, as the translation from the ambiguous "*jamais*" (never) can also mean "yes."

The *Recueil* illustrations mapping the progression of the maidservant Francisquina's rise from "used-up slut" to the powerful maid who runs the household and the men within it is a powerful testament to the importance that her role acquired in the commedia del'arte repertoire. Over time, this role parallels and sometimes eclipses that of the *prima* and *seconda donna* whom she serves. My last example is a key speech by the wily Ruchetta, from Scala's full-length play *Il finto marito* (*The Fake Husband*) (1618), since it shows a maid speaking with supreme confidence about affairs of the heart.

Ruchetta's Speech against Virginity in *The Fake Husband*

As the long-time mistress of Demetrio (the Pantalone character) who is fully aware of her place in the social hierarchy, Ruchetta intrigues against him to protect her young mistress Giulia. Aware that Demetrio is about to force Giulia into an unwanted marriage with his old crony Gervasio, she encourages Giulia to give her virginity to her young suitor Flavio first:

> RUCHETTA: E che credete, voi, d'aver a campar cento anni in questa vostra fiorita etade? Voi v'ingannate: non è cosa che più presto passi della gioventù. Sia pur benedetta l'anima di mia madre, che quando vidde ch'io sapeva masticar la carne, mi diede a conoscer il nerbo e licenza di procacciarmene piacendomi! Voi vi lamentate della fortuna e non avete ragione, perché la buona e cattiva fortuna ce la facciamo con la prudenza noi istessi. Non v'ha ella posto innanzi un giovene nobile, ricco, virtuoso, bello e gentile, e che v'ama al pari della via sua, che è Flavio? ... E ogni volta che il povero giovene vi viene innanzi, vi ponete a piangere, a sospiare e a dolervi di lui. Perdonatemi, a dirvela, queste son cose da far passer l'amore ad un cane, il quale, per bastonate che se li diano,

non lascia mai di seguitar la cagna. Bisogna credere che, essendo Flavio gentiluomo, debba parimente con voi proceder secondo la sua gentilezza e il merito vostro. Ah, ah, voi sospirate perché vi dico il vero, eh?

RUCHETTA: What were you thinking to have spent a hundred years in your virginal state – you're fooling yourself – nothing flies by faster than youth. Blessing on the soul of my mother who when she saw that I knew how to eat meat, gave me the strength and the freedom to procure my pleasures! You're complaining about your luck without any reason, because good and bad luck are in our control. First of all, haven't you picked out a young, handsome, rich, virtuous, well-bred nobleman who loves you as much as life ... And every time the poor man comes around you cry and moan for him. Excuse me for saying it, these are actions that would turn a dog off love; from the beatings you give him, he would never chase after a lady dog again. You need to know that since Flavio's a gentleman, he has to treat you with the respect your noble status deserves. Ah, ah, you're sighing because it's true, yes? (act 1, scene 4).[52]

Presented as someone who understands and enjoys her sexuality, Ruchetta helps to manoeuvre her young mistress Giulia into a loving marriage arrangement with Flavio by giving her some tips on abandoning her virginity to him before she can be forced into an unwanted marriage with an old man. Her celebration of sexual pleasure gives her a certain power as a female who knows where her bread is buttered. Her actions typify her as the female who understands that, although she herself is outside the marriage market, her mistress in the *prima donna* role needs to manage her exchange value very carefully if she wants to get a partner of her choice.[53] In chapter 3, I consider the roles of the *prima and seconda donna,* showing how they, in contrast to the maidservant, played characters whose desirability was not as closely attached to their sexual availability, but instead to their refined impersonations of upper-class gentlewomen. Their great eloquence and beauty became the source of the worship they inspired. With strong connections to the honest courtesan class, this new group of actresses marketed their skills as performers to attract large groups of followers who regarded them as celebrities.

Chapter Three

Iconic Prima Donnas

If the *serva* role spectacularized the female body as a sexual object, the *prima* and *seconda donna* performers offered a more complex mediation on female sexual identities by selling their images rather than themselves. This chapter examines connections between the first great actresses and their courtesan roots, explaining where they acquired the exceptional skills they needed to improvise dramatic characters. Since the class of actresses who took the *prima donna* roles demonstrated the kind of aristocratic education and artistic refinement necessary to play the idealized court lady, it has been argued that they probably were drawn from the new class of *cortegiane oneste* (honest courtesans) who emerged to supply the market demand for elegant city companions to aristocratic male courtiers.[1] Taviani and Schino have employed this claim to explain the arrival of the first wave of distinguished actresses who joined the companies in the 1560s.[2] They note the similarities between these actresses and the accomplished "honest courtesans" who were celebrated in literature and poetry by an elite circle of devoted patrons.[3] While resisting any absolute statements about the influx of these gifted salon performers into the troupes as a result of the new laws enforced by the Council of Trent, Taviani and Schino contend that

> the great actresses, in the cultural panorama, *found themselves* in the position of the "honest courtesans," inheriting the culture and the art of translating themselves into public figures. They rushed into the vast market of persons disposed to buy the theatre of this same culture, these same specialties that had been previously reserved for restricted circles capable of supporting their own courtesans. In return, they were able to free themselves from selling their own private selves.[4]

The commedia dell'arte as part of its marketing strategy capitalized on the mass appeal of this new class of talented women whose training imitated that of the honest courtesan, who had previously been out of reach of the general public both economically and culturally. Highly prized and fetishized by the public, these beautiful and well-known courtesans provided models that actresses could emulate in their stage practices. Virtuosic actresses thus gave audiences privileged glimpses of female performers not previously seen outside the private salons of the cultured patrons who could afford their services. Actresses taking these roles were well aware that their courtesan-style training intensified the erotic effects that their performances of the chaste, elegant, idealized court lady had on their audiences. Initially what the actresses brought was not so much the ability to improvise theatrical scripts, but their *facondia* (eloquence) as improvisers of lyric love poetry. The praise accorded to several of the first great actresses for their *virtù* in the practice of this erudite art form shows that they transferred it into their stage performances, appearing "like poets in action, like professional composers of improvised speech."[5] This tradition of poetic composition was a highly sophisticated technology aimed at seducing its intended audiences into contemplating the mysteries of love. Delivered with great oratorical skills by the actresses, these improvised speeches were embellished with passionate emotional flourishes that captivated spectators by bringing the action to life.

The records of the performances given by Flaminia of Rome and Vincenza Armani during the summers of 1567 and 1568 in Mantua portray these actresses as well-established artists and company directors, who quickly became the centre of attraction in the city. It is probable that both actresses were touring widely during the early 1560s: Vicenza's wide circuit included Rome, Florence, Siena, Lucca, Milan, Brescia, Verona, Vicenza, Padua, Venice, Ferrara, Mantua, Parma, Piacenza, Pavia, and Cremona.[6] In the commentary documenting their activities, there is proof that they fulfil the criteria of celebrity as outlined by Roach. They acquired the "public intimacy" that gave their audiences the illusion that they were close to them, evidenced by the fact that they were referred to by their first names, as if they were intimately known. By appearing on stage, actresses made themselves emotionally accessible to their audience members as they revealed the intimate feelings of the characters they were portraying. For example, in theatre impresario Leone de' Sommi's description of Flaminia's "unique" stage performance, she is portrayed as connecting directly with each audience member through her expressive speech and actions:

> When she is on the stage the audience gets the impression not of a play composed and finished by an author, but rather of a series of real events taking shape before them. She so varies her gestures, tones, and moods in accordance with the diverse nature of her scenes that everyone who sees her is moved to wonder and delighted admiration.[7]

In fact, each of these two actresses acquired a group of followers who were so ferocious in their loyalties that the city was split into rival camps, leading jurisconsul Antonio Ceruto to report that all that people could say to each other was "*I'm for Flaminia: and I'm for Vincenza*: and both houses are filled with parties of friends."[8] The ducal secretary, Luigi Rogna, describing the excitement generated at performances of the two rival companies on 1 July 1 1567, comments on their need to outdo each other in attracting a larger crowd:

> Today two plays were performed in competition with each other: one in the usual place by Signora Flaminia and Pantalone, who were accompanied by Signora Angela, the one who jumps so well. The other in the Purgo (near San Andrea) in Lanzino's house, by Signora Vincenza, the lover of Signor Federigo da Gazuolo. Each company attracted a big audience and huge crowds of fans; but Flaminia, more of the nobility, and she did the tragedy of Dido, adapted into a tragicomedy and brought it off quite well. The others, from what I've heard, were pretty weak. They will keep up this competition with a certain amount of jealous rivalry, in an effort to see who can bring in the larger crowds, much like professors in university towns vying for the greatest number of students.[9]

Rogna's account captures the sense of "public intimacy" with which the actresses were regarded, even naming Armani's lover.[10] He makes it clear that both had mass appeal, but also has the insider knowledge to identify Flaminia's fan base as coming from a higher class than Vincenza's. More specifically, Rogna's knowledge that she appealed to "gentlemen and women, judges, lawyers, and doctors"[11] shows the extent to which the public scrutinized them. In this particular run, it seems that Flaminia's company succeeded in drawing the bigger crowds, since Vincenza's company left for Ferrara on 15 July, while Flaminia's remained until September.[12]

Their close proximity and daily appearances provided a basis for audiences to become fully engaged in weighing the merits of each.[13] While these opinions might alter depending on which actress outshone the other on a particular occasion, they indicate that audiences were knowledgeable about the level of skill the actresses exhibited and awarded their praise accordingly. The kind of celebrity status that Flaminia and Vincenza inspired fits best into the category of what Rojek describes as *achieved* celebrity, which is awarded by the public to individuals who "possess rare talents or skills," where such talents have been put to the test of open competition and measured according to certain standards.[14]

Rogna's commentary applies just such a measurement when, in judging Vincenza's tragic performances to be less successful, he restricts his praise to her musical abilities and beautiful costumes. However, he pays equal attention to the dazzling technical effects that each company put forth for the competition of their *intermedi.*

> Then yesterday, both companies competed against each other by performing *intermedi* concurrently. In Vincenza's *intermedio* Cupid appeared and rescued the nymph Clori who had been turned into a tree. Jove was seen hurling a thunderbolt from above, destroying the tower of a giant, who had imprisoned several shepherds; a sacrifice was made. Cadmus sowed his teeth, and saw warriors spring up and do battle with each other. The responses of Phoebus were revealed, and then Pallas Athena appeared in her armour, and finally the city began to be built. Flaminia then, having decorated the space very nicely with gilded leather and having found very beautiful nymph's costumes, brought to Mantua those forests, mountains, meadows, rivers and fountains of Arcadia. For the *intermedio* of the play, she introduced Satyrs, and then certain magicians, and then performed some *moresche* [dances in the Moorish style], so that now no one can do or speak about anything else but these actresses. Some praise the gracefulness of the one, while others extol the genius of the other, and that's how we pass the time in Mantova.[15]

Both Flaminia and Vincenza exhibited their abilities to transfer their skills in poetic composition to their stage roles. Through the very process of measuring the success of their performances, their audiences acknowledged that they were in the presence of creative artists whose elusive originality fits Benjamin's description of the "aura."[16] This "auratic" quality has been further explained by Gell as emanating from artwork that has the power to enchant us. He argues that art that eludes our grasp fills us with awe at the unique vision it expresses.[17] Rogna's discussion of Flaminia's "genius" in adapting Dido into a tragicomedy recognizes that she and her troupe were both knowledgeable about current erudite versions, and proficient enough to adapt them.[18] Playing Dido as an *innamorata*, Flaminia would have been able to reinterpret her both to engage her audience's emotions and to show off her technique.[19] Similarly, Flaminia composed and performed her own tragic material from the Marganorre episode of Ariosto's *Orlando Furioso*, in an extreme portrayal of the avenging heroine Drusilla.[20]

> The day before yesterday Flaminia was praised for some *lamenti* that she performed in a tragedy with her troupe, extracted from Ariosto's story that treats of Marganorre. The bride, played by Flaminia, over the body of her first husband who had been murdered in the previous scene, took her revenge by giving her new husband, Marganorre's son, poison to drink after having drunk it herself, whereupon they both died over the dead husband's body. And the father, who wanted to kill all women as a result, was then stoned and killed by the women.[21]

Known to the crowds as the leading *prime donne* and chief performers of their companies, Flaminia and Vincenza acquired reputations that extended beyond their existence as private individuals, as "images" of them circulated among their fans. Although such "images" may have existed in the imaginations of their audiences more than in printed materials, they had become what Roach labels as "abnormally interesting personae" in the public eye. Beyond their private selves, they had been transformed into role-icons in the sense that their fans had preconceived ideas about them that extended beyond any specific role they might play. Thus, no matter what role they were playing at a particular time, they were always considered as existing as individuals with exceptional, "auratic" qualities.[22] As a result they come to be regarded as mythic figures who could not be extinguished by death. Such was the case with Armani, who was likely poisoned at the hands of a rival or jealous lover in Cremona on 11 September 1569, when her lover and fellow actor Valerini wrote her *Orazione* to immortalize her.[23] Delivered shortly after her death, it captured the contribution that Armani had made to shaping the commedia dell'arte, and, as such, provides valuable information for our understanding of the importance of the actresses' contribution. In praising her ascent to the divine as arising from her sublime eloquence, Valerini uses language that is similar to that of Barthes several centuries later when he describes the greatness of Garbo: "her nickname, *the Divine*, probably intended to suggest less a superlative state of beauty than the essence of her corporeal person, descended from a heaven where things are formed and finished with the greatest clarity."[24] Like Garbo, Armani was in possession of the magical "It-effect" or charisma, as Max Weber named the unique qualities that are vested in certain individuals, giving them miraculous powers to influence, inspire, and heal others.[25] For Valerini, Armani's extraordinary personal qualities, such as her natural beauty and great intellectual accomplishments, are legendary and made her into an object of worship. Her classical humanist education in the liberal arts included the canonical male curriculum of grammar, logic, rhetoric, music, and sculpture. She was fluent in both Latin and Tuscan, with an artistry in speaking and composing that was in his estimation exceptional. Ultimately, her talents and skills take on a supernatural quality: Valerini remarks that her greatest talent of all, the "eternal light of her luminous Eloquence" ("lume immortale de chiara Eloquenza") (33), exceeds any use of language before or since.

Eloquence, with its alchemic power to transform listeners, is the source of Armani's supernatural appeal.[26] Valerini returns many times to praise her now silenced eloquence, drawing attention to her special gift of improvising: "O immensa forza d'eloquenza, o rara grazia d'accorte maniere, o ineffabil soavità d'armonia" (Oh great power of speech, oh rare gift of witty delivery, oh ineffable harmonious sweetness) (35). This, too, is a mark of her extraordinary skill, as the Academy of the Intronati credited her as being better at improvising her speeches than the greatest writers who had thought out their words beforehand.

Valerini comes closest to capturing the supernatural quality of Armani's stage performances when he describes her ability to transfix her viewers. In the following passage, he recalls her different treatments of Comedy and Tragedy, and remembers how she enchanted the audience so that they felt everything she felt:

> Se nella Comedia facea veder quanto ornamento abbi un dir famigliare, dismostrava poi differentemente nella Tragedia la gravità dell'Eroico stile, usando parole scelte, gravi concetti, sentenze morali degne d'esser prononziate da un Oracolo; e se occorreva sopra di qualche suo Amante o parente, di vita spento, lamentevolmente ragionare, trovava parole e modi sì dolorosi che ognuno era sforzato a sentirne doglia vera, e ben spesso anco lagrimare, benché sapesse certo le lagrime di lei esser finte.

> If in Comedy she made visible how much ordinary speech is embellished, she then demonstrated differently the gravity of the heroic style in Tragedy, using appropriate words, weighty conceits, moral judgments worthy

> of being pronounced by an oracle; and if it was necessary to deliver a lament over a dead lover or relative, she found words and ways so sad that everyone was forced to experience genuine grief listening to them, and frequently to also be moved to tears, even though they knew for certain that her tears were false. (36)

He saves his deepest praise for her contribution to the new pastoral genre, describing her performance as transformative in creating an illusionary world. His commentary indicates that Armani's performances were made believable by her ability to suit her acting style to the rules of the different genres. Henke has noted that Armani's attention to the rules governing the genres is what made her acting verisimilar. This ability to create believable characters who conform to the expected norms of Comedy, Tragedy, and Tragicomedy actually heralds a revolution in acting that Henke calls "mimetic," in contrast to the "virtuosity" of the buffoon style, which was also practiced by the actress.[27] Valerini brings this mimetic quality to life even more so in his recounting Armani's every glance, gesture, blush, and nod in her pastoral performances. That quality translates into a live performance that made an indelible impression on her spectators:

> Che dirò delle Pastorali da lei prima introdotte in Scena, le quali de così vaghi avenimenti intesseva che di troppo meraviglia e dolcezza ingombrava gli ascoltanti; e se di trovar qualche limpido fonte mostrava esser bramosa per estinguer la sete ardente, induceva a gli uomini il medesimo desio di bere, e di riposo se di qualche arbore bramava l'ombra per riposarsi, e se, per gustar i liquidi cristalli, all'ombra assisa chinava le labra, chinavano anch'essi il capo, accompagnando i suoi movimenti, come se del suo corpo fossero stati l'ombra, tanta forza avean le parole con che ella descriveva or questo or quell'affetto.
>
> What shall I say of the pastoral plays that she was the first to introduce on the stage, which she spun out in such charming incidents that she also engulfed her spectators with a superabundance of sweetness and astonishment? And if, on finding some clear fountain, she demonstrated a yearning to slake her burning thirst, she induced her audience to have the same desire to drink, and to rest, if she yearned to take a rest under some shady tree, and if, to taste the crystal liquid, she sat in the shade and bent her lips over to drink, the spectators also bent their heads down, accompanying her movements, as if they had been her shadow. Such was the force of the words that she used to describe this or that affect. (36)

Valerini's capturing of Armani's "it" effect and its continuing magical appeal even after her death lifts her to cult status, since the afterimage of her performances remains vivid in the public memory. Marvin Carlson has described this phenomenon as "ghosting," when audiences retain sensory memories of celebrity actors from roles they have seen them play.[28] Valerini's *Oration* immortalizes her in more than words by leaving unforgettable images that keep her alive in the collective memory. In ending with the blessings that her "soul" can now impart on all her followers, he attributes to her the immortal qualities of the divine.[29] The endurance of her fame is attested to in Garzoni's tribute of 1585, sixteen years later.

> Della dotta Vicenza non parlo, che, imitando la facondia ciceroniana, ha posto l'arte comica in concorrenza con l'oratoria e, in parte con la beltà mirabile, parte con la grazia indicibile, ha eretto uno amplissimo trionfo di se stessa al mondo spettatore, facendosi divulgare per la più excellente comediante di nostra etade.

> Of the learned Vincenza I won't speak except to say that she, imitating Ciceronian eloquence, has put the art of comedy into competition with oratory, and, partly with her astonishing beauty and partly with her ineffable grace, has created a huge success for herself with audiences everywhere, establishing herself as the most excellent comedienne of our age.[30]

Two other outstanding actresses included in his list, Isabella Andreini (the subject of chapter 5) and her greatest rival Vittoria Piissimi, were also praised for their abilities to transfer their oratorical skills as neoplatonic love poets to their mimetic character portrayals of *innamorate* on the stage. Whether or not Garzoni's superlatives are part of the standard rhetoric, the praise he reserves for Piissimi stands out as exceptional. As "the perfect actress" she has the looks and the bearing, the gestures, the vocal qualities, in fact everything necessary to enchant her audiences and make them fall in love with her as a star performer.

> Ma sopra tutto parmi degna d'eccelsi onori quella divina Vittoria che fa metamorfosi di se stessa in scena, quella bella maga d'amore che alletta i cori di mille amanti con le sue parole, quella dolce sirena ch'ammaglia con soavi incanti l'alme de' suoi divoti spettatori; e senza dubbio merita d'esser posta come un compendio dell'arte avendo i gesti proporzionati, i moti armonici e concordi, gli atti maestrevoli e grati, le parole affabili

e dolci, i sospiri ladri e accorti, i risi saporiti e soavi, il portamento altiero e generoso, e in tutta la persona un perfetto decoro, qual spetta e s'appertiene a una perfetta comediante.

But above all worthy of outstanding honour, in my estimation, is that divine Vittoria who metamorphoses herself on stage, that beautiful enchantress of love who entices the hearts of a thousand lovers with her words, that sweet siren who bewitches with pleasing incantations the souls of her devoted spectators; and is without doubt worthy of being considered as a compendium of the art, with her proportioned gestures, smooth and harmonious movements, masterful and pleasing actions, sweet and affable speech, roguish and cunning sighs, sweet and spicy laughter, her tall majestic bearing, [who has] in her entire person a perfect decorum, that looks and belongs to a perfect actress.[31]

Although the historical evidence to build a substantial profile is lacking, we do know that Piissimi was probably a member of the Gelosi in 1570 and played with them in France for Charles IX in 1571.[32] It is also likely that she took the role of Silvia in their command performance of *Aminta* under Tasso's direction, presented to the Este family at Belvedere island in Ferrara in 1573. Her reputation was great enough to attract the attention of Charles IX's successor, Henri III, who on his return from Poland to take the French crown insisted that "La femme appelée Vittoria" be summoned to Venice in 1574 to perform for him. Although she may have been in France for the second Gelosi tour of 1577, her name is only occasionally associated with them after 1579, the year after Francesco and Isabella Andreini joined the troupe. Despite speculation that she left the company because of the rival presence of the younger Isabella, the evidence points to her departure, along with other members, as an upward move connected with her formation of her own company, the Confidenti. As we shall see, Isabella wrote a leading part for Vittoria as a rival nymph in *La Mirtilla* in 1588, and competed against her with a rival comedy at the 1589 Medici wedding. Whatever their relationship was, they maintained parallel careers over a long stretch of time and sometimes performed with each other's companies, as indicated by the records in 1590 of Isabella playing with the Confidenti in Parma while Vittoria was with the Gelosi.

Piissimi and Andreini may have performed together before the former left the Gelosi, or Scala could have chosen to put them together in a fictional encounter. In any case, they appear together in "Il ritratto"

(The Portrait, Day 39),[33] which pits an actress named Vittoria against an *innamorata* Isabella. The only scenario of the fifty that includes professional actors in the list of characters or, for that matter, an actress character named Vittoria, it has invited speculation as to whether Scala wrote it to highlight their real-life rivalry.[34] In any case, this outstanding theatrical tour de force reveals Scala's insider knowledge as a company director of the kind of upheavals that occur when a diva brings her theatre troupe to town.[35] As we shall see, all of the characters playing the townsfolk are pushed into defining themselves in relationship to the visiting players.[36] At the centre of their concern is the dominating presence exerted by the lead actress, played by a character named Vittoria. The ways in which Vittoria takes over the stage and invades the lives of the townsfolk enact the mysterious effects that celebrities have on their audiences and suggest that Scala was aware of the phenomenon created by stars even in the sixteenth century. Celebrity theorist Quinn explains how their extra charisma separates them from their fellow performers, so that we are always aware of their star presence existing alongside the roles they are playing. The actress-character Vittoria, especially if played by Piissimi herself, even from her offstage position in act 1 exerts this paradoxical illusion of having an "absolute presence" and remaining an "irreducible human being."[37]

In the fictional stage world, the diva character Vittoria's presence is established through an incident that sets off a chain reaction. It concerns a courtesy visit paid to her by the young cavalier Orazio, and introduces her as the main attraction. Such visits to the antechambers of leading actresses were established protocol and reflect the ambivalence towards the sexual status of the actress, since they also offered the potential for making assignations. The portrait that gives the play its name is a miniature of a beautiful woman, and is stolen by Vittoria from the gold locket she removes from Orazio's neck during his audience with her.[38] She puts it on display in her rooms as part of her trophies, which leads to its identification by the old patriarch Pantalone as a painting of his wife Isabella, and results in Vittoria naming Orazio as the person from whom she obtained it.

Vittoria's triumphant display of her dominant status through her possession of the portrait has, of course, the side effect of revealing Isabella's adulterous relationship with Orazio. This theme of female deception is given greater prominence by the fact that Flaminia, the *seconda donna,* is also cheating on her old husband Graziano, by having an affair with Flavio. Their duplicity helps to set up the metatheatricality of the scenario by alerting the spectator to what is actually happening behind the scenes in the fictional world of Parma. If the characters are deceiving each other, then the spectators need to be wary about the nature of theatrical mimesis itself. Just as the portrait remains a runaway object that is never found, Vittoria's entrances draw attention to the illusory properties of the *mise en scène* and tantalize the audience with her intrusion into it from a more "real" offstage place. Still unseen throughout the first act, "she" looms larger than life in the conversations of the other characters as they discuss "her" reputation as a sex goddess, as we have heard Piissimi to be.

Thus, act 1 opens with Isabella's lament to her servant Pedrolino about her husband Pantalone's rage at having discovered her portrait in the hands of the visiting actress – who claims to have received it from Orazio. When Isabella rants that her lover Orazio must have fallen in love with the actress, and sends Pedrolino to retrieve the portrait, a new chain of desire for an elusive love object is set in motion. Since having possession of the portrait signifies a certain privileged relationship to the one portrayed, the search for it and the unsuccessful attempts to reclaim it throughout the entire play serve as a reminder that falling in love with a diva comes with a price. Each of the characters is introduced as having some opinion about Vittoria's visit. For example, Capitano Spavento plans to have sex with her before she leaves Parma. Arlecchino, on the other hand, is not so sure, telling Capitano "che perderà tempo, poiché simil donne non si ottengono come l'uomo si crede" (that he's wasting his time, because such women are not as easy to have as some people think) (act 1, 399).

The fight over the missing portrait heats up again towards the end of the act when Isabella descends from her window to confront Orazio over its absence and complain about the dangerous situation it has put her in with Pantalone. She exits in a rage, insisting that Orazio's actions prove he is in love with the actress and has been frequenting the theatre to enjoy her. Orazio laments to Pedrolino and the audience about his own behaviour and "dell'arrivo di quella compagnia de i comedianti, dicendo ogni male di loro, e, per ultimo, maledice quella Vittoria, venuta per suo danno in quella cittade" (the arrival of that company of actors, saying terrible things about them, and above all, cursing that Vittoria for coming to town and causing him so much trouble) (act 1, 400–1). Keeping the focus on the theatre as a hot topic, Capitano wraps up the act: "dicendo la comedia esser trattenimento nobile e che quella Signora Vittoria è donna onorata" (saying that the theatre is a noble form of entertainment and that Signora Vittoria is a respectable woman) (act 1, 401). Punctuated with constant brawling and threats of dueling to the death, act 1 sets the scene for Vittoria's physical entrance in act 2.

When Vittoria makes her appearance at the top of the second act, the diva incarnate with her rich clothing and jewels, she brings her offstage world with her:

> Vittoria comica, vestita riccamente, con catene d'oro, con braccialetti di perle, con diamante e rubini in dito, accompagnata da Piombino, lodando la città di Parma, il Duca e tutta la sua corte, trattando dell'infinite cortesie che giornalmente riceve da quei signori parmegiani.
>
> The actress Vittoria appears, richly dressed, with golden chains, pearl bracelets, diamond and ruby rings, accompanied by Piombino, praising the city of Parma, the Duke and all his court, speaking of the endless courtesies that she receives on a daily basis from the gentlemen of Parma. (act 2, 401)

Drawing all eyes to her larger-than-life presence, she takes over the stage, using her status to command the favours of Pantalone and Graziano, the two leading householders. Isabella, restricted to watching from her window, is powerless to do anything but turn her gaze on Pantalone when he tries to pay court to Vittoria. Vittoria's fleeting visit adds a new dimension to the desire for her now that she has been seen – she is the lure that connects the gaze to what we wish to see, drawing attention to herself as an actress who understands the way that theatrical illusion plays with our desire for tangible presence.[39] As a tangible presence, she evokes the desires of her spectators by her irresistible appeal. Quinn describes this magnetic draw that celebrities have as arising from the sense of plenitude they exude in contrast to the viewers' feelings of unfulfilled desires.[40]

Vittoria's doubled sexual appeal as the character and the actress becomes the primary topic of conversation in act 2, arousing the extreme jealousy of Isabella, who accuses her lover Orazio of being in love with "quella puttana errante" (that roving whore) (act 2, 402). In sparking these debates, Vittoria's allure provides the occasion for setting up the major ruse on which the resolution of the comedy depends, as Pedrolino uses Pantalone's and Graziano's lust for seeing Vittoria perform to provide the opportunity for the adulterous visits of Orazio and Flavio to the old men's wives. If Orazio and Flavio are willing to turn away from Vittoria and the theatre in order to have sex with their mistresses, Isabella and Flaminia, Lesbino, the transvestite page, is not so lucky in dissuading Capitano from pursuing Vittoria. "His" accusation echoes Isabella's defamation of the actress as whore when she warns Capitano against "l'amare una comediante vagabonda, la cui professione è solo di far star questo e quello" (loving a vagabond actress, who spends her life dumping one lover after another) (act 2, 404).[41]

When Vittoria takes the stage at the top of act 3, her diva status again precedes her. However, this time, in her address to the audience, she and Piombino let the illusion of her transcendent power slip as they talk about her need to capitalize on her fame while it lasts:

> Vittoria: dicono che, essendo stati a desinare a casa d'un gentiluomo suo innamorato, hanno avuto di buoni donativi, toccando, sopra questo particolare del donare a' comedianti, molte cittadi principali d'Italia, nelle quali ella è stata favourita di molti presenti, e finalmente com'ella si burla e ride di quelli amanti che non li donano. Piombino l'essorta a non s'innamorare di nessuno, ma che attenda a far della robba per la vecchiezza.
>
> Vittoria (and Piombino) enter, saying that they had been to dinner at the house of a gentleman admirer, and that they have received beautiful gifts, then they touch on the practice of giving gifts to comedians, [mentioning] most of the principal cities in Italy, where she has been favoured with many gifts, and finally about how she teases and laughs at those lovers who give them. Piombino urges her not to fall in love with anyone but to concentrate on amassing some wealth for her old age. (act 3, 405)

This admission is tested in the fictional world of the play when Vittoria demands favours from Pantalone and Graziano and sets off a chain of responses that erupt in a confrontation with Isabella, who comments to Vittoria that "se li fusse onore mettersi con una comediante simil a lei, che le insegnerebba a procedere" (if it wasn't beneath her to have anything to do with an actress such as herself, she would tell her where to go) (act 3, 405). Vittoria, left alone on the stage after Isabella exits, appears to have the last word: "se ne ride, dicendo che, dove arrivano compagnie di comedianti, le donne maritate il più delle volte stanno a bocca secca" (she laughs about it, saying that when the acting companies arrive, married women often find themselves left panting for it) (act 3, 405–6). It is in this showdown that "Isabella" asserts her celebrity status as "Vittoria's" rival. With Andreini commenting directly on their

Figure 3.1. Scene from *Recueil Fossard* of abduction of Lady Cornelia by Pantalon, Harlequin, and Zany (prototype of Vittoria's abduction). Photo © Nationalmuseum, Stockholm.

profession, the fight between them for supremacy breaks into the stage fiction.

What follows in act 3 positions Isabella to take over from Vittoria, possibly signalling Andreini's ascendancy in the Gelosi. As the result of a brawl that breaks out during a performance, Vittoria is forcibly removed from the fictional world of the play and from the stage itself.[42] Falling victim to the rivalries she has stirred up among her many suitors, she seeks protection from Pantalone and Graziano, but is is captured by a gang of bravados who "escono fuora le spade ignude, cercano Vittori; la vedono in messa a Pantalone e Graziano, danno loro delle piattonate, li levano Vittoria, e la conducono via" (come out with their swords drawn looking for Vittoria. They find her with Pantalone and Graziano, beat them with the flat of their swords, and take her away) (act 3, 408). Figure 3.1 provides a pictorial example of a similar abduction. With Vittoria's disappearance, even Capitano gives up on her, excusing his infatuation because "quella comediante l'aveva affatturato" (that actress had bewitched him) (act 3, 409). A unique treatment of the diva and her transcendent powers, "The Portrait" also reveals that Scala and his actors were well aware that her appeal was precarious and dependent on keeping her patrons satisfied.

In this chapter we examined the records concerning four outstanding actresses to demonstrate their vital importance in transforming the commedia dell'arte into a legitimate new theatrical art form. We have seen what this new class of actresses, trained as singers, dancers, and musicians and equipped with exceptional oratorical skills, brought to the creation of the *prima* and *seconda donna* roles. Through their eloquence they created emotionally convincing characters with whom audiences could identify, and in the process introduced a new mimetic dimension to their performances. A select number of them became star performers whose loyal fans fought for their favours, as "The Portrait" reveals. In the next chapter I discuss an extension of the *prima* and *seconda* roles: the transvestite heroine role.

Chapter Four

Transvestite Heroines

In addition to contesting class and status divisions within female sexual identities, when commedia dell'arte actresses took over the transvestite page roles they also questioned the very process of gendering that hierarchized male and female sexual differences. These roles, developed in the all-male erudite theatre, feature the exploits of renegade female characters who adopt male costumes and personae in order to usurp male prerogatives. Dressing up in the sumptuous clothing of the male courtier, and impersonating the ideal traits and accomplishments of this new social elite, the actresses were positioned to tease the spectator with their sexual ambiguity and phallic power. In showing off their skill as male impersonators, they also increased their charisma for audience members impressed with their gender ambiguity. Since the practice of female transvestism became one of the hallmarks of the commedia dell'arte, it is important to begin by looking at early modern transvestite practices both on the stage and in Italian society.

When females took over the transvestite heroine roles originally performed by young aristocratic males in the erudite theatre, they were empowered to represent "real" females as desiring subjects. In this period, as gender theorists have noted, wearing the clothing of the opposite sex created a strong fetishistic reaction in the audience. In their analysis of transvestism on the all-male English stage, Jones and Stallybrass propose that treating gender representation as dependent on revealing or concealing sexual parts through costuming suggests that audiences must have viewed notions of gender itself as a fetish:

> The actor is both boy and woman, and he/she embodies the fact that sexual fixations are not the product of any categorical fixity of gender.

> Indeed, all attempts to fix gender are necessarily prosthetic: that is, they suggest the attempt to supply an imagined deficiency by the exchange of male clothes for female clothes or of female clothes for male clothes; ... But all elaborations of the prosthesis which will supply the "deficiency" can secure no essence. On the contrary, they suggest that gender itself is a fetish, the production of an identity through the fixation on specific parts.[1]

Their argument rests on the fact that no female parts could be found under the boy actors' costumes on the English stage, and women in male costumes on the Italian and other continental stages worked in a similar prosthetic fashion. If boys could impersonate women by exchanging male for female clothes and women could supply a similar deficiency by putting on male clothes, then spectators who accepted these impersonations were also automatically supplying the lack in both cases.[2] Female and male transvestite performers no doubt evoked a range of complex and diverse responses that were connected to both theatrical conventions and cultural practices. On the public stage, to a greater extent than in the erudite theatre, the transvestite disguises of both boy and female performers carried extra significance by referencing their offstage sexual availability and vulnerable social status.

For the many – both boys and women – who found themselves circulating in the new urban marketplace, transvestism was a mark of sexual availability practised by both sexes to entice customers.[3] Lisa Jardine argues that the *dependency* governing the practice of transvestism in the marketplace was mirrored in the stage representation of the transvestite who enters into private service in a household:

> In the early modern period, erotic attention – an attention bound up with sexual availability and historically specific forms of economic dependency – is focused upon boys and upon women in the *same* way.
>
> So that, crucially, sexuality signifies as *absence of difference* as it is inscribed upon the bodies of those equivalently "mastered" within the early modern household, and who are placed homologously in relation to that household's domestic economy. In this household, I shall argue, dependent youths and dependent women are expected to "submit" under the order of familial authority, to those above them.[4]

Economically dependent adolescents of both sexes entering into household service needed to please their masters in whatever ways were required. David Herlihy, in his study of early modern Florentine households, describes the constant "drift of young persons," both distant kin or non-kin who went in and out of service in the homes of wealthier households for some period of time during their adolescence.[5] While adolescents who could claim some degree of kinship to their masters may have had some advantage in obtaining a permanent place in the household through a marriage alliance, the far larger number of servants and apprentices of both sexes remained in a very precarious position. The suggestion that the transvestite page character was one step away from prostitution is echoed in the association between the actresses who took the roles and the courtesan practice their disguise evoked. For example, Cesare Vecellio describes the Venetian prostitute's common practice of wearing

> a somewhat masculine outfit; silk or cloth waistcoats adorned with conspicuous fringes and padded like young man's vests, especially those of Frenchmen. Next to their bodies they wear a man's shirt ... Many of them wear men's breeches ... and one instantly recognizes them for what they are because of these trousers and certain little round pieces of silver they use as ornaments.[6]

If transvestite disguise increased the erotic appeal of the actress by suggesting her availability, it might also suggest her sexual ambiguity. The well-known 1590 engraving (fig. 4.1) shows a fashionable Venetian courtesan wearing a full-length gown that is lifted up in the second panel to reveal men's breeches focusing attention on her laced-up and padded genital area, where cupid's dart is aimed.

The suggestion that she is equally alluring whether male or female also carries with it the implication that she could offer herself as either. Such ability to fulfil the sexual fantasies of those seeking both same and opposite sexual pleasure is captured in Pietro Aretino's letter to a courtesan from Pistoia, praising his good fortune in having been able to have sex with her

> the first time as a woman dressed like a man and the next time, as a man dressed like a woman. You are a man when you are chanced on from behind and a woman when seen from in front ... You talk like a fair lady and act like a pageboy ... even the clothes which you wear upon your back, and which you are always changing, leave it an open question whether my she-chatterbox is really a he-chatterbox, or whether my he-chatterbox is really a she-one.[7]

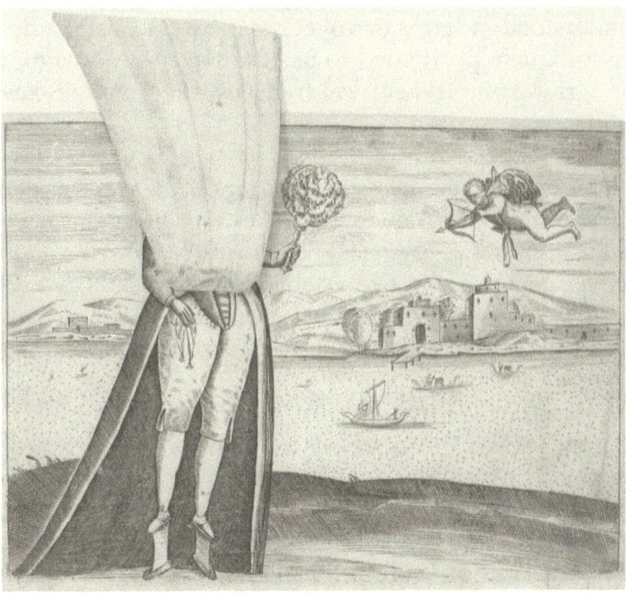

Figure 4.1. Venetian woman of fashion with moveable skirt. Publisher: Ferrando Bertelli (1563). Engraving, sheet: 5 ½ × 7 7/16 in. (14 × 18.9 cm) The Elisha Whittelsey Collection, The Elisha Whittelsey Fund, 1955 (55.503.30). The Metropolitan Museum of Art, New York, NY, US. Image copyright © The Metropolitan Museum of Art. Image source: Art Resource, NY.

That the professional actresses were metonymically linked with the courtesan means that their transvestite performances signified their potential as sexually available and of ambiguous sexuality. On the stage, such figures could evoke a range of desires in spectators that extended the erotic possibilities for imagined couplings with same- and opposite-sex partners even beyond those suggested by an all-male transvestite stage.[8] Arriving on the stage just at the time when the edicts of the Council of Trent were being enforced, the actresses' transvestite performances deliberately flouted the church's attempts to police sexual behaviours.[9] The ambiguous sexuality of the lovers is captured in the detail reproduced in fig. 4.2.

Actresses taking the transvestite roles might well have evoked complex discourses that reflected the intersection of many different cultural anxieties across a range of categories, since, as Carole-Anne Tyler notes, "relations between members of one class or race and another, like relations between members of different genders, are desiring relations and can be understood in terms of voyeurism and fetishism"; the actresses thus were uniquely positioned to use the stage to play with these desires.[10] In writing about theatrical transvestism, Traub makes the case that

> the donning of masculine dress enacts the logic of the supplement through the displacement of the body to the clothes. Signifiying the independent use of a woman's always possibly inordinately endowed clitoris, cross-dressing not only masculinizes but eroticises the female body. Such a displaced equivalence gives a more situated, more *embodied* meaning to many critics' current understanding of female transvestism as a strategic appropriation of the phallus.[11]

Treating the transvestite actresses as imposters who *embody* the phallus offers many possibilities for seeing them as destabilizing their roles as fetish objects for spectators. In Lacanian terms, the woman has to *be* the phallus in order for the man to *have* it and make up his lack.[12] But since "she" must masquerade as the phallus so that "he" can parade his lack, Lacan suggests that the woman "appearing" to have "it" masks the fact that the phallus is lacking in both. Tyler develops this Lacanian explanation to build the case for the kind of displacement that occurs when the male not only "projects his lack onto woman and then disavows it through the fetishistic transfer of phallic value to another part of her body, some item of her clothing, etc., thereby distancing himself

Figure 4.2. Ambiguous lovers, detail from *Lucia and Trastullo,* anonymous artist, Bologna, ca. 1590. Reproduced by permission from Museo teatrale alla Scala.

from lack, ... [but] also maintaining a belief that the phallus is the penis – a fetishistic belief."[13] What emerges as significant is that fetishism is based on imposture; hence, the displacement of lack from the subject to the object is never fully accomplished with the result that male viewer and female spectacle remain bound in reversible positions. As the actresses taking the transvestite roles appear to "have the phallus," they also know how to put it in play.

In this early modern period, when the shifting dynamics between the members of the new bourgeois household were being represented on stage, the fluidity of sex, gender, and class identities proved to be an irresistible topic, as Giannetti has so effectively demonstrated. The frequency with which female cross-dressing and transvestite disguises were adopted attests to their centrality as stage conventions. In Scala, my main reference here, female cross-dressing occurs in over one-third of the fifty scenarios in the collection.[14] His depiction of such strong female performers and characters in such a range of different dramatic genres brings them to life as active subjects testing out the restrictions imposed on them by their class and gender roles.[15] Since respectable female characters were restricted by social conventions from appearing in public places unaccompanied, the device of adopting male dress for reasons of mobility also helps to explain why cross-dressing was such a popular device.[16] While it is likely that the appearance of women in male dress for whatever reasons had erotic significance for spectators, here I will distinguish between the terms "cross-dressing" and "transvestism," in order to clarify the connection to instances of female fetishism. In fact, the authors of *The Tradition of Female Transvestism in Early Modern Europe* explain that the 119 cases of female cross-dressing they describe were primarily cases of gender disguise rather than examples relating to the pursuit of sexual pleasure.[17] Thus, for the purposes of this chapter, I adopt the distinction between cross-dressing and transvestism made by Robert Stoller: "the term transvestism should only be used to describe fetishistic cross-dressing, that is erotic excitement induced by garments of the opposite sex."[18] While female transvestism as an erotic practice has not been as fully examined as male transvestism in early modern society, representing it on stage certainly catered to the voyeuristic pleasure of the spectators and would have induced erotic excitement of various kinds arising from the transgressive female presence and the range of ambiguous sexual attractions it featured.

Below I focus on Scala's representations of Andreini as the male page Fabrizio in selected scenarios that provide compelling examples of the ways in which female transvestism worked as a stage device in the commedia dell'arte. It seems likely that Scala was paying tribute to Isabella's popular success in playing the male page Fabrizio by including five scenarios showing her sustained impersonations of this signature role. He sets her in a range of highly inventive plot situations that complicate the erotic reception of the erudite theatre's transvestite heroine, and shows her as Fabrizio self-consciously referencing the homosocial/homosexual subculture of the erudite theatre, as well as the hierarchical divisions separating the society by gender, sexuality, class, and cultural status. Andrews, noting that the name "Fabrizio" is borrowed from the transvestite heroine's brother in *Gl' ingannati (The Deceived)*, comments that Scala likely created such scenarios to give Andreini "a chance to display a different dramatic range."[19] While we cannot know the degree to which Andreini was involved in creating these scenarios, it becomes apparent that she had established herself as a role-icon or, in Roach's definition, as a performer so exceptional that she existed in the minds of her audience as someone always worth coming to see, no matter what role she was playing.[20] As a celebrity, she was never completely eclipsed by her fictional role, so audiences were always aware that she was simultaneously the star actress and the character Fabrizio.[21] Her charismatic allure was further enhanced by her transgression of gender boundaries.[22]

Fabrizio, the transvestite page, makes a sustained appearance in Days 14, 16, 25, 26, and 30, often as the central figure, usurping male power and destabilizing heterosexual desire. In each of the five, she appears in plot situations that lead to her speaking directly to the audience about her character's plight and the need to avoid detection in order not to be severely punished for transgressing the social and legal norms extending into the world outside the play. Since Andreini's personal qualities are never completely transformed into her Fabrizio impersonation, her actions and dialogue require the audience to see her as the ultimate source of meaning. The effect of this self-referential performance intensifies the desire for her because, as a celebrity, she gives the illusion of being what Quinn describes as the actor/character who is in possession of a higher truth.[23] My close readings of three of these (Days 14, 25, and 30) showcase a range of situations where Andreini uses her Fabrizio disguise to tease the spectator with her display of phallic power. As will become evident, in all three scenarios "Fabrizio" signals that "he" is also Isabella in ways that showcase Andreini's uncanny ability to move in and out of any fixed sexual identity.

"The Faithful Loving Pilgrim"

In the Scala scenario "Il pellegrino fido amante" (The Faithful Loving Pilgrim, Day 14), Isabella sustains her male alias as the malcontent page Fabrizio for the duration of the action.[24] Here she performs the role of the antagonist who has fled from her lover (the faithful pilgrim), and uses her disguise to express her vehement hatred of romantic love. The spectator's pleasure in watching her performance comes from her success in disguising her identity so completely that no one suspects she is a woman. The argument sets her up as a sexual outlaw who has run away from Milan and adopted a transvestite disguise in order to avoid the marriage her father Dottore has arranged with her suitor Flavio. The explicit statement that she fled from her father creates a profile for her as a renegade who refuses to accept her proscribed female duties, since we are told that "quella essere totalmente contraria al suo disegno, e quello non già perché ella Flavio odiasse, ma solo perché nell'animo fisso teneva una certa contrarietà d'amore, per la quale abborriva l'esser moglie, et il sottoporsi al marito" (she was totally against his plan – and this not so much that she hated Flavio, but just because she had fixed in her mind a certain abhorrence towards love, which made her loathe the idea of being a wife and submitting herself to a husband) (argument, 149). Scala's choice to showcase Isabella Andreini's star transvestite turn suggests that her very presence probably invited the worship of her fans familiar with her virtuosity as a male impersonator.

When Fabrizio appears in act 1, "he" has established "himself" as page to the young nobleman Orazio in Genova, far from home. A compelling presence, despite "his" servant status, "he" sets the play in motion when "he" responds to Orazio's protestations of love for Flaminia with an eloquent rant itemizing all love's evils. Although the dialogue is not included in the scenario, the script indicates that a set speech would have been added here. A sample from "Sopra il biasimo d'Amore" (On the Condemnation of Love) offers a sense of the kind of virtuosic bravado such a situation requires:

> Io voglio brevemente descrivervi la maligna natura d'amore, accioche voi sappiate come governarvi: Voi dunque, che lo sequitate, e che avete lasciato ogni vostro diletto, e perduta la vostra libertade, ascoltate le humane dolcezze, e l' humana natura di questo vostro Dio, che voi chiamate amore: egli è un tiranno accorto, un Re senza fede, un Principe senza honore, un Monarca infedele, un falso Dio senza giustitia, un Profeta bugiardo,

amico finto di chi lo seque, l'esempio del male, il modello del vizio, la regola, e il compasso della malizia, impaziente, audace, imperioso, pieno di sospetto, di crudeltà, d'audacia, malizioso ingannatore, i suoi piaceri non sono altro, che vento, il suo riposo non è altro, che vento, il suo riposo non è altro, che paura, e per ricompensa di ben servire dona ad' altrui la perdita di se medesimo accompagnata da un lungo pentimento.

I want briefly to describe the malignant nature of love to you, so that you will know how to behave yourself: you then, who follow him, and have left your every pleasure, and lost your liberty, hear about the humane goodness and kindly nature of this your God, whom you call Love: he is a cunning tyrant, a faithless king, a prince without honour, an unfaithful monarch, a false unjust God, a lying prophet, a false friend to those who follow him, an evil example, the model of viciousness, the rule and the compass of malice, impatient, audacious, imperious, full of suspicion, of cruelty, of audacity, malicious deceiver, his pleasures are nothing other than air, his repose nothing other than fear, and to repay good service he gives to others the loss of themselves accompanied by a long repentance. (*Fragmenti,* 97)

Fabrizio's speech unleashes a chain of responses on the pros and cons of love and who is a worthy object of desire. As the gentleman scholar Orazio is measured against the soldier Capitano, who is also vying for the love of Flaminia, the scene descends into jokes about which profession is the nobler and who has the better equipment to satisfy a lover. Pedrolino's and Franceschina's unmistakable gesturing to the superiority of the sword of the military man draws attention to the phallus as the sought-after object – which the mysterious Fabrizio may or may not have. Fabrizio keeps "himself" at the centre of the action by setting Flaminia and Orazio at each other's throats so that "he" can continue his pontifications on the evils of love.

Fabrizio se ne ride, Orazio lo sgrida, et egli li dice come Flaminia non l'ama, ma che lo simola, e che ne faccia la prova. Orazio, per chiarirsene, dice a Flaminia aver finto d'amarla, ma che non l'ama. Flaminia, querelandosi di lui lo chiama amante falso e traditore, e piangendo se n'entra in casa. Orazio brava a Fabrizio, essendo pentito di quanto ha detto; e, sdegnato seco, si parte. Fabrizio, ridendo, racconta le miserie de gli amanti, dicendo in uno male d' Amore.

Fabrizio laughs at them, Orazio calls him out, and he tells Orazio that

> Flaminia doesn't love him, but that she is faking it, and that Orazio should put her to the test. Orazio, to clear it up, tells Flaminia that he has pretended to love her, but does not. Flaminia, counterattacking, calls him a false lover and a traitor, and exits into the house crying. Orazio threatens Fabrizio, regretting what he has said, and, annoyed with him, exits. Fabrizio, laughing, recites stories of the miseries of lovers, speaking of the evil of love in each case. (act 1, 151–2)

Left in possession of the field like a malevolent cupid, Fabrizio once again delivers a diatribe on the vagaries of love – another occasion for Andreini to display her ability to perform a masculine persona. That Fabrizio is at least temporarily in possession of the phallus in word and deed is reinforced at the end of the act when "he" has to break off from reciting "his" litany against love to deal with Arlecchino's interference:

> ARLECCHINO: vestito da furfante li dà una mentita, e fugge. Fabrizio di nuova torna a dir mal d'Amore. Arlecchino fa il medesimo, e fugge. Fabrizio caccia mano alla spada, e li corre dietro.

> ARLECCHINO: dressed as a rogue calls him out for lying, and runs away. Fabrizio returns to saying bad things about Love. Arlecchino does the same thing again and runs away. Fabrizio draws his sword and chases after him. (act 1, 152)

As act 1 ends with Fabrizio's brandished sword punctuating "his" phallic power, the scene is set for "his" corresponding relinquishing of the same in act 2. This occurs when "he" encounters "his" rejected lover Flavio, who has taken on a pilgrim's disguise in order to search for the Isabella who deserted him so long ago. Fabrizio is so overwhelmed by Flavio's excessive devotion that "he" abandons "his" hatred of love and makes this confession to the audience:

> FABRIZIO: narrando la sua istoria, discorre sopra la possanza d'Amore, li chiede perdono, rendendosi vinta, loda il suo amante …

> FABRIZIO: telling her story, speaks about the power of Love, and asks love for forgiveness, acknowledging that she has been defeated, and praises her lover ... (act 2, 154)

At this point, the set speech Andreini would have inserted, such as this one from "Delle lodi d' Amore" (In Praise of Love), expresses her desire:

> Se le cose ornate di celeste bellezza, di singular virtù, d'onorate creanzė, di costume nobile e d'altri eccellenti e segnalati doni, dolce Signor mio, si debbono amare, voi, che di tutte queste doti nobilissime siete adorno, meritate ch'io v'ami, anzi pur (se m'è lecito il dirlo) ch'io v'adori. E se niun è tenuto alle cose impossibili, a me certo è impossibile il non amarvi e 'l contradir ad Amore; dunque, non son tenuta a farlo. (Marotti and Romei, *La commedia dell'arte,* 192)

> If objects decorated with celestial beauty, singular virtue, honoured breeding, noble habits, and other excellent and remarkable gifts, my sweet Sir, ought to be loved, you, who are endowed with all these most noble gifts, then you deserve to have me love you, better still (if it is permitted to me to say) that I adore you. And if no one is beholden to impossible things, and for me certainly it is impossible not to love you and contradict love, then, I am not held to do so.

As powerful in her expression of awakened desire as she was in its denial, Andreini is equally at ease in her manipulation of Petrarchan motifs and devices in both the male and female voice, and performs "the ėlision between the roles of lover and beloved ... blurring what was left of the boundaries between male and female."[25]

In the final act, after putting both her father Dottore (who has also arrived in Genoa) and Flavio to the test by circulating rumours of her death, Fabrizio steps out to identify "himself" as the missing Isabella. In the last scene when she reveals herself to Orazio, she takes her celebrity bow and brings the action to an end.

> FABRIZIO: [DOTTORE, PELLEGRINO et ARLECCHINO]. Si scopre per donna a Orazio, qual si meraviglia; Pellegrino il simile; tutti s'abbracciano. Arlecchino chiede Franceschina. Pedrolino salta in campo dicendo: "Chi la vorrà se la guadagnerà con l'arme in mano." Arlecchino subito gliela cede, il simile fa Pantalone; fanno le nozze.

> FABRIZIO: [DOCTOR, PILGRIM, and ARLECCHINO). She reveals herself to be a woman to Orazio, who is amazed; the Pilgrim also reveals himself; everyone embraces. Arlecchino asks for Franceschina, Pedrolino jumps into battle, saying, "Whoever wants her will have to win her with their

weapons in hand." Arlecchino gives her to him instantly, as does Pantalone; the marriages are arranged. (act 3, 156)

"Isabella's Jealousy"

In "La gelosa Isabella" (Isabella's Jealousy, Day 25), the "jealousy" of the "incomparable" Andreini as a transvestite performer is given even greater prominence (2:249–57). The scenario works off the literal premise that Isabella's "jealous" reaction to her lover Orazio's presumed flirtation with the maid Franceschina leads her to seek revenge. In this case, her revenge takes the shape of her putting on male attire so that she can challenge him to a duel. For the first half of the action until the middle of act 2, the play concerns itself with drunken revelry and brawls that break out between oppositional characters. Isabella is caught in the middle and witnesses an apparent love scene between the maid Franceschina and Orazio that puts her into an impassioned rage and provides the stimulus for her to decide to adopt a male disguise. At this point the action shifts as a new plot line is laid over the first with the unexpected return of Isabella's long-lost twin brother, Fabrizio, who had been taken away from their father, Pantalone, at birth and raised by relatives. His as yet unknown presence has enormous consequences for the fate of Isabella, since Pantalone has negotiated a marriage contract for her with his old friend, Graziano, who is willing to take her without a dowry, until it can be definitely proven that Fabrizio is dead and not in need of an inheritance.

For contemporary audiences it would have been obvious that these new developments borrow very closely from certain details found in the earlier popular classic Intronati play *Gl'ingannati* (*The Deceived*), wherein a transvestite heroine, Lelia, dons the disguise of a male page, Fabio, to enter into the service of her former lover, Flamminio, in order to win him back and thwart his new relationship with a more eligible heiress, Isabella.[26] In *The Deceived*, similar terms of the dowry are detailed at the top of the play and are used to create the very high stakes that Lelia plays for: not being bargained off to her father's aging, libidinous friend Gherardo (214). The daring, sexually savvy, transvestite heroine Lelia/Fabio made *The Deceived* a popular hit that was translated into several languages and performed all across Europe.[27] Lelia/Fabio proves to be so irresistibly alluring with her androgynous beauty that Isabella falls madly in love with "him" when "he" woos her on behalf of "his" master. The solution to this doomed female-female romance is the surprise return of Lelia/Fabio's long-lost brother Fabrizio, whose identical appearance (he even sports the same white suit) leads to many situations where the twins are mistaken for each other and assumptions about male and female sexual differences are tested. The climactic act that brings the play to its solution comes about when Fabrizio is thrown into bed with Isabella because he cannot be distinguished from Lelia/Fabio.

A staple of erudite theatre, the work was originally performed by the aristocratic all-male amateur actors of the Siennese Academy of the Intronati and written for one actor to play both the roles of Lelia/Fabio and Fabrizio, since they are never seen on stage together. Inevitably, in such a performance the ultimate referent underneath the female clothing would always have been the male body. With the same male actor playing both twins, the questions that the play raises about the ambivalent nature of erotic desire and sexual difference leads ultimately back to a confirmation of the homosocial and homoerotic bonds that typify the all-male aristocratic theatre of the time.

When Andreini similarly played both Isabella in male attire and her twin Fabrizio across a spectrum of female-maleness, there may well have been an implied competition with the erudite theatre concerning the execution of the transvestite performance. We do not know exactly what Andreini looked like in her Fabrizio alias, but her great success as a transvestite performer suggests that she may also have earned the same kind of comment about her androgynous appeal that is given to Fabio in *The Deceived*:

> Remember that you are just a young dandy, and you don't really understand how lucky you are. But this fascination with you isn't going to last forever, you know. You're going to grow a beard, your cheeks aren't going to remain so fresh, your lips so red. You won't always be so sought after by everyone – no, sir. (229)

In "Isabella's Jealousy," Andreini's identity-swapping between the female character Isabella in male disguise and the returned male twin Fabrizio works as a prolonged in-joke that is created for the pleasure of her spectators. The manner in which she uses her imposture to work the fetish – by never fully transferring "the displacement of lack from the subject to the object ... with the result that male viewer and female spectacle remain bound in reversible positions"[28] – is directed to her audiences, since they alone respond to her impersonation of Fabrizio as separate from her appearances as "Isabella dressed as a man." For the other actors on stage, she is never other than Isabella wearing a male disguise; an effect that opens up questions about how sexual differences can be discerned or defined. For example, when Fabrizio first appears part way through act 2, "he" immediately causes confusion. "His" first encounter with Capitano and Arlecchino, who both think "he" is Isabella disguised in men's clothes, results in Capitano approaching her as if she were sexually available: "la prega amorosamente" (makes amorous advances to her) (act 2, 254). When Fabrizio draws "his" weapon, as a man would in the circumstances, they simply run away on the grounds that they do not fight with women.

In fact, nothing Fabrizio does, including making a full confession identifying "himself" as Pantalone's long-lost son when "he" arrives at Burattino's inn, works to convince the other characters that "he" really exists in the dramatic fiction. Even after "he" tells the innkeeper Burattino the whole story of "his" long absence, Burattino waits until Fabrizio has gone inside before declaring that he thinks he has been talking to Isabella but that she has gone crazy because of her father's bad habits. In this way, the joke that no one believes in Fabrizio's existence but always perceives "him" as Isabella sets up a discourse that plays on the concept of the sexualized body as a prosthestic production. Once there are two male versions of Isabella on the stage, the audience has to take them both into account: immediately following this scene, Isabella appears "vestita da uomo, avendo trovata la comodità di quell'abito adoperato in una rappresentazione fatta tra loro donzelle" (dressed like a man, having found the costume because it was used in a play that she had put on with the other girls) (act 2, 254). When she calls attention to her attire, by changing into her male disguises in full view of the spectators, she invites a very close look at the body parts she needs to conceal. What happens over the next two acts is an oscillation back and forth where "Isabella in male attire," out looking for Orazio, is mistaken over and over again for "Fabrizio" who finds "himself" forced to fight off the attempts of Pantalone and Graziano to bring "him" to heel. Since Andreini presumably was dressed almost identically in both roles, the comparison between her representation of "Isabella in male attire," where she draws attention to transvestism as a stage device, and of Fabrizio, where she is in her male persona, forces the spectator to attend to the interplay between the stages of dressing and undressing used to represent the different degrees of masculinity. Jones and Stallybrass note this as a stage practice that reveals gender representation "as a process of fetishizing which is conceived both as a process of fixation and as indeterminable."[29]

What results from the gender-crossing on stage is an ongoing guessing game with all the expected ambiguities and disavowals drawing attention to the missing body parts, as in the following sequence where "Isabella in male attire" makes a hasty exit to avoid seeing her father Pantalone, and then reappears as Fabrizio. When Pantalone and Graziano berate Fabrizio for dressing as a man and failing to accept that she is to be married to Graziano, "he" reacts as a man and responds by being deeply offended that "his" masculinity is in question. If the dialogue that takes place resembles the same conversation in *The Deceived*, it probably includes Fabrizio's scandalized reaction to Graziano, who, thinking "he" is Isabella, tries to marry "him."[30] After this altercation, Fabrizio calls for help and is rescued by Orazio, who drives Pantalone and Graziano away. However, when Orazio, who also thinks Fabrizio is Isabella, tries to repair their relationship, Fabrizio laughs at him, denies any knowledge of who he is, and retreats to the inn.

When "Isabella in male attire" appears at the top of act 3, she makes sure to distance herself from Fabrizio by telling Capitano when he questions her about insulting him that she doesn't know what he is talking about. The lengthy explanation she launches into about adopting the costume in order to be able to challenge Orazio to a duel pushes her masculine impersonation to the limit as she actually promises to marry Capitano – if she survives the duel. Even her father rails against her performance of masculinity:

> ISABELLA: arriva, Pantalone subito la vede, et in collera, li domanda la cagione dell'esser in quell'abito. Ella arditamente dice esser stata un tempo innamorata d'Orazio, e che, per un torto ch'egli le ha fatto, s'è posta in quell'abito per voler con l'armi far quistion seco, e via.

> ISABELLA: enters, Pantalone sees her immediately, and angrily asks her why she is dressed in this way. She audaciously replies that she was once in love with Orazio and that because of a wrong he did her, she has put on this dress in order to challenge him to a duel, and she exits. (act 3, 255–6)

This encounter leads to the climactic moment when Isabella exits and Fabrizio emerges from the inn and is mistaken for her, so that when Graziano's daughter Flaminia invites Fabrizio into her home, she has the full approval of Pantalone, who has failed to notice any differences between them:

> FLAMINIA: dice Fabrizio (ingannandosi) che, se bene ha occasione d'esser in collera seco, li dispiace vederla in quell'abito, essendo donna, e, se non vuole andare in case di suo padre, che vada in casa sua con lei. Fabrizio domanda al vecchio se si contenta. Pantalone: di sì. Et essi, abbracciati, entrano in casa.

> FLAMINIA: says to Fabrizio (mistaking him) that although she has reason to be angry with her, it upsets her to see her dressed like that since she is a woman, and if she doesn't want to go into her father's house, that she can come with her into hers. Fabrizio asks Pantalone is that's all right with him. Pantalone says yes. And they wrap their arms around each other and go inside. (act 3, 256)

The explosion that results when Franceschina rushes out of the house screaming that "Isabella è diventata uomo" (Isabella has become a man) (act 3, 256) is followed with a prolonged voyeuristic glimpse into what went on in Flaminia's room, as Franceschina reveals to Graziano that she "aver trovato un giovanotto abbracciato con Flaminia sua figlia" (has found a young man embracing his daughter) (act 3, 256). Almost a direct steal from the same discovery scene by Pasquella in *The Deceived*, Franceschina's shocked response would have reminded spectators of these famous lines of Pasquella:

> After a while I decided to go in to see what was up, and I found them hugging and kissing! So I decided to find out whether it was a man or a woman. My mistress had the person down on the bed, and she called me to help her while she held his hands. And he was letting her win, so I opened the front of his clothes, and all of a sudden I felt something slap my hand, and I wasn't sure whether it was a large pestle or a big stick or that other thing. But whatever it was, it was in great shape. And when I saw how big it was, I took off, sisters, and locked the door behind me! (267)

In possession of the phallus, Fabrizio, chased out of the house by Graziano, is at last recognized by Pantalone as his son and given permission to marry Flaminia. Through the sheer power of her transvestite performance as Fabrizio, Andreini has demonstrated that the phallus is up for grabs – for both sexes.

To fulfil the requirements of the dramatic fiction, "Isabella in male attire" takes her moment of revenge for his infidelity by drawing her sword on Orazio and demanding satisfaction for his betrayal. By keeping Fabrizio offstage and leaving us with an image of "Isabella in male attire" in full possession of the field, Scala pays tribute to Andreini's abilities to make us believe in the fantasy that sexual identities are mutable – at least on stage. A complete star turn for Andreini, "Isabella's Jealousy" was probably developed to showcase Andreini's charismatic appeal for fans familiar with her Fabrizio impersonation and eager to see her perform it again and again.

"The Disguised Servants"

The other scenario that echoes *The Deceived* by featuring a transvestite heroine who has disguised herself to pursue her lover is "Li finti servi" (The Disguised Servants, Day 30, 2:305–15). Isabella, who fell in love with Orazio when he was visiting her in Genova, disguises herself as the male page Fabrizio and pursues Orazio to Florence when he returns to his father Pantalone's household. As Fabrizio he obtains employment with Orazio's family in an effort to be near him. As the plot goes, the disguise is so successful that Orazio fails to recognize "him," and instead, "he" attracts the attention of Orazio's sister, Flaminia, who falls madly in love with "him." To push this case of mistaken identity to an extreme, Scala begins the action with Flaminia very pregnant and mistaken in believing that Fabrizio has fathered the child she is carrying. (The explanation that she has been impregnated by Isabella's brother Cinzio, who accompanied her into exile, is shared with the audience part way into act 1, but is not known by the other characters until the final scenes. Cinzio, who is employed as a servant in Graziano's household, secretly visits Flaminia's bed at night in the dark and successfully impersonates Fabrizio between the sheets.) For most of the play, the action revolves around Andreini's sustained male impersonation and the inability of the other characters to recognize that "he" is really Isabella.[31] In another star turn for Andreini, whose Fabrizio was well known to the spectators, she nods to their ability to appreciate her skill by making them alone privy to her disguise. Flaminia's fantasy of union with Fabrizio regardless of "his" sexual identity is presented as a distinct possibility. If Andreini's celebrity presence fuelled her fans' dreams that they too might be united with her in sexual union, her transvestite disguise would have fed their fantasies, regardless of their sexual identities.

The scenario begins with Fabrizio playing a love scene with the distraught Flaminia as "he" tries to reassure her that the messenger her father has sent to Genova to investigate "his" pedigree will return with the information that "he" is worthy of her hand, at which point "he" will marry her and save her from the shame of her out-of-wedlock pregnancy. Until well into the third act, and even after Flaminia has given birth, the other characters respond to Fabrizio as if "he" is the man who has fathered her child. Traub's observation that "cross-dressing not only masculinizes but eroticises the female body"[32] is taken to an extreme in "The Disguised Servants" because Fabrizio presents as unassailably male.

Andreini's success at impersonating Fabrizio means that all her efforts to signal to Orazio that she is really a woman are ignored and misread as homoerotic. Fabrizio finds "himself" playing out a long scene in which "he" repeatedly attacks Orazio, displaying "his" jealous rage. While Orazio remains oblivious to Fabrizio's real identity, he becomes increasingly fascinated by the way his favourite page is acting and finds that he "lo tien guardato molte volte" (can't stop looking at him again and again) (act 1, 308). When Fabrizio finally departs, Orazio comments to Pedrolino: "se Fabrizio fusse donna, crederebbe ch'ella fusse innamorata di lui" (if Fabrizio were a woman, he'd think she was in love with him) (act 1, 308). Pedrolino's cryptic reply "Dunque voi non sapete ancora chi sia Fabrizio?") (Then you still don't know who Fabrizio is?) (act 1, 308) underlines the strange fascination that Fabrizio has, showcasing Andreini's ability to play between male and female sexual identities. It is only in the final scenes of the scenario, after the truth comes out that Isabella's brother Cinzio is the father of Flaminia's baby, that Fabrizio reveals her true identity as Isabella: "dopo molti timori si discopre per Isabella, figlia di Leone Adorni Genovese" (after a lot of hesitation, reveals herself to him as Isabella, the daughter of Leone Adorni of Genoa) (act 3, 313).

These three scenarios featuring Isabella as Fabrizio provide examples of the kinds of transgressive roles available to the actresses to perform as transvestite heroines. I have argued that we can explain the extreme popularity of the transvestite heroine role by relating it to both theatrical and social practices concerned with the exploration of questions of sex and gender differences of interest to early modern society. Transvestite roles not only permitted the actresses to showcase their great acting skills as part of their celebrity appeal, but also offered the chance to stage scenarios in which masculine privilege was challenged and the social hierarchy subverted. As the actresses showed what it meant to have the freedom to act with male agency, they offered spectators a chance to view sexual identities as having a certain fluidity that allowed for greater social mobility. Although Andreini's Fabrizio has provided the examples here, she is only one of the many who appeared in male disguise. It is, however, a measure of her exceptionality that she is such a prominent figure in Scala's unique collection of all-star performers. In chapter 5 I evaluate her life and work in the context of her rise to international diva status.

Chapter Five

Isabella Andreini: The Making of a Diva

The records relating to Isabella Andreini depict her as an actress and musician of astounding range and skill who became the *prima donna* of the Gelosi at a very early age and continued to perform with them, often co-directing the company with her husband Francesco.[1] In addition to her acting, she won recognition in court and academic circles as a scholar, poet, playwright, and author of note.[2] Through these circles she acquired a wide base of dedicated followers whose praises amounted to cult worship. All of this evidence qualifies her as having what Roach calls "the multifaceted genius of It" through her public intimacy, the illusion she gave of shared experience with her audiences, and the It effect itself through her mass appeal and cult following.[3] With such a wide range of other accomplishments, she exceeded the fame accorded to her fellow-actresses who vied with her for honours on the stage, but about whom little is known. Although Armani and Piissimi and other early actresses have also been credited with the same charismatic gift of divine eloquence, we are not able to flesh out their celebrity status in the same way that we can with Andreini because of the records we have of her. In understanding her celebrity status, we need to measure the superhuman persona against the ordinary mortal from which she transforms.

Celebrity theorist Dyer argues that a star's charisma depends on the public having knowledge of his/her offstage existence as an *authentic* flesh-and-blood mortal. He suggests that it is only by knowing there is a living person behind the superhuman qualities that the public is able to authentic her fame.[4] Andreini's "authentic" offstage existence included being known as a wife and mother and as a scholar, poet, and *literata*. Her "authenticity" works on stage to make her appear as always "herself" no matter what roles she took, and so references both the real person and the superhuman "authentic presence" of the celebrity who had transcended her origins.[5]

Most of the information that makes up Andreini's fame narrative stressed the great obstacles she had to overcome. Andreini herself fed the rhetoric during her lifetime, and after her death it was stoked by her husband and son, who portrayed themselves as members of a theatrical dynasty.[6] The "rhetoric of authenticity" that grew up around her also locates the source of her fame in her great striving to achieve excellence. Hers is what Rojek calls an *achieved* celebrity – "in the public realm they are recognized as individuals who possess rare talents or skill."[7] I propose that Andreini's rise to fame operates in the context of her exceptionalism as a female artist struggling to overcome the obstacles of her humble birth and possible connections to the courtesan class. It is also affected by the challenges she faced as a wife and mother who had to earn her living by touring with the Gelosi and satisfying her patrons. In part 1, I discuss how Andreini's rise to diva status is framed through the rhetoric "authenticating" her as a *prima donna,* wife and mother, aspiring *literata,* and academician. Part 2 deals with the traces of her "authentic presence" as celebrity-artist as it is manifested in her poetry collected in the *Rime;* her pastoral *La Mirtilla,* which she both wrote and performed in; and in her famous mad performance of *La pazzia* at the Medici wedding gala of 1589. In part 3, I show how her legend lived on after her death, mainly through the efforts of her husband.

Part 1: The Rise to Diva Status

Isabella Andreini's lowly birth in Padua in 1562 as the daughter of one Paolo Canali and an unknown mother indicates that she had to make her own way in the world. Her extensive classical education and training in the fine arts and her skills as a poet and musician are more consistent with the traditional upbringing of an honest courtesan than of a woman from a respectable family. The first record concerning her dates from 1576, when her son Giovan Battista was born in Florence, followed by her marriage to Francesco Andreini in 1578 or 1579.[8] They soon became star members of the company and, as their careers in the Gelosi flourished side by side, seemed to have worked hard to establish themselves as worthy of membership in an upper-class elite. Giovan Battista's record of life in their household ("which was always full of noble and literary figures, who if they entered with delight, left with marvel") defends his young mother as a prodigy "who astounded even the most erudite with her great learning."[9]

Records of their private family life are full of accounts of the great love of Francesco and Isabella, a narrative that Francesco shares with the public in intimate detail after her death. At the same time, their public profile as a respectably married couple carried with it the duty of childbearing.[10] Since she was pregnant at least eight times over their twenty-eight years of marriage, she must often have performed on stage while visibly pregnant. Such pregnancies were proof of her fidelity and seem to have strengthened her appeal. Roach suggests that in the case of the great stars, their vulnerabilities, which he labels "stigmata" in contrast to their "charismatic" marks of genius, work to deepen our attraction to such individuals.[11] It seems that such was the case for Isabella, since her aging body and frequent pregnancies never diminished her stage appeal, even up to her death in Lyon. Her children's lives also mark her with both charismata and stigmata. Giovan Battista, her firstborn, was not only a famous actor but also a very successful playwright, helping to build the family's theatrical reputation. Her son Domenico served as army captain under Ferdinando Gonzaga, and another son, Pietro Paolo, became a Vallambrosian monk in Pavia. What became of her four daughters is less clear, although they may have ended up in nunneries in Mantua.[12] The two letters that we have, written by Isabella to place two of her daughters in the courts of Mantua and Florence, indicate that she was not able to provide for them and maintain her career as a travelling performer.[13] Such harsh economic realities concerning her own daughters underline the high costs of success and the disadvantages of being born female.

Presenting herself as a woman with a lifelong desire for education and learned conversation, Andreini built a reputation for herself. Her work began to appear in different anthologies as early as 1587, indicating that she was gaining recognition for her poetry in certain literary circles and academies that she frequented.[14] One of the crowning achievements of her career was her acceptance into the Academy of the Intenti in Pavia in 1601, after a long association with several of its illustrious members, many of whom were devoted fans.[15] Her emblem, created to mark her entry into the Intenti under her chosen name, *L'Accesa* (Lit-One), celebrates her as a unique artist but also underlines her struggle for acclamation, since the image she chose draws attention to her artifice (fig. 5.1): the rocket shooting up over the city is from an artificial source of fire. Her motto, *Elevat Ardor* (The Flame Rises), describes her own ascent to the heavens.

LETTERE
D'ISABELLA
ANDREINI
PADOVANA,
COMICA GELOSA,
ET ACADEMICA INTENTA
NOMINATA L'ACCESA.
DEDICATE
AL SERENISSIMO DON CARLO
EMANVEL, DVCA DI SAVOIA, &c.
Con Priuilegio, & Licentia de' Superiori.

IN VENETIA, Appreſſo Marc'Antonio Zaltieri. MDCVII.
Ad inſtantia di Gieronimo Bordon.

Figure 5.1. *L'Accesa*, Isabella Andreini's emblem. Engraving from frontispiece in her *Lettere*, Venice, 1607. Reproduced by permission from Bibliothèque nationale de France, 97C221914 16° 24052.

However deserving Andreini was of her celebrity, she has never escaped the suspicion that her reputation may have been enhanced by the fervent efforts of dedicated and well-placed fans. One notable admirer, the Albanese poet Gherardo Borgogni, a fellow member of the Intenti, expressed such intense devotion that he appears to have been in love with her.[16] Nor was Andreini above encouraging his praise for her impersonation of the nymph Filli. Borgogni's championing of her lyric verse in many anthologies, including the seventeen poems he wrote to her, played a significant role in building her cult. On the eve of the publication of her *Rime,* he described her in a dialogue that idolized her as a "donna di gloriosa fama e di gran nome nell'arte comica, e nella poetica meravigliosa ai tempi nostri, et un vero e stupendo miracolo della natura stessa" (woman of glorious renown and great reputation as an actress, and a marvellous poet of our times, and a real and stupendous miracle of nature herself).[17] Borgogni and his circle proved their idolatry of her by their determined effort to bring her to the attention of Torquato Tasso.

The attempt to associate Andreini's name with Tasso's demonstrates Andreini fans' cultish desire to align her with one of the greatest talents of their time.[18] Even today, Italian scholars remain sceptical about the legendary relationship between Andreini and Tasso, as shown in Taviani's well-known article "Bella d'Asia: Torquato Tasso, gli attori e l'immortalità."[19] Ultimately, Taviani dispels the doubts about the two most important links between them: the poetry contest in which Isabella came second to Tasso, and the attribution of his "Bella d'Asia" sonnet to her. We know that in 1592 Borgogni wrote a *canzonetta* to Tasso, imploring him to write a poem in praise of "Signora Isabella Andreini, comica Gelosa, intesa per Filli" using echoes from her madrigal in his own *canzonetta* to remind Tasso that she had helped to get him out of jail.[20] The *canzonetta* also contains Borgogni's offer to Tasso that if he does write for her, Borgogni and other distinguished poets, including Cinzio Aldobrandini, would help Tasso achieve his dream of being crowned with laurel at the Campidoglio.[21] This dream of Tasso's may have come true, if the description of Tasso's winning the poetry contest at the Roman banquet is to be believed. The event records the presence of Andreini as an honoured guest who came second to Tasso in the featured poetry competition. It also describes how her bust was similarly crowned with laurel:

> Trovandosi in Roma questa virtuosa comica fu non solo dipinta, ma coronata d'alloro in simulacro colorito tra il Tasso, e il Petrarca, allorché dopo

una mensa fattale dall'Eminentissimo Cardinal Cintio Aldobrandini gran mecenate de' virtuosi, dove erano per commensali sei Cardinali sapientissimi, il suddetto Tasso, il Cavalier de'Pazzi, Antonio Ongaro, ed altri poeti chiarissimi tra il quali in bella gara scrivendo e improvvisando sonetti l'Andreini spiritosamente dopo il gran Torquato ne riportò il primo vanto.[22]

This virtuosic actress, finding herself in Rome, was not only painted but crowned in effigy between portraits of Tasso and Petrarch, after a banquet offered to her by the Most Eminent Cardinal Cintio Aldobrandini, great patron of artists, where at table there were six learned cardinals, Tasso, the Cavalier de'Pazzi, Antonio Ongaro, and other very famous poets, writing and improvising sonnets in a poetry contest, in which Andreini with sparkling wit came second only to the great Tasso.

Even if the contest has something fabled about it, the sheer magnitude of the claim that Andreini was also crowned after Tasso has caused most Tasso scholars to dismiss it as a deliberate fabrication.[23] Even Taviani, who cites evidence that the event did occur, finds it necessary to explain that the crowning-with-laurel ceremony must have been some token offering, and that Andreini's bust was probably not an actual image of her but an allegorical depiction that showed her as a Muse, so that no direct comparison to Tasso could be made.[24] Whether or not Isabella was present at the dinner and did improvise her way to second place may be of less importance than the fact that the public believed it to be true. Such a legendary tale means that images of her were in circulation during her lifetime, and proves that she was regarded as an "effigy" in the public imagination.[25]

The other significant connection with Tasso was his sonnet "Per la Signora Bella d'Asia," which appeared among the tributes and epitaphs from other famous poets at the beginning of Andreini's posthumous *Lettere*.[26] Considered to be one of the foundational tributes on which her fame rests, its contested attribution draws attention to the precarious nature of celebrity worship.[27] Taviani, after considerable debate, comes to the conclusion that Tasso wrote the sonnet to her, probably in 1587, shortly after his release from Sant' Anna. After this time, we can assume that she was known to Tasso through both her poetry and her stage career, which included playing the male lead in his *Aminta* and writing her own pastoral, *La Mirtilla*, in response to his. The sonnet, written in the mystical form of an *impresa*, memorializes all aspects of the "beauty" that (Isa)bella's "name" can be made to yield.[28] Thus, in the octave he brings her "mortal spoils" to life through the dazzling figures of speech – the flowers, roses, jewels, stars, and perfumes he (on behalf of Mother Nature) collects to compose her:

Quando v'ordiva il prezioso velo
L'alma Natura e le mortali spoglie,
Il bel cogliea, si come il fior si coglie,
Togliendo gemme in terra e lumi in Cielo:
E spargea fresche rose in vivo gielo,
Che l'Aura e 'l Sol mai non disperde, o scioglie,
E quanti odori l'Oriente accoglie;
E, perché non v'asconda invidia o zelo,

When fostering Mother Nature fashioned
Your precious veil and mortal spoils,
She sought out beauty and gathered it like a flower,
Taking jewels from the earth and stars from the Heavens:
And spreading fresh roses in flowing ice,
So that the Dawn and the Sun could never melt or disperse them,
And collecting so many perfumes from the Orient;
And because she hid no envy or zealousness in you,

In the sestet, where all her beauty and honours are made manifest in her "name,"[29] Tasso goes further to imprint the god Love himself into her image, endowing her with the power to transform her audiences forever through the understanding of "Love" she brings:

Ella, che fece il bel sembiante in prima,
Poscia il nome formò, che i vostri onori
Porti e rimbombi e sol bellezza esprima,
Felice l'alme e fortunate i cori,
Ove con letter d'oro Amor s'imprima
Nell'imagine vostra e' n cui s'adori.

She, who first made your beautiful semblance,
Then made your name, so that it would sound and echo
Your honours and express only beauty,
Happy the souls and blessed those hearts,
Where with letters of gold Love has stamped
His name on your image and in which he is adored.

Tasso's sonnet, like many of the other tributes Andreini received, treats her as having the supernatural powers that mark artistic genius. Around the time this sonnet appeared, Garzoni also described her unparalleled mastery of her art form. This suprahuman display of artistry (Gell calls such displays "the technology of enchantment") drew fans to her.[30] Garzoni's praise reflects the reputation that she had already acquired as a young *prima donna*:

La graziosa Isabella, decoro delle scene, ornamento de' Teatri, spettacolo superbo non meno di virtù che di bellezza, ha illustrato ancor lei questa professione in modo che, mentre il mondo durerà, mentre staranno i secoli, mentre avran vita gli ordini e i tempi, ogni voce, ogni lingua, ogni grido risuonerà il celebre nome d'Isabella.

Gracious Isabella, adornment of the stage, ornament of the theatre, a superb spectacle no less of *virtù* than of beauty, [who] has also made her profession so illustrious that while the world lasts, while the centuries unfold, while time and laws endure, every voice, every tongue, every cry will echo the famous name of Isabella.[31]

Part 2: The Celebrity Artist

Andreini's desire to be known as more than a famous performer is captured in her *Rime*, published in two volumes (*parte prima* in 1601 and *parte seconda* in 1605). In figure 5.2 we see an engraving of her that suggests, from her rich clothing and hairstyle, that she has achieved the stature of a court lady. In keeping with the legend that her ability to improvise beautiful verse had led to her coming second to Tasso, Bartoli described her poetry as "non in punto inferiori ad altre de' più famosi Poeti di quel Secolo istesso" (in no way inferior to those of the most famous poets of her century).[32]

Collected from the repertoire of lyric verse that she had been preparing over many years, the *Rime* poems show her ability to write in many genres.[33] They attest to her membership in different academic and courtly circles, as some were included in exchanges with noble and royal patrons.[34] The first sonnet in the *Rime* is addressed to the reader and offers one of the few statements she made connecting her stage performances to her poetic compositions. In it she cautions the reader not to be fooled by the great passions she expresses on the stage or to think they are any more "real" than those she is now recording on the page. Instead she claims that every emotion she has acted on stage is "faked," that her grand gestures expressing love, madness, desire,

Figure 5.2 Portrait of Isabella Andreini. Engraving from frontispiece in her *Rime*, Milan, 1601. Courtesy of Thomas Fisher Rare Book Library, University of Toronto.

and despair were "lies":

S'Alcun sia mai, che i versi miei negletti
Legga, non creda à questi finti ardori,
Che ne le Scene imaginati amori
Usa à trattar con non leali affetti:
Con bugiardi non men con finti detti
De le Muse spiegai gli alti furori:
Talhor piangendo i falsi miei dolori,
Talhor cantando i falsi miei diletti. (*Rime* 1, 1)

If anyone ever reads my forgotten verses,
Do not believe in these feigned passions
That I have used to stage imaginary loves
With faithless sentiments.
With lies, no less with deceitful words,
I have portrayed the high furour of the Muses:
Sometimes crying for false sorrows,
Sometimes rejoicing for false delights.[35]

In the sestet, she describes herself as a performer who transcends gender boundaries, shifting easily between male and female roles just as she moves the art form beyond the rules governing both nature and art:

E come ne' Teatri hor Donna, ed hora
Huom fei rappresentando in vario stile
Quanto volle insegnar Natura, ed Arte.
Così la stella mia seguendo ancora
Di fuggitivia età nel verde Aprile
Vergai con stil ben mille carte.

And just as in the Theatre, I sometimes played women
And sometimes men, representing them in varied style,
As Nature and Art would teach us.
So following my star once more
in the verdant April of my fleeting life,
I have penned with varied style a good thousand pages.

Setting herself up as an artist who strives for technical mastery in both her acting and writing, Andreini introduces the reader to the "good thousand pages" that she has penned in the *Rime* as proof of her poetic range. As MacNeil notes, her poetry reflects the "'public' compositional strategies of one who performs on stage, either as an actor or an orator."[36] Delivering Petrarchan love poetry as part of a stage performance as a *prima donna* invited audience members to respond as if they were being directly addressed.[37] In stressing her technique, she intentionally draws her audience's attention to the cleverness of her conceits while at the same time offering them a visceral experience. The connection created between Andreini and each of her spectators thus creates the illusion of intimacy and shared emotion that is part of the diva's appeal.

Andreini's ability to captivate her audiences by composing in a variety of styles in prose, poetry, and song is likely to have included occasions where she followed the popular practice of inserting actual lines from Petrarch into her own work to display her ability to alternate between her own writing and that of Petrarch.[38] She has left two examples of *centoni*, a challenging genre very much in vogue requiring the author to use only materials from Petrarch that were reassembled to create striking new meanings.[39] Listeners could delight both in hearing the words and in recognizing the skill with which they had been assembled.[40] To give a sense of the way that the insertion of a *centone* might embellish a performance, I include below her poem "Amor m'ha posto come segno a strale" (*centon* 2, *Rime* 1:152), wherein each line has been carefully chosen from the opening lines of different Petrarchan sonnets. Imagining Andreini delivering it on stage gives a sense of the emotional impact:

Amor m'hà posto come segno à strale,
Pasco il cor di sospir, ch'altro non chiede,
E qual è la mia vita ella se' l vede,
E quinci, e quindi il cor punge, ed assale.
In questa breve mia vita mortale
Lasso, ch'io ardo, ed altri non me 'l crede;
Veggio à molto languir poca mercede.
O viva morte, ò dilettoso male.
Non veggio, ove scampar mi possa homai;
E vo' contando gli anni, e taccio, e grido,
O speranza, ò desir sempre fallace.
Primavera per me pur non è mai.

Pascomi di dolor piangendo e rido;
E sol di lei pensando hò qualche pace. (*Rime*, 1:152)[41]

Love has set me up like a target for arrows,
I feed my heart with sighs, it asks for nothing else,
And what my life is, she sees herself,
And from both sides pierces and assails my heart.
In this my brief mortal life.
Alas, I burn and I am not believed,
I see little reward for so much yearning,
O living death, O delightful harm.
I don't see where I can escape anymore.
And I go counting the years and I am silent and cry out,
O hope, o desire, always deceptive.
Spring for me still never comes.
I feed on pain, weeping I laugh,
And only thinking of her do I have any peace.

At the same time, however, Andreini is speaking in the borrowed words of Petrarch himself, and therefore drawing attention to her technical mastery of this elegant experimental form. Experiencing Andreini reciting her *centone* on stage drew her audience in emotionally, and at the same time reminded them of the brilliance of her powers of invention in assembling her lines from familiar Petrarchan sonnets. Perhaps this effect resembles cultural sociologist Jeffrey Alexander's explanation of the way that worshippers regard celebrity icons as transitional objects who mediate between internal and external reality and, as such, are often "introjected" by fans and made into part of themselves.[42]

The *Rime*, published when she was at the pinnacle of her fame, shows Andreini participating in the creation of her own legend, offering glimpses of her private self, even as she maintained the secrets of her artistic process. James Wyatt Cook finds the *Rime* full of "evidence of her wit, her self-respect both as an artist and woman, her skill at verbal fencing and sarcastic repartee, and her quick intelligence."[43] The woman who writes and acts from both masculine and feminine subject positions in what Ray calls her "hermaphroditic register"[44] had also shown her deep understanding of prevailing misogynistic attitudes when she wrote *Mirtilla* in response to Tasso's *Aminta*. Andreini was positioned to "negotiate the competing and contradictory definitions of her own significance as a celebrity sign." Thus her presence as the poet-performer in *Mirtilla* carried with it an interrogation of "the active construction of (female) identity in the social world."[45]

La Mirtilla

La Mirtilla, published in 1588 when Andreini was only twenty-six, enjoyed a long and successful print run and was probably performed frequently during that time.[46] Figure 5.3 reproduces the portrait of Andreini that appeared in the frontispiece.

Recent studies, notably Lisa Sampson's *Pastoral Drama in Early Modern Italy* (2006) and Virginia Cox's *The Prodigious Muse* (2011), have explored the contributions made by other women writers to the pastoral genre and put in question whether *La Mirtilla* was the first to be published.[47] But if Andreini was not alone, or perhaps even the first woman to write a pastoral, she still stands out as the first and only female performer to do so.[48]

Andreini, like many other commedia dell'arte actresses, became well known for playing in pastorals, and on occasion took the male role of Aminta, as we can see in this verse by Borgogni, conflating her Aminta with Filli, the nymph role she was most identified with:

> Al tuo partir cadeo
> Il gran teatro, e la famosa scena,
> Già d'alta gioia piena,
> Per grave duol si feo
> Men lieta e men serena.
> Né qui si vide Aminta
> Ch'avea nel volto allor Filli dipinta.
>
> When you left
> The great theatre collapsed, and the stage,
> Which used to be full of joy,
> Turned less happy and less peaceful.
> For the great sorrow.
> Nor did we see Aminta ever again
> Speaking through Filli.[49]

Andreini, then, was familiar with *Aminta* and its treatment of gender roles and sexual violence. When she came to write *Mirtilla* as a tribute to Tasso, she put her improvisational skills to good use, both in the

Figure 5.3. Portrait of Isabella Andreini. Engraving from frontispiece in her *Mirtilla*, Verona, 1588. Courtesy of Thomas Fisher Rare Book Library, University of Toronto.

composition and staging of dramatic scenes with eloquent speech and song and in the introduction of rougher comic elements taken from the commedia dell'arte repertoire.[50]

In order to show how *Mirtilla* disrupts the traditional model requiring female submission to male desire, I focus on Andreini's presence as the "poet-performer" in control of the aesthetic vision, which she most often expresses through her iconic role as the nymph Filli. Quinn observes that celebrities have an "absolute presence" as individuals when they appear on stage and hence are never eclipsed by the roles they play. Andreini's multifaceted functions as actor, character, and author draw attention to her ultimate aesthetic control.[51] Andreini's appearances, first as the goddess Venus in the prologue and then as the seminaked nymph, Filli, might well have carried an extra erotic change for spectators aware of her authorial role.[52] Playing on her sexual attraction as a celebrity figure, Andreini modelled her pastoral around the exploits of her female nymph protagonists and their search for love.[53] No longer in Tasso's world where Amore can hide from his mother, Andreini speaks as Venus herself, who has returned to bring her wayward son to heel. In her fictional world, the hymeneal rule of Venus will be restored and everyone, except Satiro, will find his or her place coupled in consensual married bliss.

Andreini copies Tasso's trope of having Amore punish chastity, but diverts the thrust of the plot away from the fulfilment of male desire, offering instead rival female protagonists who already know the depths of love and passion that Tasso wants to teach Sylvia. In the series of contests that ensue, the characters are measured against each other in various ways. Three key plot strands will illustrate how Andreini showcases her female protagonists and adds new twists to the *Aminta* plot: Filli and Mirtilla's rivalry for Uranio's love; Filli's encounter with the satyr; and Ardelia's falling in love with her mirror image.

As a nymph who knows the pain of unrequited desire and the pull towards death, Filli models the art of rejection with exquisite sensibility, setting the mood for the other characters to follow.[54] Her opening lament reveals her special insights into what the other characters are experiencing:

> e misera e perduta
> per gli ermi boschi e pei solinghi campi,
> indarno Uranio chiamo e mentre chieggio
> al ciel s'ei mi sarà spietato sempre,

dai cavi sassi accresce il mio tormento
Eco, ch'al mio parlare risponde sempre …
e vivendo in tal morte, ecco le stelle
veggio sparire ad una ad una, e sola
restar nel cielo l'amorosa stella;
la qual, mentre da me tardi si parte,
umilmente prego ch'al mio male
qualche termine ponga, se non ch'io
diverrò di me stessa acerba Parca.

Miserable and lost
in the lonely forests and desolate fields,
I call to Uranio in vain. When I demand of
heaven if it will always be so unmerciful to me,
Echo, who always responds to my speech
from the rocky hollows, increases my torment …
And living in such death, I see the stars
vanish one by one, until only
the amorous star remains in the sky.
While it belatedly departs from me,
I humbly pray that it puts some end
to my misfortune; otherwise, I
will become a bitter Parca to myself. (1.2.565–70; 575–81)

The constant reminder that Andreini as Filli mediates the dramatic fiction is echoed by the presence of another famous diva and stage rival, Piissimi, for whom Andreini wrote the role of Mirtilla. As Andreini's creation, Piissimi as Mirtilla is always seen in relation to Filli, which, while drawing attention to the celebrity status of both and heightening the competition, still leaves Andreini in control. Having made her appearance as Filli in act 1, Andreini gives act 2 to Mirtilla to play out the star turn that begins with her confessing her burning desire for Uranio, and sets up the three-handed scene with Uranio where Mirtilla pleads for his love and he scorns her for Ardelia, who in turn scorns him. The brilliance of the fast-moving witty repartee, delivered as if it were being improvised, ends with Piissimi as Mirtilla capping off the act with the final lament.

As rivals for the love of Uranio, Filli and Mirtilla appear together in act 3 in a singing contest that is based on Virgil's third ecologue, but with the protagonists changed from male to female. The scene contains similarities to Guarini's contest between Corsica and Amarillis in *Il pastor fido,* but rather than ending badly with Corsica's plot to kill Amarillis, here Mirtilla and Filli are judged by the old shepherd Opico to decide who deserves to win Uranio.[55] This display of their rivalry in love captured in a contest of rivalry in art underlines Andreini's conscious paralleling of the two, ending with Opico declaring them to be equals.[56] A sample of a few of the verses captures the virtuosity they display in attempting to best each other by improvising inside the required rhyme. The ensuing contest was intended to impress and delight the spectators as they heard the singers deliver their competing stanzas with surprising new interpretations and ornamentation.[57]

MIRTILLA
Amo Uranio crudele e non me'n pento.
che la beltà, ch' a tutti gli occhi piace,
mi fa lieta gioir d'ogni tormento.
FILLI
La neve al sole si dilegua, e 'l foco
strugge la cera, e a me lo sdegno e l'ira
d'Uranio il cor consuma a poco a poco.
MIRTILLA
Giovan l'erbe agli agnelli, a l'api i fiori:
a me sol giova contemplar d'Uranio.
nel vago viso i bei vivi colori.

MIRTILLA
I love cruel Uranio and do not regret it,
for his beauty, which pleases all eyes,
makes me happy to rejoice in every torment!
FILLI
The snow melts in the sun, and the fire
melts the wax, and, as for me, the disdain and anger
of Uranio consume my heart little by little.
MIRTILLA
The sheep benefit from grass,
as do the bees from flowers,
but the only thing that benefits me is to contemplate
the beautiful face and vivid colouring of Uranio! (3.5.1769–77)

If the contests allowed both actresses to share the stage, the centrepiece of the play belongs to Filli and her encounter with the satyr. Her Satiro resembles Tasso's in his menacing threats, swearing that:

> E s'ella al mio voler non sarà presta,
> le farò mille oltraggi.
> Né sua bellezza voglio che le giovi,
> né gli altri gridi o'l domandar mercede!"
>
> And if she won't surrender to my will,
> I'll do her a thousand outrages!
> Neither her beauty nor her loud cries
> or her request for mercy will help her! (3.1.1285–8)

However, when Filli falls into his trap, a scenario is presented that is very different from Tirsi's (Tasso's mouthpiece) narration of the nymph Silvia's brutal treatment and humiliation. Instead Andreini's scene borrows more from Beccari's *Il sacrificio*.[58] It may also have been influenced by Guarini's *Il pastor fido*, which had been in circulation since 1585, as well as sharing some common elements with other female-authored pastorals of the time.[59] But only *Mirtilla* and *Amorosa speranza* by Miani go to such extremes in their physical humiliation of the satyr.[60] Here Andreini's Filli engages with the satyr physically in a scene that showcases her co-option of its usual sadomasochistic overtones for her own instructional purposes. We can only speculate on the erotic effect the beautiful young actress in her semi-naked nymph costume might have had as she played the cruel dominatrix. For Quinn, moments when a celebrity offers an iconic enactment of a scene such as this feed the fantasies of the spectators who witness it.[61] The shared intimacy in playing such an intensely erotic scene by acting it out together step by step makes it very different from Tirsi's voyeuristic narration after the event had taken place.

After Satiro lays out the standard script of his plans to tie up her naked body and torture her to death, Filli begins her reverse seduction by reacting to his monstrous appearance with flattery as she looks right into his "begl'occhi" (beautiful eyes). Filli's vow, by Satiro's "robuste braccia / e per la vaga tua cornuta fronte" (robust arms / and by your charming horned brow") (3.2. 1334–5), that she is not mocking him puts the two in close proximity. By her fearless response, Filli gradually disarms him and turns Satiro into the one who is being wooed. Once he has become the submissive in a bondage-domination script, a new, cruel side of Filli emerges. She begins by getting him to let her tie him up, "ch'io ti leghi / le braccia, perché tu da la dolcezza / che sentirai baciandomi / tanto non mi stringessi" (so that you, from the sweetness / that you experience kissing me, / won't embrace me so tightly) (3.2.1382–4). As he agrees, she winds the cords around his arms, all the time talking him through her love for him, even thanking the tree – in a reference to Tasso's branch that helped in Silvia's rape – for keeping "poiché fermo terrai colui che tiene / l'anima mia legata in sì bel nodo" (fast the one who keeps / my soul tied in so beautiful a knot) (3.1.1396).

And when he complains that she has pulled the cords too tight, she keeps to her role as dominatrix: "Datti pace / e soffri per un poco: / perché quanto più stretto / ti lego, tanto più sicuramente / ti bacierò dipoi" (Calm down, and suffer for a moment: because the more tightly, I tie you, the more safely / I will then kiss you) (3.2. 1398–1401). As the satyr begs her for the kiss, she holds him off again by pretending that her modesty is at stake. She becomes more and more physically violent, first by pulling his beard when she gets him to bend down for the kiss and then twisting his neck and pinching his nipples until he begs her to stop. To maintain the illusion that at any point he could break free and turn on her, she pretends to cry, as they both speak in asides to the audience. With everything ending up focused on the actual kissing of his "quella cara e dolce bocca" (dear and sweet mouth) (3.2.1475), Filli gives Satiro his final punishment by feeding him a bitter herb to sweeten his breath.

Filli's final speech to the tied-up Satiro taunts him on behalf of all women:

> O malaccorto
> or hai pur finalmente conosciuto
> ch'io mi beffo di te, qual donna mai,
> benché diforme e vile, si compiaque
> d'amar sì mostruoso, orrido aspetto?
> Or vedi ch'io ti colsi, resta pure
> schernito, come meriti, ch'io ti lascio.
> Così volesse il ciel che fosti preda
> d'orsi rabbiosi e d'affamati lupi;
> perché innanzi mai più non mi venisse
> codesta tua sì brutta e a me tanto
> noiosa odiatissima sembianza.

O foolish one,
now you finally understand
that I have been mocking you! What woman,
even if deformed and vile, could take pleasure
in loving so monstrous and horrid a countenance?
Now you see that I have caught you! Remain here,
mocked, as you deserve to be, while I leave you.
Would to heaven that you were prey
of rabid bears and hungry wolves
so that I would never again encounter
your ugly face, which to me is
the most annoying and odious. (3.2.1488–96)

Overturning the male-authored outcome where the dishevelled naked nymph is saved at the last minute, Andreini leaves Filli in charge and Satiro at her mercy:

Filli, Filli, ove vai? Fermati, ascolta,
slegami almeno, acciò ch'io non diventi
de l'altre come te spietate ninfe
scherzo, favola e gioco.
Ohimè, che non può fare
femina risoluta d'ingannare?

Filli, Filli, where are you going? Stop, listen,
at least untie me so that I do not become
a joke, a tale, and a game
for other pitiless nymphs like you!
Oh me, what can't a woman do
when she is resolved to deceive? (3.2.1498–1504)

Andreini's other major innovation occurs in the scenes where Ardelia falls in love with her own image. Although there is no record of who took this role, it is also a part for a virtuosa-celebrity and would have complemented the appearances of Andreini and Piissimi as part of Andreini's pro-feminist dramaturgy. Ardelia's reluctance to accept Uranio's advances turns into an inquiry about female beauty as a male construction. There are obvious echoes of Tasso's treatment of Silvia's gazing at her reflection in the water that Daphne and Tirsi discuss when they are trying to determine her innocence. Andreini reprises the scene with Ardelia, who first appears beside a spring, looking at the flowers and thinking about "tessere ai crini miei vaga ghirlanda" (weaving a pretty garland for my hair) (2.1.795), using it as a prelude to a much longer scene in act 4, where Ardelia is revealed gazing at herself as Silvia had done. Andreini has Ardelia share her experiences directly with the audience for greater theatrical impact. Emily Wilbourne treats a similar scene in a later play as full of linguistic clues that allow us to both hear and see the actress's embodied expressions of her sexual responses.[62] Thus, our voyeurism – rather than being reflected through Daphne and later Tirsi – is unmediated, as we watch and listen to Ardelia marvelling at her reflection as she bends down to drink from the spring. Her inability to communicate with her image awakens such longing that she is overwhelmed with a burning desire that escalates into gasps and sighs as she pleasures herself by making love to her image:

troppo a quest'occhi piaccion gli occhi miei,
e 'l proprio viso e 'l proprio seno e troppo,
ah finalmente, a me medesma piaccio:
e s'io vo' far vendetta
di chi m'offende, incrudelir conviemmi
contra me sola; oh sventurato amore!
. . .
ahimè, ahimè, che per maggior mia doglia
mentre piango il mio male, il pianto istesso
è del mio mal ministro,
poiché turbando l'acqua
mi toglie di goder di me medesma.

Too much these eyes please my eyes,
this face, this breast, too much;
in the end, I love myself!
So if I want to have revenge,
on the one who offends me, I must use cruelty
against myself; oh, unlucky love!
...
Alas, alas! [I see] that for my great suffering,
while I cry over my misfortune, the weeping itself
is the cause of my distress –
because disturbing the water
deprives me of the pleasure of myself! (4.4. 2576–90)

If there is a certain comic self-mockery built in to Ardelia's love for her own beauty, what Doglio referred to as her doomed "lesbian passion,"[63] this scene also stands as an interrogation of female beauty being more than a lure for male desire. Beyond the Narcissus myth, Ardelia also plays her own Echo, responding to her beauty with lust and passion that continues to consume her until the end of the play, when Uranio wins her only by reminding her of the fleeting nature of her beauty.

In act 5, when all the lovers have been taught their lessons and abandoned their blind attractions, they come before Venus to celebrate her rule, paired up in sanctioned consensual unions that have been interpreted as Andreini's advocating an end to the male sexual freedom that Tasso expounds in *Aminta.*[64] On the other hand, since she has shaped the pastoral form to give Filli and Mirtilla and Ardelia strong voices to express their own desires and to confront male sexual violence, *Mirtilla* still reads as a witty exposé of pastoral sexual politics and a celebration of sexual passion, which the wise shepherd Coridone describes. More frank in its praise of reciprocal lovemaking than other female-written pastorals, *Mirtilla's* sophisticated pro-feminist sentiments bring Andreini alive as both a performer and a playwright of note.

La pazzia

The celebrity status of Andreini and the Gelosi is confirmed by their presence at the wedding gala held to celebrate the marriage of Grand Duke Ferdinando de' Medici to Cristina di Lorena in May 1589, just a year after *Mirtilla* was published. Apparently, the duke was sufficiently impressed by them that when he learned of their arrival in Florence he issued a last-minute invitation to contribute to the wedding festivities. According to the Bolognese envoy, Guiseppe Pavoni, "Sabbato, che fù alli sei, ritrovandosi in Firenze li Comici Gelosi con quelle due famosissime Donne la Vittoria & l'Isabella, parve al Gran Duca, che per trattenimento fosse buono far, che recitassero una Commedia à gusto loro" (Saturday, at six, on learning that the Gelosi were in Florence with their two most famous leading ladies Vittoria and Isabella, it seemed to the Grand Duke that it would be good to have them perform a comedy of their own choosing).[65] Specifically, he was endorsing their admission into the magnificently appointed Uffizi Grand Sala where he and his wedding party would preside over the spectacle, featuring the official dramatic entry *La pellegrina* (*The Female Pilgrim*) performed by

Gl'Intronati.[66] But he went beyond paying them the compliment that they could compete with the aristocratic theatre, by also arranging for their performances to be accompanied by the six fabulous *intermedi* designed for the occasion.[67]

Consistent with the fabled professional jealousy between Vittoria and Isabella as competing celebrities, the actresses apparently could not agree on which piece to perform: "Così vennero quasi, che à contesa le dette Donne fra di loro, perche la Vittoria voleva si recitasse la Cingana, & l'altra voleva si facesse la sua Pazzia, titolata la Pazzia d'Isabella, sendo, che la favorita della Vittoria è la Cingana, & la Pazzia, la favorita d'Isabella" (The said two ladies almost started a quarrel because Vittoria wanted to perform *La zingana* [*The Gypsy*], and the other one wanted to do *La pazzia* [*The Madness*], since Vittoria's favourite role is *The Gypsy* and *The Madness* is Isabella's). The decision they finally arrived at was that both plays would be performed on separate occasions; *The Gypsy* on 6 May and *The Madness* on 13 May) (lxxiii).[68] It is a measure of the public fame they had achieved that such information always preceded them as part of their mystique.[69] On this occasion, Vittoria's *La cingana*, probably based on Giglio Artemio Giancarli's famous play or a scenario derived from it, received this brief but highly complimentary praise: "et così recitarono detta Cingana con gli Intermedi istessi, che furono fatti alla Comedia grande: ma chi non hà sentitio la Vittoria contrafar la Cingana, non hà visto, ne sentito cosa rara, & maravigliosa, che certo di questa Comedia sono restati tutti sodisfatissimi" (and so they performed *La Cingana* with the same *intermedi* that were given with the great Comedy: but anyone who has never heard Vittoria's impersonation of the Cingana has missed out on seeing and hearing a rare and marvellous thing, for it is obvious that everyone has been utterly delighted by this Comedy) (lxxiii). Piissimi earned the delighted praise of the Grand Duke himself as he remarked on her "delle grandi inventioni recitate dalla Vittoria in persona della Cingana, che gli parve una meraviglia, non che intelletto di donna" (astounding skill in impersonating the gypsy, considering it something of a marvel, let alone the product of a woman's brain) (lxxiii).[70]

Pavoni's much fuller description of Andreini's performance of *La pazzia* a week later (on 13 or 15 May) began with this advance notice: "Un altra volta faranno poi *la Pazzia*, e toccarà à l'Isabella à far la Pazza: il valor della quale, & la leggiadria nell'esplicare i suoi concetti, non occorre hora esplicarlo, che è già noto, & manifesto, à tutta Italia le sue virtudi" (Another time they will do *La Pazzia* and it will be Isabella's turn to play the mad woman: the merit of which and the beauty with which she handles her conceits, it's not necessary to speak about now, given that her virtuosity is already known and proclaimed throughout Italy) (lxxiii). As a celebrity figure, Andreini was never completely eclipsed by her dishevelled mad persona. Thus, her outbursts of impassioned speech imitating the divine madness that Plato outlined in the *Phaedrus* would have highlighted the learning that she was famous for and underscored her genius in impersonating madness.[71] Unfortunately, the script is lost and we are dependent on Pavoni's plot summary, briefly outlined here.[72] The cause of her madness is a betrayal in love. Her father forbids Isabella to marry her lover Fileno, but her plans to elope with him are overheard by Flavio, who then abducts her by taking Fileno's place under cover of darkness. Stolen from her home by a man she does not love, she finds her chance for happiness destroyed, along with her reputation as a virtuous maiden. Such betrayal sets off her descent into madness:

> L'Isabella in tanto trovandosi ingannata dall'insidie di Flavio, ne sapendo pigliar rimedio al suo male, si diede del tutto in preda al dolore, & così vinta dalla passione, e lasciandosi superare alla rabbia, & al furore uscì fuori de se stessa, & come pazza se n'andava scorrendo per la Cittade …

> Meanwhile Isabella finding herself deceived by Flavio's machinations, not knowing where to find a remedy for the harm he had done, let herself fall prey completely to her sorrow, and thus conquered by passion, and letting herself be overcome with rage and fury, she went completely out of herself, and like a mad woman went running throughout the city … (lxxv)

In establishing with the audience that the main subject under discussion was the power of love – the neoplatonic theme resonating throughout the entire event in recognition of the nuptials of the ducal couple – Andreini was gesturing to the majesty of the occasion and taking her audience on a sacred journey of ascent and descent. Rojek notes that to replace the loss of religious faith, "celebrity culture has developed a variety of ceremonies of ascent and descent to symbolize honorific status and the loss of it."[73] Elevated above the crowd by her acknowledged fame, Andreini takes a risk in descending into madness, which enhances the sense of public intimacy experienced by her audience as they watch her in a dishevelled and semi-naked state running erratically around the stage. Stripped down before them, in much the same way that religious figures often appear, she had a similar magical effect on them as both "touchable and transcendent."[74] In addition, she showed her charismatic powers by "speaking in tongues" in a mangled mixture of all the languages of the foreign envoys in attendance,[75]

> fermando hor questo, & hora quello, e parlando hora in Spagnuolo, hora in Greco, hora in Italiano, & molti altri linguaggi, ma tutti fuor di proposito: & tra le altre cose si mise à parlar Francese, & à cantare certe canzonette pure alla Francese, che diedero tanto diletto all Serenissima Sposa, che maggiore non si potria esprimere.

> stopping first this person and then another, speaking now in Spanish, now in Greek, now in Italian, and many other languages, but always without making any sense. And among other things, she began to speak French and to sing certain songs (also in French), which gave inexpressible pleasure to the Most Serene Bride. (lxxv)

Her invention of these language distortions marks her descent into insanity as she has lost her command of pure Tuscan and instead creates a strange new comic language through the clash of several foreign tongues that she mangles together. In mimicking the babble of different languages that were spoken all around her, she temporarily erased the linguistic barriers separating the guests and brought them together in a shared enchantment.[76] The effects on audience members, both Italian and foreign, seem to have been a mixture of awe and delight, especially in the case of the Grand Duchess Christina when Isabella ended by singing to her in French.[77]

When Andreini returned to the stage, her descent into madness took another turn, as she now appeared to disintegrate further by shifting in and out of her body to mimic the speech and gestures of each member of her company:[78]

> Si mise poi ad imitare li linguaggi di tutti li suoi Comici, come del Pantalone, del Gratiano, del Zanni, del Pedrolino, del Francatrippe, del Burattino, del Capitan Cardone, & della Franceschina tanto naturalmente, & con tanti dispropositi, che non è possible il poter con lingua narrare il valore, & la virtù di questa Donna.

> After that she started to imitate the dialects of all her fellow actors – Pantalone, Gratiano, Zanni, Pedrolino, Francatrippa, Burattino, Captain Car-

done, and Franceschina – so naturally and with so many absurdities, that words alone cannot describe the value and virtù of this woman. (lxxv)

As a true diva, having taken her audience to the extremities of her madness, she must ascend again as part of the ritual of redemption and transcendence. She regains her sanity by drinking a magic potion. She then offers an eloquent discourse on the transcendental powers of love, likely addressed (as were her earlier songs) to the bridal couple themselves.[79]

Finalmente per fintione d'arte Magica, con certa acque, che le furone date à bere, ritornò nel suo primo essere, & quivi con elegante, & dotto stile esplicando le passioni d'amore, & i travagli, che provano quelli, che si ritrovano in simil panie involti, se fece fine alla Commedia; mostrando nel recitar questa Pazzia il suo sano, e dotto intelletto; lasciando l'Isabella tal mormorio, & meraviglia ne gli ascoltatori, che mentre durerà il mondo, sempre sarà lodata la sua bella eloquenza, & valore.

Finally, by the art of Magic, she returned to her first self with the help of certain waters that she was given to drink and here in an elegant and learned style, explaining the passions and travails of love that all undergo who find themselves ensnared in similar nets, she ended the Comedy; demonstrating in the performance of her Madness her sane and learned intellect, Isabella left her audiences murmuring and marvelling so that as long as the world lasts, her beautiful eloquence and worthiness will always be praised. (lxxv)

If Pavoni's comments on the audience response are to be trusted, Andreini appears to have transfixed them by performing madness as a ritual of ascent, descent, and magical redemption. Her magic, in this case, offered in the form of the potion with its classical precedents, was also a symbol of her transformational powers. In performing the magical feat of restoring herself to sanity, she became part of the magic in the public perception. In this way, as part of the spillover effect, she came to be perceived as "a magical cultural colossus," as Pavoni's superlative comments suggest.[80]

Part 3: Celebrity Death and Posthumous Fame

In the last few years of her life, Andreini's status as "a magical cultural colossus" was in full operation as she won recognition in several public venues. *La Mirtilla* continued to be reprinted, and her *Rime* went to a second printing in Paris in 1603. For some of these crucial years, we have a record of her rise to fame in her correspondence with the Belgian humanist Eyricius Puteanus, professor of rhetoric at the Palatine School in Milan and a member of the Intenti, whose youthful devotion to her helped to solidify her reputation as an academician.[81] Her company was in great demand, and the documents indicate engagements back and forth between Mantua and Milan, in particular during 1601 and 1602, before the Gelosi went to the French court for a long engagement between 1602 and 1604. During their extended stay in France, the company moved back and forth between Fountainebleau and the Hôtel de Bourgogne in Paris, performing for both the court and the public.[82] Pierre Matthieu, the official historian of this period, comments on her great success in the French court:

> La bande d'Isabelle Andreini recita devant le Roy et la Reyne. C'estoit une femme Italienne scavante en poesie, qui n'avoit encores trouvé sa pareille en l'elegance, promptitude et facilité de toutes sortes de discours convenables à la scène. Si elle eust vescu en Grece au temps que la comedie estoit en vogue, on lui eust donné des statues, et eust recu sur le theatre autant de couronne de fleurs, comme le mauvais ioüeurs-y recevoient de coups de pierres.[83]

> Isabella Andreini's company performed for the King and Queen. She was an Italian woman learned in the art of poetry, whose equal has never been found in the elegance, ease, and facility she had in creating speeches for the stage. If she had lived in Greece when comedy flourished, she would have had statues made to her, and received crowns of flowers in the theatre, just as the bad actors received blows from stones.

Beyond the court, her popularity with the Parisian public also became part of the mythography:

> Elle feust veüe et escoutée avec un grand applaudissement, et la comedie utile aux moeurs, et souvent utile aux princes pour amuser le people, comme disoit un bouffon à l'empereur Auguste, estoit le charme des vaines pensees et le divertissement des inutiles actions de Paris.

> She was seen and heard with great applause, and provided theatre that

> was morally instructive and frequently found to be useful to the prince in keeping the public amused – as they say the Buffoon said to the Emperor Augustus [about the ability of comedy] to charm the idle thoughts and divert the Parisian crowds from their boredom.

Having achieved such recognition through her extended performance run in both Paris and at the court, Andreini became so firmly entrenched in the public imagination of the French that her sudden death in Lyon on her return voyage to Italy became an occasion for a state funeral and a great outpouring of public grief. Every detail connected with her tragic demise became part of the legend that circulated around her, as her family, fellow actors, and fans sought to preserve their connection with her by clinging to the remaining vestiges of her life and work. Even the royal letters written by Henry IV and Marie de' Medici that had failed to protect her became important relics for her family, followers, and biographers.[84] The stigmata associated with dying unexpectedly at the age of forty-two after making the difficult journey through the Alps from Paris, from complications giving birth to her eighth child, only seems to have enhanced her charismata, since the city of Lyon rallied around to give her the unprecedented honour of a state funeral:

> ed alla sua morte fu favorita dalla Communità di Lione di Francia d'Insegne e de mazzieri, e con doppieri da' signori Mercanti accompagnata: ed ebbe un bellissimo Epitafio scritto in bronzo, per memoria eternal, come ne fa fede il Signor Pietro Mattei istorico e Consigliere del Re Cristianissimo.[85]

> and at her death she was favoured by the Community of Lyons in France with its insignia and maces and accompanied with candles by the Merchants; and she was given a most beautiful Epitaph inscribed in bronze for eternal memory, as borne witness by Signor Pietro Mattei, historian and counselor of the most Christian King.

Francesco, as her chief mourner, fed the frenzy for personal details of her last moments after her body was interred in the chapel of the cathedral of Sainte-Croix. Her official epitaph formalized her passing: "D.O.M. ISABELLA ANDREINI Paduan Woman of great virtue. Honest ornament, wife; modest in adornment, eloquent of speech, fecund of mind, religious, pious, Muses' friend, and Theatre artist, lies here awaiting resurrection. Of a miscarriage died 10 June 1604, aged 42 years."[86]

But in a second informal version – "D.O.M. Dearest Wife, sweetest Isabella, your Francesco makes for you this monument: if it lacks gems, it does not lack tears, for with me all the citizens of Lyons wept. Let your body rest in the tomb, and your soul in heaven" – Francesco turned her tomb into a place of public mourning.[87] Isabella's death, like that of other celebrities, did not end her relationship with her followers, who continued to treat her relics as blessed. Rojek describes this worship of the celebrity's relics as resembling both rites of initiation and worship in shamanistic practices, where certain cultures believe that the bones of the dead possess the healing powers of *mana*.[88] Her grave site, according to Giovan Battista, became a place of pilgrimage, at which followers could acquire a commemorative medal to remember her by[89] (fig. 5.4): "ed ogni giorno, pellegrine genti non solo da così famosa città passando vanno (mercé loro) ad ononar il selpolcro di quella con preghiere e celebrala con lodi, ma cercano di quelle medaglie possedere" (and every day pilgrims passing [voluntarily] through this famous city not only go to honour her grave with prayers and celebrate her with praise, but also to seek for those medals).[90]

The medals, struck in bronze, gold, and silver, provided fans with their own personal relic of Isabella, who appears in effigy on both sides of the coin. Memorializing her as all-powerful, the coin represents her on one side in the guise of a Roman emperor and on the other as the goddess Fame herself, wearing a laurel crown and holding two trumpets, blowing the one held in her right hand and holding silent the one in her left. Still recognizably human in the imperial pose that has her name, profession, and date of death inscribed on it, she acquires godlike status on the other, which endows her with eternal fame. As magical objects that capture Isabella's transcendence, the coins acknowledge the tragedy of her death through the presence of the second idle trumpet that symbolizes her stigmata.

After Isabella's death, her husband Francesco gave up his life on the stage and swore to devote the rest of his life to her memory. In the theatrical dialogue he wrote to address his "defunta Fillide" in his pastoral role as Corinto, he vowed to bring her the glory and honour she deserved.[91] From this point on, the "rhetoric of authenticity" supporting her celebrity status is mediated through Francesco and Giovan Battista. The legend that Francesco and Isabella had been so much in love that he could not bear to go on the stage without her drew attention to her tragic absence and fed the public desire to reach out to her beyond the grave.[92] As her chief mourner, Francesco encouraged the cult worship

Figure 5.4. Commemorative medallion of Isabella Andreini. Paris, 1604. Both sides, 38 mm. Reproduced by permission from Bibliothèque nationale de France, Argent (Cabinet de France), 95 A 73 141–2.

of her entombed remains, addressing her dead body as the source of *mana* he so desires: "Ma ora, che tu se' rinchiusa dentro a freddo Sasso, avendo teco rinchiuse le Virtù tutte e le bell'opere, s'è talmente cangiato il mio Destino, ch'altro non mi rimane che la memoria d'averle vedute et amate" (But now that you are closed up in cold stone together with all your virtues and accomplishments, my lot is so changed that nothing remains to me but the memory of having seen and loved them). For him, her sepulchre is the only place he wants to be, "le mie ossa con le sue ossa, la mia cenere con la sua cenere" (my bones with her bones, my ashes with hers).[93]

Lettere

In 1607, three years after his wife's death, Francesco Andreini's *Lettere* appeared in print. The dedicatory letter (dated "Di Venezia, 14 marzo 1607") to Carlo Emanuele Duca di Savoia was signed by his "umilissima e divotissima serva Isabella Andreini," as if she were still alive.[94] The formal portrait that she had commissioned from Raffaello Sadeler (fig. 5.5) appeared in the frontispiece.

In it "she" describes her struggles to cheat death by "speaking" again from the printed page:

> Intenzion mia dunque fu di schermirmi quanto più io poteva della morte, ammaestrata così della Natura. Perciò non doverà parere strano ad alcuno, s'io ho mandato e se tuttavia mando ne le mani degli uomini gli scritti miei, perché ognuno desidera nataurαlmente d'avere in se stesso e nei suoi parti, se non perpetua, almen lunghissima vita.
>
> My intention then was to shield myself from death as much as I could, as nature teaches us. Thus it ought not to seem strange to anyone if I have sent and still send my writings into the hands of men, because everyone naturally wants to have for themselves and their labours, if not perpetual, at least very long life.[95]

For Francesco then, the *Lettere,* which he framed with two more letters from a grieving husband, were intended to bring her memory back to life. In "Della morte della moglie" (On the Death of His Wife) (*Lettere,* 266–8) he swears that he lives for nothing else but "darti nella sua memoria vita, e renditi certa, che l'oblio perderà per me il suo nome" (to give life to your memory and convince you that I will never forget you) (267).[96] His decision to publish her *Lettere* reflects his awareness that the

Figure 5.5. Portrait of Isabella Andreini, after the engraving by Raffaello Sadeler, 1602. Reproduced by permission from Musei Civici Padova, 3482.

letters would help to augment the literary reputation she had acquired with *La Mirtilla* and her *Rime*. Packaged to locate her in a culture that placed a high value on collections of *Lettere*,[97] her letters are different from most others of the period in their lack of shared personal information between the author and addressee.[98] Missing the names and dates of specific exchanges, they are reworked records of love scenes she had inserted into her stage performances and bear the traces of her "ghostly" presence.[99] Once turned into polished literary forms, they showed her ability, as she had claimed in her opening sonnet to the *Rime*, to move back and forth between stage and page and to shift with ease from male to female subject positions.

Francesco's publication of the *Lettere* indicates that he regarded Andreini's "hermaphroditic abilities" to speak beyond gender boundaries to fans of both sexes as a key element of her celebrity status. In fact, since "generic, fictionalized letters" came increasingly into vogue at the turn of the century, Andreini was at the forefront in responding to a changing market for a growing body of readers in search of epistolary models of all kinds.[100] In addition, the anonymity of her letters encourages the reader to imagine that he or she is the one for whom the letter is intended. Andreini, as the implied sender, would thus be able to speak directly to her readers on the most intimate matters relating to love. In this way the volume recreates the sense of the "public intimacy" and "shared experience" that her performances had once brought.

Andreini invites her readers to interact with the sender of her letters in "Delle lettere che si scrivano" (On the Letters That We Write) (*Lettere*, 42–3), when the young woman, sequestered in a country villa, writes to her lover about how much happier she would be "se'n vece di legger la vostra lettera havessi udita la vostra voce" (if instead of reading your letter I might have heard your voice). Anyone can identify with the young woman in wanting to "hear" the letter as if it were being spoken aloud. Such a direct appeal invites the readers to experience the letters as if they were providing the response, even if their voices are never directly heard. In this way the letter form, with its implied but silent addressee, resembles the relationship between the actor and the audience at a stage performance. For early modern audience members, eager to share in the refined sentiments of Bembist court culture, hearing such passionate discourses on the powers of love spoken by Andreini would resonate in a personal way.[101] A few lines from "Della forza d'Amore" (On the Power of Love) (*Lettere*, 36–8) show how desire can become palpable when it is fed by gazing on the beautiful beloved:

> Ma s'amore è possente, non meno è possente la vostra bellezza, poich'ella non men d'amore in ogni parte comanda, anzi, che la vostra bellezza è quella che sola può superar Amore, poich'egli nasce dalla bellezza d egli stesso non è altro che un desiderio di bello. (Marotti and Romei, *La commedia dell'arte,* 171–2)

> But if Love is powerful, your beauty is no less powerful, since it no less than Love rules everywhere, indeed your beauty is the only thing that can exceed Love, since he was born from beauty and is himself nothing other than the desire for beauty.

The *Lettere* memorialize Andreini in performance, but also record her compositional techniques in speaking about love and the emotional and philosophical questions it raises. Her fictionalized treatment telling lovers how they might respond to all kinds of situations they face (from falling in love to dealing with rejection, jealousy, desperation, and so on) provided readers with models of witty exchanges that they could apply to their own lives. As the first of its kind to speak about love from both male and female positions, the collection includes many letters exploring emotional states as they affected both sender and addressee, with titles such as "In Praise of Love," "Against Love," "Desperation," "Conversations between Lovers," and "Being Far Away." In providing a blueprint for exploring the new role that romantic love was supposed to play in equalizing male-female relationships, Andreini's letters give women, whose voices had been traditionally silenced, a chance to enter into the exchange.[102] In so doing, the letters open up opportunities for contesting conventional attitudes towards the female sex and showing that women were just as capable of witty repartee. Thus, in a highly codified treatment of the topic "Della pudicizia della donna" (On Modesty in Women) (*Lettere,* 139–40), the female speaker responds to her suitor's letter by telling him "a me sarebbe impossibile soddisfar al vostro desiderio, senza preguidizio della mia fama, il che me sarebbe con ragion più della morte acerbo, perché sol vive reputo quelle donne, delle quali è salva la pudicizia" (it would be impossible for me to satisfy your desire without prejudice to my reputation, which [losing] would rightly be more bitter than death for me, because I think that the lives of women are protected only by their modesty) (139). But when she launches into a long list of precautions a woman needs to take to avoid falling into lascivious thoughts, Andreini's "speaker" reveals that she is fighting off such feelings herself.

> Per vivere dunque eternamente al dispetto dell'istessa morte, bisogna usar ogni arte, ogni ingegno, et ogni forza, per non sommergersi nel pericoloso mare de gli indegni, vani, e lascivi pensieri d'Amore, sotto la tirannia di cui tante infelici piangon le loro sventure.

> Then in order to stay alive in the face of this same death, it is necessary to use every art, every wile, every force, in order not to sink yourself in the perilous sea of shameful, vain and lascivious thoughts of Love, under whose tyranny so many unhappy souls cry over their misadventures. (139)

The playful wit on both sides is captured in many of the letters, which show abrupt shifts in the argument as they move from one emotional state to its opposite. An example from "Della disperazione" (On Desperation) (*Lettere,* 22–3) begins with the male "I" paying lip service to his unfaithful love, but moves into his recognition that she is not worth it:

> In virtù di quella fede con la quale (infedelissima donna) v'ho gran tempo amata, credei così fermamente al vostro mentito amore, che mi parea che voi nelle mie proprie pene vi struggeste, onde molte volte m'ingegnai di chiuder il mio dolor nel seno per non vedervi turbata; ma ora conosco che gli atti vostri, a guisa del cuore, furono simulati e finti. (Marotti and Romei, *La commedia dell'arte,* 169)

> By virtue of that faith, with which (unfaithful woman) I have so long loved you, I believed so strongly in your lying love, that it seemed to me, that you shared in my terrible suffering; thus many times I cunningly hid my love painfully away in my breast, so that it wouldn't upset you; but now I know that your acts, like your heart, were fake and false.

On the other hand, in another letter, "Delle lodi feminile" (In Praise of the Feminine) (*Lettere,* 229–30), the lover begins with a lament about his suffering but then launches into a full-blown neoplatonic tribute to his beloved:

> Ma che parl'io? chi può aggiunger all'infinito? Prima che voi veniste ad arrichir il Mondo del vostro bellisimo sembiante: che cosa era bellezza? ella altro non era, che un nome senza affetto, un sogno de gli amanti, un disegno, del quale voi siete l'opera, overo un'ombra della quale voi siete il

> corpo, onde bisogna conchiudere, che ciò, ch' è bello in voi, e ciò che non è in voi, non è bello, per la qual cosa io conosco, che tanto meriterei biasmo non amandovi, quanto merito lode servendovi, dunque voglio amarvi, e servirvi, mentre che averò vita; volendo il contrario, non potrei, perché nacqui per amarvi.
>
> But what am I saying? Who can add to the infinite? Before you came to enrich the world with your beautiful image: what was beauty? It was nothing but a name without feeling, a lovers' dream, a model of which you are the work, or else a shadow of which you are the body, from which it is necessary to conclude, that beauty is in you, and that what is not in you is not beauty. From this I know how much censure I would deserve for not loving and serving you as long as I am alive. Wishing otherwise is not possible because I was born to love you. (230)

The *Lettere* achieved Francesco's purpose of keeping her memory alive and providing a record of her pro-feminist side. I will mention three examples here that use specific situations to comment on ways in which women are mistreated in the society. The first, "Biasimo de i vecchi innamorati" (A Cursing of Old Male Lovers) (*Lettere,* 35–6) contains a list of the man's repulsive attributes and a warning to him to stay away from women altogether:

> Com'è possible che, nella vostra età cadente, non vi siate vergognato di mettervi all'impresa d'amar donna tanto dall'esser vostro dissimile? Com'è possible che non abbiate scorto che a quella fronte rugosa, a quel ciglio irsuto ed a quella faccia pallida poco, anzi nulla, si convien amore? (Marotti and Romei, *La commedia dell'arte,* 170–1)
>
> How is it possible that in your declining years, you're not ashamed to be setting out to make love to a woman who is so much your opposite? How is it possible that you don't know that in this wrinkled forehead, these bristling brows, this colourless face, there is little, rather nothing, suited to a lover?

The second example, "Dei pensieri onesti di giovanetta da marito" (On the Honest Thoughts of a Young Marriageable Woman) (*Lettere* 223–5), takes up the discourse on marriage and its evils from the point of view of the young woman forced to marry against her will.[103] While she moans about every disgusting detail regarding her bridegroom to build the comedic effect, she also opens up a space in the discourse around unwanted marriage, in a manner that considers what it means to be female:

> Ohimè, che l'esser donna, e non altro, è cagione de' miei dolori. O sesso calamitoso, e misero, sesso pieno d'affani, e di tormenti, sesso noioso a te medesimo, non che ad altrui. Oh non foss'io mai nata, o se pur nascer doveva (ch' essendo nata pur troppo i' dovea nascere) foss'io nata o sterpo, o sasso falso. Pensando di dovermi accompagnare con un'uomo pieno di mancamenti, per la soverchia doglia, sento scoppiarmi il cuore.

> Alas, to be a woman and not otherwise is the cause of my suffering. O calamitous and wretched sex, sex full of worries and torments, the sex that is annoying not only to others but to you yourself. Oh that I had never been born, or if I had to be born (since unfortunately being born means that I had to be born) that I had been born a stick or a rock. Thinking of having to be partnered with a man who lacks everything, I feel as if my heart is breaking from the overwhelming pain. (*Lettere*, 224)

The third and most important example, "Del nascimento della donna" (On the Birth of a Woman) (*Lettere*, 30–3),[104] is addressed to a man to chide him for expressing his disappointment on the birth of his daughter.[105] An eloquent discourse that defends the female sex, it exposes the paradoxes underlying the ideological biases against women, often with bitter irony.

> Quasi che per esser tale, ella non sia vostra carne, vostro sangue e vostr'ossa, non men di quello che sarebbe stato un maschio, et è possible che voi, che siete uomo di tanta esperienza, non vogliate pigliar con allegrezza d'animo quell che vi manda Iddio sapientissimo, Facitor delle cose?

> Almost as if by being such, she was not your flesh, your blood and your bones, as much as a son would be; and is it possible that a man of such great experience as you would not want to accept with a joyful heart that which is sent to you by God the most wise, Maker of all things? (Stortoni and Prentice Lillie, *Women Poets*, 226–7)

After setting up the standard arguments claiming that it is much easier to raise daughters because of their obedient and docile natures, she turns the argument into a catalogue of the abuses such apparent acquiescence masks. In a series of rhetorical questions implying that they had little choice, she lists the numbers of girls who "senz'alcuna replica si rinchiudono per sempre tra solitarie mura?" (lock themselves up forever within solitary walls without protest?); who "sopporre il collo al giogo maritale?" (submit their necks to the marital yoke in order not to displease others?); who "con quanta pazienza sopportano poi la maggior parte de' defetti insopportabili de i mariti?" (with what patience later bear the greatest part of the unbearable faults of their husbands?) (Stortoni and Prentice Lillie, *Women Poets,* 228–9). In this powerful example, Andreini shows her pro-feminist stance, aligning herself with those who took the pro-woman side in the debates on the "woman question" raging at the time. Her concluding arguments mention the long list of famous women from history and mythology whose outstanding examples had became part of the proof that women were exceptional.[106]

Fragmenti di alcune scritture della Signora Isabella Andreini

In 1620, Francesco published a collection of Isabella's stage dialogues, dedicated "alla felice memoria d'Isabella comica, ed Accademica Intenta, mia moglie: delle quale m'è parso servirmene a gloria sua, per non lasciarle in poter della fortuna" (to the blessed memory of my wife Isabella, actor, and member of the Accademia Intenta; with which it seems to me I can serve her glory by not leaving them in the hands of fate).[107] He also implies that they will allow her to "speak" through him – "che i morti sono quelli che fanno parlar i vivi" (that it is the dead who make the living speak) (10) – and in some sense bring her to life again. Francesco's project proved successful in that the thirty-one *contrasti* (dialogues) in the *Fragmenti* enrich our knowledge of Andreini's stage performances immeasurably. Typical of the kinds of scenes that the *innamorati* would have inserted into their trysts with each other, they provide fictional models for a range of situations that lovers might encounter and, while they repeat the same themes found in the *Lettere* and sometimes the same words, are full-fledged dialogues requiring equal participation from the male and female characters partnered in each of them. Formalized to the extent that a male and female with different classical names present each dialogue, they were likely written and performed by Andreini during her years with the Gelosi. They address a range of questions about love similar to those found in the *Lettere,* but in this case set up the sparring pair to take opposite sides on various topics: "Sopra la febre amorose" (On Love's Fever); "Fingere d'amar una, e amare un' altra" (Pretending to Love Someone While Loving Another); "Sopra le morti d'Amore" (On Those Who Died of Love); and "Sopra le passioni dell'odio e dell'amore" (On the Passions of Hatred and Love). Full of rapid-fire verbal exchanges and eloquent rhetorical flourishes, they stylized the lovers' interactions and intensified the spectators' pleasure in watching and listening to them fight each other for ascendancy. Most important, they allowed the female characters the rare opportunity to show themselves as equally passionate in their desires and often superior in their wit. Andreini's staging of the dialogues uses the intimacy of their verbal exchanges to suggest the full range of physical passion it evokes for the spectator watching the give-and-take of the exchange. In the examples below, I have included enough dialogue to show how carefully Andreini builds the contrasting arguments as each character tries to make the case for his or her side.

For example, the dialogue between Attilio and Diotima in "Amoroso Contrasto: sopra la dignità de gli amanti" (Lovers' Quarrel: Over the Worthiness of Lovers) (*Fragmenti,* 11–16) debates whether his "active" love for her is better than her "passive" love for him. Whether or not he is prostrate at her feet when he is speaking these lines, the situation has been set up for him to actively pursue her, which he does, with his words and whatever actions they suggested:

> ATTIL: In questo il mio parere è contrario à quello di V.S. & credo quanto à me, che sia migliore: Udite la ragione: tutte le cose agenti son più degne de le patienti, l'amante in amore è l'agente, e l'amata la patiente, dunque l'amante è più degno dell'amata.

> ATTIL: On this matter my opinion is the opposite to that of Your Ladyship and I am convinced that it is much better: Hear the reason: Everything that is active is better than everything that is passive. The lover in love is active, and the beloved is passive, therefore the lover is more worthy than the beloved.

Later, Diotima, having fended him off for so long, inverts the active-passive argument and takes control by her superior wit:

> DIOT: ... anzi al contrario vi dico, che l'amata è l'agente, & l'amante il patiente. E si come non è dubbio, ch' è più nobilissimo quegli, che move, che quello ch' è mosso, cosi non è dubbio, che l'amata è quella che move e genera l'amore nell'animo dell'amante.

DIOT: ... I'm telling you that it's the opposite, that the beloved is active and the lover is passive. And since there is no question that the noblest of all is the person who acts rather that the one who is acted upon; then there is no question that the beloved is the one who acts and arouses the love in the mind of the lover. (15)

Now the dominant lover, she engineers their final moments of a mutual exchange of love where it flows freely between them and makes them both active and passive, and one and the same.

In an example wherein the lovers' physicality is central to the debate, the lovers Curio and Nicostrata explore the implications of having exchanged souls. In "Sopra il cambio dell'Anime" (On the Exchange of Souls) (*Fragmenti*, 54–8), they find themselves wondering if they have also exchanged their sexual identities:

NIC: Comincio à poco, à poco à capire, & intendere queste dolci tramutazione dell'anime innamorate: Ora se l'anime sono quelle che informano i corpi, io vengo con voi à far un grandissimo guadagno; poiche di donna, ch'io era sono uomo diventata nello scambiar dell'anime, & voi siete diventato donna per l'istessa cagione, ond'io non più Nicostrata, ma Curio sono, & voi non più Curio, ma Nicostata siete.

NIC: I'm beginning to understand little by little and to realize that sweet transmutation of the lovers' souls: now if the souls are those that inform the bodies, I stand to gain tremendously from you: since from the woman that I was, I have become a man in the exchange of souls, and you have become a woman for the same reason, so that I am not Nicostrata any longer, but I am Curio, and you are not Curio any more, but Nicostrata. (55)

They realize that if this is truly the state of affairs, they won't be able to have sex because Nicostrata will be missing Curio's sexual organ – "Ma à V.S. manca quello che fà Curio esser Curio" (But Your Ladyship is missing what makes Curio Curio) – and they begin to consider the importance of their bodies rather than their souls. As Nicostrata describes what lovers really do, she also cues the passionate physical exchange taking place:

NIC: ... Quindi avviene, che gli amanti consumano il più del tempo nel badare con gli occhi, e con gli orecchi intorno all'amata, e rare volte la mente in loro si raccoglie, vagando spesso per gli occhi, e per gli orecchi, come ora facciamo noi, spendendo il tempo in parole, e nel rimirarsi l'un l'altro.

NIC: ... So it happens, that lovers spend most of the time paying attention to the beloved with their eyes and ears, and only rarely concentrating their minds, often roaming with their eyes and ears, as we are doing now, passing the time in talking and in beholding each another. (56)

Whether an actual stage direction or not, the dialogue ends with the promise of the physical satisfaction that they both want, having learned their lesson, as Curio sums it up, that "ognuno di noi rimanga con l'anima, con lo spirito, e col corpo suo, accioche meglio si possa sodisfare à gli amorosi nostri desiderii" (each of us keeps our own souls, spirits, and bodies so that we can better satisfy our loving desires) (56).

As a final example, "Amoroso contrasto sopra la commedia" (Lovers' Dialogue on Comedy) (*Fragmenti,* 58–64) is unusual in its inclusion of theatrical theory as part of the lovers' quarrel. I include it because it is likely that the role of Ersilia was written and performed by Andreini to tease her spectators with her star presence and insider knowledge of dramatic genres. Ersilia shows her hand at the beginning when she persuades Diomede, who is attending the performances of a visiting troupe, to admit to his fascination with the actresses:

ERSIL: Credo che il vostro maggiore diletto sia nel veder quelle signore comiche, le quali intendo esser molto belle e graziose.

DIOM: La natura non è stata avara nel dar loro quelle parti che più a donna convengonsi.

ERSIL: E poi intendo che vanno riccamente vestite, che suol essere di grande accrescimento alla bellezza feminile.

DIOM: Così è veramente.

ERSIL: I believe that your greatest pleasure comes from seeing the lady actresses whom I understand are very beautiful and agreeable.

DIOM: Nature hasn't been stingy in giving them those parts that suit a woman.

ERSIL: Besides I believe that they go about richly dressed which usually is a great enhancement to feminine beauty.

DIOM: That's true.

Having made her case, she issues the warning that actresses are fickle:[108]

ERSIL: Guardate pur, signor Diomede, a non v'innamorar di qualcuna di loro, perché nella loro dipartenza sentirete poi grandissimo dolore, come intendo esser intervenuto a degli altri della nostra città. (Marotti and Romei, *La commedia dell'arte,* 203)

ERSIL: Then take care, Signor Diomede, not to fall in love with one of them, because at their departure you will feel the worst pain, as I understand has happened to others in our city.

Determined to battle Diomede at every turn, Ersilia argues with him over the rules for titling a comedy, expounding on Aristotle's *Poetics* as proof that "il titolo si debbe pigliare dal nome della persona principale, intorno la quale è il suggetto di tutta la comedia" (the title must take its name from the leading character on whom the whole subject of the comedy is centred) (204). The couple then fall into sparring about the rules for writing a good comedy and whether or not Diomede is up to the task. Ultimately the debate turns into a dispute about whether his writing is good enough to impress her:

ERSIL: Tentate, tentate signor Diomede, come gli altri poeti fanno, o col poema comico, o col tragico, o con l'eroico componendo, far che questa bramata fonte getti per voi qualche soave stilla d'acqua, per rinfrescarvi l'amorosa ardura.

ERSIL: Try, Try, Signor Diomede, as the other poets do whether composing comic, tragic or heroic poems, so that this longed-for fountain may shower you with some sweet drop of water to cool your amorous passion. (205)

This prompts Diomede to admit his intention to write a play with her as the central character and have her fall in love with him:

DIOM: Io voleva, tra l'altre mie composizioni, comporre ancora una comedia ed intitolarla l'*Ersilia* dal nome vostro, essendo voi la persona principale dell'amorosa mia favola, sopra della quale doveva cadere la peripezia o tramutamento, e la ricognizione del amor mio.

> DIOM: I would still like among my other compositions to compose a comedy and title it with your name, *Ersilia,* since you are the leading amorous character in my story, on whom must fall the peripetia or transformation and the recognition of my love. (205)

The debate wraps up with a battle over the play's title. Diomede proposes *L'innamorata Ersilia,* as proof that he has made her fall in love with him. She claims the victory with the closing line, "Intitolatela pure: *Lo sventurato Diomede,* che sarà meglio" (Call it *Unlucky Diomede* instead, that will be better) (206), indicating that she will never submit.

Coda

Francesco's publication of Andreini's *Lettere* and *Fragmenti* was of central importance in keeping her memory alive and in verifying her celebrity status and enduring accomplishments. Together with their son Giovan Battista, the Andreini family established themselves as a theatrical dynasty. A sign of the great esteem they had achieved is captured in the fresco that was painted of the family in 1611 by the artist Bernardino Poccetti for the cloister of Santissima Annunziata in Florence (fig. 5.6).[109]

The fresco features life-size portraits of Francesco on one side and Giovan Battista on the other in the foreground, each dressed in the rich robes of courtiers and posing with heads bowed. They are shown in the company of many members of the Medici court, who occupy the background of the picture. In the right middle ground, surrounded by the ladies of the court, is the figure of the dead Isabella, who appears in profile with an imperial hairstyle similar to that on her commemorative coin. Illuminated somewhat more than the figures near her, she dispenses her mystical *mana* to all around her, reminding the viewer of her sacred place in the trinity of her famous family.[110]

I have presented an overview of the life and works of Isabella Andreini to establish "the rhetoric of authenticity" on which her ascent to diva status was based. My consideration of contemporary Italian and Anglo-American scholarship reflects on this rhetoric and the suspicion with which it has been regarded. While more traditional scholars tend to query the unqualified praise she received, feminist scholars seek to reclaim her as an innovative artist distinguished by her unique "hermaphroditic register." My coverage of her rise to diva status brings her to life as a living-and-breathing mortal who actively cultivated her

Figure 5.6. Fresco of Isabella, Francesco, and Giovan Battista amid Medici court. Bernardino Barbatelli Poccetti, Santissima Annunziata, Florence, 1611.

relationship with the public. As such, her achievements have been re-examined to foreground ways in which the records give us access to her subjective voice. While this is a somewhat speculative task, given that we do not know for sure how much of her written work was actually used in her stage performance, her career trajectory is impressive. What caps her international diva status is the fame accorded to her in death and the preservation of her memory in the posthumous publications of her writings for the stage found in the *Lettere* and *Fragmenti*.

Chapter Six

Conclusion

In 1625, when Giovan Battista Andreini proclaimed in *La ferza* that the most marvellous feature of the commedia dell'arte was the miraculous presence of the actresses, they had been established members of the companies for over sixty years.[1] As I traced their status on the stage from their earliest appearances on the mountebank stages to their achieving the status of revered divas, my goal has been to look at the ways in which actresses' stage performances commented on the formation of early modern female sexual identities. As noted above, these identities were shaped on the commedia dell'arte stage in response to the erotic desires of the male spectators. Because the arrival of actresses on the professional stage was connected to the rise of market capitalism, and the need to sell a theatrical product, I have deployed various theories of the fetish to explain their appeal. Using feminist interpretations of fetishism, I have sought evidence of the ways in which actresses taking female roles had to actively engage in improvising their responses to the situations in which they found themselves and in the process could articulate their own subject positions as fetishized objects. Because the commedia dell'arte implicates the spectator in shaping the action, the actresses were in a position to show the spectator what kind of choices were available to them. As I have shown, the actresses embodying the roles of the maidservant, *prima* and *seconda donna,* and transvestite heroine acquired the self-knowledge to speak and act with agency in their performances. So at least in the fictional world of the stage, actresses were positioned to reflect back their desires to their audiences.

In particular, the gifted stratum of actresses who had strong connections to the honest courtesan class acquired the status of role-icons.

Breaking the taboo against the public appearance of women, they attracted large audiences who were eager to see them perform in the beautiful, often revealing clothing worn by the court ladies they impersonated in the *prima donna* roles. Known by their first names, or the names of the characters they played, they gave an "illusion of availability" to the public who flocked to see commedia dell'arte performances. As we have seen from the records of the performances of Flaminia of Rome and Vincenza Armani from 1568 in Mantua, all the conditions that Roach lists as signs of celebrity are present. In addition to the "public intimacy" of being known on a first-name basis, their fans also "shared vicariously" in the theatrical experience. Most important, both this first generation of great actresses and the second, Piissimi and Andreini, all exhibited "the It-effect: the personality-driven mass attraction" that is part of their "multi-faceted genius."[2]

The fame accorded to the commedia dell'arte actresses derives from their exceptionality as female artists. It fits into the category that Rojek describes as *achieved* celebrity that is based on the "perceived accomplishments of the individual in open competition."[3] The actresses, as we have seen, were always pitted against each other in well-publicized competitions. The virtuosity that their roles required on stage, where they had to display their talents as musicians, dancers, singers, and rhetoricians able to improvise in any situation, is well documented. Evidence that many of their spectators knew the level of skill involved in creating their performances can be found in the glowing praise showered on them in the many tributes they received. To understand what made female performers objects of worship, I have followed the thinking of the celebrity theorists who propose that their power to enchant derives from their artistic genius. Endowed by their audiences with the illusion of "absolute presence," which Quinn defines as a belief in their superhuman qualities, they become "magnets" of desire.[4]

As celebrities, the actresses were also the product of the commercial theatre and, as such, dependent on mobilizing public desire in order to keep audiences interested in returning. Rojek argues that celebrities are commodities who *humanize* desire, but at the same time are vulnerable to the constant need for change that the market demands. If the actresses mobilized the desires of the audience for the idealized Petrachan love object on stage, they were also aware that they were selling a product. In performing these roles, they enhanced their desirability by showing off their skills as multitalented artists who knew how to manipulate their audiences. Thus the actresses developed their professional skills as artists in response to the demands of their audiences. As Campbell has observed, their performances of the chaste, obedient, beloved gentlewoman were always qualified by their connection to their courtesan training, which emphasized their *sprezzatura*, eloquence, charm, musical skills, and abilities to flatter and deceive.[5]

As divas in charge of expressing their own desires and reflecting those of their audiences, they performed the female roles in ways that challenged female sexual identities. Alexander Doty observes that "divas ... are about troubling and breaking out of their 'proper' culturally assigned sex, gender, sexuality, class," and the early Italian divas challenged these categories especially when they took the transvestite heroine roles.[6] Taking these roles over from the all-male erudite theatre where young males had played them, the actresses were empowered to represent females who used their transvestite disguises to challenge male privilege and notions of sexual differences. Played self-reflexively, the transvestite roles showcased the actresses' skill as male impersonators and increased the range of desires experienced by their audiences for sexual liasions with both same- and opposite-sex partners.

Of the four great early actresses featured here, Flaminia, Armani, Piissimi, and Andreini, Andreini has been given the most attention. If we follow Dyer's dictum that a star's charisma can only be accorded when the public has knowledge of the star's offstage authentic existence, only Andreini has left sufficient evidence to fit the profile. Her range of accomplishments as poet, performer, *literata*, musician, playwright, and author, and the attention that was devoted to establishing her reputation, through both her own efforts and those of family members, gives us enough information to create a rhetoric of authenticity around her. Finally, the stardom she achieved as a role-icon led to her immortalization after death. Her fame was such that her name became synonymous with the *prima donna* role. Her youth and exquisite beauty are suggested by a Carnavalet portrait (fig. 6.1) that for many centuries was thought to be of her. The painting is now known to depict the Gelosi from a much earlier period before Andreini toured there. However, the speculation has persisted that it is she.[7] Since the portrait also spawned many variations over time, all featuring an Italian actress touring France with her company, we know that this image remained in circulation long after her death, as a sign that she lived on in effigy. In the centuries to come, both images and tributes kept her memory alive. In one of the many sonnets written to her memory, Giovanni Battista Marino acknowledges her divine gifts:

Figure 6.1. *Italian Comedians on Stage*. Oil on canvas, circle of Ambrose I Francken (anon French), 1570s. Reproduced by permission from SAEML Parisienne de Photographie © Musée Carnavalet / Roger-Violliet. All Rights Reserved.

Piangete, orbi Teatri: invan s'attende
Più la vostra tra voi bella Sirena
Ella orecchio mortal, vista terrena
Sdegna, e colà donde pria scese, ascende.
Quivi, ACCESA d'amor, d'amor accende
L'eterno Amante; e ne l'empirea Scena,
Che d'angelici lumi è tutta piena,
Dolce canta, arde dolce e dolce splende.
Splendono or qui le vostre faci intanto,
Pompa a le belle esequie; e non più liete
Voci esprima di festa il vostro canto.
Piangete voi, voi che pietosi avete
Al suo tragico stil più volte pianto;
Il suo tragico caso, orbi piangete.

Cry empty Theatres: still waiting in vain among you
for your beautiful Siren
She disdains mortal ear and earthly sight
and there where she once descended, ascends.
Here, LIT with love, with love inflames
the eternal Lover; and on the Heavenly Stage
filled with angelic lights, she sings sweetly,
loves sweetly and shines sweetly.
Now here meanwhile your torches shine,
trappings for her beautiful funeral rites;
and no longer happy voices express your festive song.
Cry, you who have so often wept
sorrowfully at her tragic style;
Cry, blind theatres for her tragic fate. (*Lettere*)[8]

Marino's poem to Andreini could be read as a tribute to all great actresses of the period, whose presence changed early modern European theatre by making female performers a central attraction in the centuries to come.

Notes

Introduction

1 Kathleen M. Lea provides a list of seventy-three actresses who took the *innamorate* roles, and twenty-four *fantesche*. See appendix E in *Italian Popular Comedy*, 2:499–505.

2 I am referring to the professional stage, as there is evidence of a considerable presence of non-professional female performers from the 1500s on. See Brown and Parolin, *Women Players in England*.

3 While fetish theory can connote exclusive male agency connected to Freudian-Lacanian phallocentrism, I am working with feminist interpretations of the three main types of fetish as a means of exploring the marketing of female performers as erotic commodities. For an outline of the critical discourses on this topic, see Gamman and Makinen, *Female Fetishism*, 1–50.

4 During, *Modern Enchantments*, 1–2.

5 Pietz, "The Problem of the Fetish, I"; "The Problem of the Fetish, II"; "The Problem of the Fetish, IIIa."

6 The word *fetisso*, which came into usage to describe the emergence of the fetish, is derived "from the Portuguese *feitiço*, which in the late Middle Ages meant 'magical practice' or 'witchcraft' performed, often innocently, by the simple, ignorant classes. *Feitiço*, in turn, derived from the Latin adjective *facticius*, which originally meant 'manufactured'" ("Fetish, I," 5).

7 "Fetish, II," 24, 27, 29.

8 Gamman and Makinen, *Female Fetishism*, 34.

9 Stratton, *The Desirable Body*, 3.

10 Flaminio Scala, *Il teatro delle favole rappresentative*, vol. 1.

11 Ilya Parkins makes an important argument, which I have condensed here,

stressing how "the enormous critical potential of the concept of commodity fetish can offer insights both into the complexities of historical subjects, and the complexities of our own historical methodologies – our ways of conceptualizing the project of writing history." Understanding the fetish as a conceptual entity shifts our understanding of the relationship between materiality and agency and opens up the potential for "feminist historians to think materiality in productive ways, and to make connections between materiality and agency that will not only inform the history that is produced, but – perhaps more crucially, and perhaps more excitingly – how it is written" ("Notes on a Relationship," 90).

12 McCallum, *Object Lessons*, 45.

13 McCallum, *Object Lessons*, 47.

14 Female performers took over the *prima* and *seconda donna* roles on the professional stage, except in the Papal States, where they were forbidden to do so. Some male actors continued to play the maidservants' roles alongside female performers. But if this practice complicated the referencing to (or of) an actual female body, it did not necessarily cancel out the representation of the maidservant as consciously responding to her sexual objectification.

15 For ways to read plays to identify shared values promoted or queried by different characters, see McConachie, "Using the Concept of Cultural Hegemony," 37–58.

16 There is a large body of work dealing with celebrity culture. Some important studies are: Rojek, *Celebrity*; Marshall, *Celebrity and Power*; and Dyer, *Heavenly Bodies*.

17 The rationale for locating the modern concept of fame in the eighteenth century is based on the conviction "that celebrity is above all a media production" and that only in the eighteenth century did "an extensive apparatus for disseminating it emerged" (Luckhurst and Moody, *Theatre and Celebrity in Britain*, 3).

18 It should be noted that Roach acknowledges his Anglo-American bias and suggests that the definition of "it" in Renaissance Italy was probably Castiglione's *sprezzatura* (7).

19 For connections between performance and print, see Henke, *Performance and Literature in the Commedia dell' Arte*.

20 Roach, *It*, 3. This fascinating work has been extremely important to my project in these pages because it traces the rise of celebrity worship back to the late 1660s on the English stage, and thus makes connections with the arrival of professional actresses at that time, one hundred years after their appearance in Italy.

21 Roach, *It*, 3.
22 Roach, *It*, 29.
23 See States, "The Actor's Presence," 22–42. He discusses the collaborative mode as the second mode.
24 Bruce Wilshire's description of the ways in which our identities as persons are shaped through our identification with actors standing in for characters through whom we interpret the "world" – and the possibilities it offers for human interaction – has provided an underlying model for my readings of the scenarios. See his *Role Playing and Identity*, 23–5.
25 Roach, *It*, 3.
26 Roach, *It*, 12.
27 Rojek, *Celebrity*, 54.
28 Barthes, "The Face of Garbo," 56.
29 Rojek, *Celebrity*, 17–18.
30 Quinn, "Celebrity and the Semiotics of Acting." 156.
31 Gell, "The Technology of Enchantment," 51–2.
32 Gell, "The Technology of Enchantment," 48, 56–9. Gell's term "art object" can be applied to the actor's embodied performance.
33 Benjamin, "The Work of Art," 221–3.
34 Roach notes that the "it" effect is intensified "when a charismatic performer takes over the typifying marks of gender from the opposite sex" (*It*, 11).
35 Cesare Vecellio depicts the Venetian prostitute's common practice of wearing male breeches to signal her trade (*Habiti antichi*, qtd. in Lawner, *Lives of the Courtesans*, 20).
36 Lorraine Daston and Katharine Park note that female transvestite disguise was becoming increasingly associated with hermaphroditism, tribadism, and female presumption ("The Hermaphrodite," 430–1).
37 That is, the transvestite could be equally desirable whether male or female, which served the sexual fantasies of those seeking both same- and opposite-sex experiences.
38 Referencing the English stage, Ann Rosalind Jones and Peter Stallybrass propose that – in this period where costuming conceals missing body parts – gender itself was treated as a fetish ("Transvestism and the 'Body Beneath,'" 216–17).
39 Traub, "The (In)significance of 'Lesbian' Desire," 156.
40 Marshall comments: "In its simultaneous embodiment of media construction, audience construction, and the real, living and breathing human being, the celebrity sign negotiates the competing and contradictory signs of its own significance" (*Celebrity and Power*, xi).
41 Rojek, *Celebrity*, 14–15.

42 As Rojek sets it out, capitalism requires consumers to develop an abstract desire for commodities that can never be satisfied if the market is to keep expanding, and therefore is well served by celebrity figures who, as animate objects, embody desire in ways that allow for deeper levels of attachment and identification than inanimate objects do. As such, celebrities *humanize* desire (*Celebrity*, 189, original emphasis). It is interesting that Rojek's explanation of how desire is mobilized leads him back to psychoanalytic theory and the unconscious, referencing the process the male child undergoes when transferring his oedipal desire towards a replacement love object. Ultimately, Rojek believes that the ideology validating the supreme value of romantic love becomes the driving force behind societal desire.

1 The Early Female Peformer as Marketplace Fetish

1 These crucial documents are collected in Taviani, *La commedia dell'arte*. They remain for the most part untranslated into English. I have provided a sampling of translations throughout the book to make the information available for English readers and to augment those in Richards and Richards, *The Commedia dell'Arte*.
2 Molinari, "L'Arte," 67.
3 Henke, *Performance and Literature*, 6.
4 See Molinari, *Commedia*, 67–70, for a discussion of the complex meanings of the term *arte* and its references to both the profession and the technique.
5 Cocco, "Una compagnia comica nella prima metà del secolo XVI," 57–8. For a copy of this first existing contract, see Richards and Richards, *The Commedia dell'Arte*, 44–6.
6 Croce, "Intorno alla commedia dell'arte," 507–9. Unless otherwise noted all translations are mine.
7 Taviani and Schino, *Il segreto*; Tessari, *La commedia dell'arte nel Seicento* and *Commedia dell'arte*.
8 Ferrone, "La vendita del teatro," 35–72.
9 Tessari, *Commedia dell'arte*, 31–47.
10 Henke, "The Italian Mountebank," 2. This very informative article looks at a range of mountebanks of both genders who set up their stalls across the marketplaces of major Italian cities. It gives special insight into the *cerretani*, since this label was assigned to a whole class of legendary quack performers, known as unscrupulous thieves who could wring money and sympathy from audiences by parading their false illnesses and injuries as theatrical spectacles.

11 Tessari, *Commedia dell'arte*, 37, 40.
12 During, *Modern Enchantments*, 1.
13 Moryson, *Shakespeare's Europe*, 465.
14 Katritzky, "Italian Comedians," 246. For further discussion of the connection between Carnival and the commedia dell'arte, see Richards and Richards, *The Commedia dell'Arte*, 18, where they debate the inconclusiveness of the literary and iconographic evidence for an exact transfer between the masked Carnival figures and the characteristic commedia dell'arte masks, but concede the complexities of the interconnections between popular materials and improvised drama. See also Toschi, *Le origini del teatro italiano*, who examines the intersections of pagan, Christian, and popular fertility rituals performed at Carnival. His tracing of the underworld origins of the Zanni, Arlecchino, and Pulcinella masks and his insistence that the commedia dell'arte borrowed many performance traditions from Carnival in its improvised use of lazzi, acrobatics, burlesque, and obscenity bring to light the pagan antecedents of these kinds of performance that the post-Trentine church also condemned.
15 See Katritzky, *Women, Medicine and Theatre*, 61–85.
16 Procacci, *History of the Italian People*, 187. For further discussion, see Bossy, "The Counter-Reformation and the People of Catholic Europe." He argues that the aim of Tridentine reform was to enforce a uniform code of parochial practice.
17 Borromeo to Mons. Giambattista Castagna, Arcivescovo di Rossano, Nunzio apostolico in Spagna, 2 November 1571, in Taviani, *La commedia dell'arte*, 18.
18 Memorandum. "Memoriale di Monsignor Illustrissimo e Reverendissimo Cardinale di Santa Prassede Arcivescovo. Al suo diletto popolo della Città e Diocese di Milano," 1579, in Taviani, *La commedia dell'arte*, 24.
19 Bascapè, "Della Settuagesima," 8 January 1606, in Taviani, *La commedia dell'arte* , 61.
20 Borromeo to Cardinal Gabriello Paleotti, Arcivescovo di Bologna, July 1578, in Taviani, *La commedia dell'arte* , 23.
21 Baldesano, "Del fuggire li teatri e le vanità de gli spettacoli," in *Stimolo alle virtù*, 1592, in Taviani, *La commedia dell'arte*, 96, 99.
22 Pietz, "Fetish, I," 5.
23 Pietz, "Fetish, I," 6, 12.
24 Baldesano, "Del fuggire," in Taviani, *La commedia dell'arte*, 99.
25 Pietz, "Fetish, I," 13.
26 Seneca, "Sulla soppressione degli spettacoli Comici," 1597, in Taviani, *La commedia dell'arte*, 115–16.

27 Gori, *Trattato contro alle commedie lascive,* 1604, in Taviani, *La commedia dell'arte,* 141.

28 The post-Trentine church instituted a policy of censorship over play scripts and performances. After the Council of Trent, the church began to dissociate itself from what it now labelled profane and immoral. Although the Jesuits would reinstitute a strong theatrical tradition to buttress their intellectual and moral training, the baroque church was no longer at ease with physical representations of sacred subjects. A new definition of what was obscene would mark degrees of acceptability. There is a famous incident in which Cardinal Borromeo finally agreed to let the famous Confidenti troupe under the highly educated actor Adriano Valerini perform in Milan after they agreed to submit their scripts for advance approval. Nicolò Barbieri describes the incident in *La supplica discorso famigliare,* 86.

29 de Pineda, *Discorso del danno,* 1599, in Taviani, *La commedia dell'arte,* 121.

30 Cecchini, *Brevi discorsi,* 16. The date is based on a remark by Luigi Riccoboni, who is alleged to have taken it from Cecchini: "It was in the time of Flaminio Scala that women were introduced into the scene, that is, about 1560" (*L'Histoire du Théâtre Italien,* 42).

31 Ottonelli, "Is the desire for the actresses reason enough to allow their public appearance?" in Taviani, *La commedia dell'arte,* 356.

32 Re, "Comedianti a Roma nel secolo XVI," 291–300.

33 Taviani and Schino, *Il segreto,* 335.

34 Scott, "*La Virtu et la volupté,*" 153n9, quoting from Lacour, *Le premières actrices françaises,* 6.

35 See Scott, "In the Beginning," 59–100. This chapter, which begins with the anecdote above, covers the activities of both French and Italian actresses in France from 1545 to 1630.

36 Smith acknowledges that female mountebanks took speaking parts as well as walking the rope, dancing, singing, and playing the lute, but believes they were "too untrained to be given important places in the academic productions, either Latin or Italian" (*The Commedia dell'Arte,* 56–7). Rosamond Gilder refers to both street performers and aristocratic women appearing occasionally from about 1513 on (*Enter the Actress,* 49–58). Another performance that included female performers whose status is not entirely clear took place in 1548, when Italian actors staged Bibbiena's *La calandra* in Lyons for Henri II and Caterina de' Medici.

37 Grazzini, "Canto di Zanni e di Magnifichi," 53–4.

38 Garzoni, "De' comici e tragedie così auttori come recitatori, cioè de gli istrioni," in *La piazza universale,* 739–40; extract in Marotti and Romei, *La*

commedia dell'arte e la società barocca, 14; translation in Richards and Richards, *La Commedia dell'Arte*, 70.

39 Garzoni, "De' formatori di spettacoli in genere, e de' ceretani o ciurmatori massime," in *La piazza universal*, 745–7; extract in Marotti and Romei, *La commedia dell'arte*, 16.

40 D'Ancona, *Origini del teatro italiano*, 2:449. Katritzky suggests that this Angela may be Angela del Re, aged twelve when her father, Maphio del Re, was murdered in Rome in 1553 (*Women, Medicine and Theatre*, 20).

41 See Henke for translations of these two notices from the *Archivo di Stato di Firenze, Mediceo Principato*, 5140, cc. 452^{v}, 466^{v} ("The Italian Mountebank," Document G, 27).

42 Henke, "The Italian Mountebank," Document G, 27.

43 Ottonelli, "Do common actresses kill souls with acrobatics done in the public theatre?" in Taviani, *La commedia dell'arte*, 385.

44 Katritzky contends that the constant presence of a Zanni figure in trestle performances suggests that the masks and plots of the commedia dell'arte were not borrowed by the trestle performers but were always part of their tradition ("Was Commedia dell'Arte Performed by Mountebanks?" 104–125).

45 Katritzky suggests that "Bragetta" is probably a corruption of "Brighella: "le Braghetta (corriger en Brighella) Italien avec sa compagnie" ("Mountebanks, Mummers and Masqueraders, 1:29n41).

46 Katritzky, "Was Commedia Performed?" 117.

47 Katritzky, "Was Commedia Performed?" 114.

48 For an English dramatic treatment, see Ben Jonson's *Volpone*, in which Volpone offers a consummate impersonation of the Italian mountebank Scoto complete with "a tumbling whore." Scoto is so successful in his sales pitch of the miraculous cure-all product he is selling that Celia responds by throwing him her knotted handkerchief from the window where she watches (2.2).

49 Katritzky, "Was Commedia Performed?" 114.

50 Ottonelli, "In what way does the common actress help the earnings of the actors or charlatans?" in Taviani, *La commedia dell'arte*, 361; translation in Richards and Richards, *The Commedia dell'Arte*, 245.

51 William Eamon discusses the enormous attraction that "secrets," supposedly unique recipes or techniques, had for the sixteenth-century populace. In addition to their nostrums and the chapbooks describing their miraculous cures, he argues that the *ciarlatani* also promoted licentious behaviours to counter the restrictions being placed on the people by church and state ("The Secrets of Nature," 234–66).

52 Marx, *Capital,* 1:165.
53 Pietz, "Fetishism and Materialism," 146.
54 Henke describes "the undercurrent of sexual thrill" in mountebank performances, including the vast range of elixirs that promised to enhance sexual activities ("The Italian Mountebank," 8).
55 Pietz, "Limits of Theory," 146–7.
56 Ottonelli, "In what way?" in Taviani, *La commedia dell'arte,* 361; translation in Richards and Richards, *The Commedia dell'Arte,* 245.
57 Ottonelli, "In what way?" in Taviani, *La commedia dell'arte,* 361; translation in Richards and Richards, *The Commedia dell'Arte,* 245.
58 He describes the time he spent with a mountebank named il Monferino who suffered at the hands of the authorities, who accused him of necromancy (Barbieri, *La supplica,* 126).
59 Barbieri, "What is a buffoon?" *La supplica,* 26.
60 "Virtuosi" has a double meaning here, both of being gifted performers and of having good morals (Andreini, *La ferza,* 518–19).
61 Barbieri, *La supplica,* 37–42. In chapter 15, "What is the reason why people go to the theatre?" he asks, "How many find themselves going to the theatre only to see if the actresses are beautiful, how young and beautiful they are and how well they perform, how many commit the sin of lust?," 37-38. In chapter 16, "It isn't true that everyone comes to see the beautiful women," he insists that it is their skill as performers that brings the crowds. 39-40. In 17, "What damage those who condemn the theatre bring," he charges that it is lustful audience members who are at fault (40–42).
62 Barbieri, "It is more natural to have females play married women than to have boy actors cross-dress as women," *La supplica,* 122.
63 Ottonelli, "Is the difficulty of performing without the appearance of women sufficient reason for legalizing their presence?" in Taviani, *La commedia dell'arte,* 349.
64 "How much and in what ways does the appearance of the common actresses injure the soul?" in Taviani, *La commedia dell'arte,* 367, 369.
65 "If prostitutes are legal, couldn't we also accept the commercial actresses?" in Taviani, *La commedia dell'arte* , 441.
66 "Is the ultimate good sufficient reason to introduce women and amorous discourse in the public theatre?" in Taviani, *La commedia dell'arte,* 398, 400.
67 Barbieri discusses the complaints against women playing love scenes with men other than their husbands as proof that the critics don't understand the imitative nature of comedy (*La supplica,* 81).

68 Pedro Hurtado de Mendoza, *Dissertazioni scolastiche e morali*, 1631, in Taviani, *La commedia dell'arte*, 87.
69 Pedro Hurtado de Mendoza, *Dissertazioni scolastiche e morali*, 1631, in Taviani, *La commedia dell'arte*, 88–9; translation in Richards and Richards, *The Commedia dell'Arte*, 252.
70 Ottonelli, "Is it worse to use young men dressed as women in the theatre?" in Taviani, *La commedia dell'arte*, 395.
71 De Mendoza, *Dissertazioni*, in Taviani, *La commedia dell'arte*, 89.
72 Andreini, *La ferza*, in Marotti and Romei, *La commedia dell'arte*, 510.
73 Pietz, "Fetish, I," 8.

2 Pornographic Bawds, Courtesans, and Maidservants

1 Thomas Laqueur notes that "the sexual body haunts society and reminds us of its fragility. Modern laments that sex is used to sell are not about some accidental and transitory association of late capitalism. They are rooted in an *almost three-hundred-year-old* history of desire, corporeal and commercial" (my emphasis) ("Sexual Desire and the Market Economy, 214–15).
2 Ottonelli, "Is the powerful attraction that is born when a female appears a valid reason to consider her profitable?" in Taviani, *La commedia dell'arte*, 341.
3 "How much and in what ways do common actresses kill souls by appearing in the theatre?" in Taviani, *La commedia dell'arte*, 371–2.
4 Stratton, *The Desirable Body*, 32.
5 Sanuto, *I diarii*, 8:414.
6 Coryate, *Coryate's Crudities* 1:264.
7 Rosenthal, *The Honest Courtesan*, 21. However, she agrees with Guido Ruggiero's suggestion in *The Boundaries of Eros* (151–3) that the numbers of courtesans and prostitutes are exaggerated in tourist reports (258n2).
8 Moryson, *Shakespeare's Europe*, 409–10.
9 Moulton, *Before Pornography*, 15. His point is well taken in that he believes that the condemnation of pornography as morally wrong and misogynist ignores some of its historical context and occludes the representation of autonomous female sexuality in the early modern period.
10 Williams, *Hard Core*, 30; Brown, "A Feminist Interest in Pornography,"10.
11 Williams, *Hard Core*, 43.
12 Katritzky examines several early records that suggest that acrobats from mixed-gendered troupes "may have been *buffoni* whose repertoire included improvised plays" (*The Art of Commedia*, 63).

13 Bruni, "La fantesca grassa. Prologo," in "Prologhi di Domenico Bruni comico," 390.
14 Bruni, "La ruffiana. Prologo," in "Prologhi di Domenico Bruni comico," 423–4.
15 Katritzky mentions a 1569 record of the Bavarian court musician Lasso being sent to Italy to find and engage new players – both male and female – for commedia dell'arte performances. One popular form of entertainment she found was self-composed, one-man playlets starring "il magnifico, Zannj, Franceschina" (*The Art of Commedia*, 63).
16 Richards and Richards, *The Commedia dell'Arte*, 33.
17 Giovanni Dotoli outlines how its risky subject matter, its theatricality, and its infinite adaptability to public demands made it irresistible to the entire city ("La rivoluzione della commedia dell'arte," 35).
18 Clubb, "Theatregrams," 27. Also see Clubb, *Italian Drama in Shakespeare's Time*.
19 In these pages I use the Italian term *innamorata/e* to designate the female lover/s.
20 Clubb, "Theatregrams," 19–20.
21 The records indicate that some male actors – alongside their female counterparts –played the maidservant roles for some time. For references to male actors in female roles see Ademollo, who records that boys occasionally took the part of "Franceschina in comedy," even in public performances in the latter half of the Cinquecento (*I teatri di Roma*, xxii–iii). D'Ancona discusses the continuing use of male actors in female parts until the end of the sixteenth century, and in the Papal States until the nineteenth. He notes that Franceschina was played by Battista Amorevoli in 1584 and by Ottavio Bernardini in 1614 (*Origini*, 1:416–17). D'Ancona also references "Carlo who plays Franceschina" in a letter dated 1591 from Drusiano Martinelli to Captain Catrani at the Mantuan Court (*Origini*, 2:504–6). Kathleen M. Lea mentions a group of Paduan actors going to Rome in 1549 who engaged Francesco, a smith's son from Concarolo, to play the women's parts. She also notes that no women are mentioned in Ganassa's troop in 1572, or in the Neapolitan company in 1575 (*Italian Popular Comedy*, 1:115, drawing from Pastor, *Nuevos datos*). Lea also provides evidence that men were still playing the role of Franceschina in Spain, citing an incident in which Puertocamera, the Spanish authority, granted permission for a woman to play the role: "Si la Francesquina es la que yo vi en la posada del Señor Cardenal, no la tengo por muchacho y ansí podra representar" (If the Franceschina is the one I saw at Señor Cardenal's inn, I do not take her for a boy and thus she may play the role) (Pas-

tor, *Nuevos datos*, 21). This permission, granted in 1587 to Los confidentes italianos, was to permit two married actresses who were accompanying their husbands to act. Prohibitions in Spain in 1614 and 1641 against women playing men's roles and vice versa suggest that cross-gendered acting was still going on in the seventeenth century (D'Ancona, *Origini*, 1:276n1).

22 Stratton, *Desirable Body*, 3, 6.

23 Lacan, *Écrits*, 312.

24 "Clinical experience has shown us that this test of desire of the Other is decisive not in the sense that the subject learns by it whether or not he has a real phallus, but in the sense that he learns that the mother does not have it" (Lacan, *Écrits*, 289).

25 Lacan describes how the woman becomes the phallic fetish: "I am not saying that it is in order to be the phallus, that is to say, the signifier of the desire of the Other, that a woman will reject an essential part of femininity, namely all her attributes through masquerade. It is for that which she is not that she wishes to be desired as well as loved. But she finds the signifier of her own desire in the body of him to whom she addresses her demand for love. Perhaps it should not be forgotten that the organ that assumes this signifying function takes on the value of a fetish" (*Écrits*, 289–90).

26 Irigaray, "Women on the Market," 171, 175, 183.

27 Homi K. Bhabha notes that "within discourse, the fetish represents the simultaneous play between metaphor as substitution (masking absence and difference) and metonymy (which contiguously registers the perceived lack)" ("The Other Question," 74–5).

28 In *The Daughter's Seduction*, Jane Gallop argues that Freudian theories leave a place for the intrusion of the maid/governess/nurse into the Oedipal family circle (144), citing Cixous' apt labelling of the maid as "the hole in the social cell" (Cixous and Clément, *The Newly Born Woman*, 150).

29 Rosemary Hennessy, in discussing the connections between the emergence of commodity culture and the formation of new female sexual identities, also notes the corresponding elevation and devaluation of middle- and lower-class women (*Profit and Pleasure*, 197).

30 Troiano, *Dialoghi di Massimo Troiano*, ff. 146v–152v, in Pandolfi, *La commedia dell'arte*, 2:79–83; translation in Richards and Richards, *The Commedia dell'arte*, 49–52. Further citations of this work in Pandolfi and in Richards and Richards appear in the text.

31 Having the courtesan's role played by one of the noblemen guests keeps the event's focus very much on male relationships and highlights the treatment of women as objects to be used and exchanged.

32 Katritzky, *The Art of Commedia*, 52.

33 Scala, *Il teatro delle favole rappresentative*, ed. Marotti. I will use "(act, page)" references to the scenarios from Marotti's edition throughout the rest of the book; the translations that follow are my own unless otherwise indicated. Readers can also find many of these scenarios in Andrews, *The Commedia dell'Arte of Flaminio Scala*.

34 Freud, *Jokes*, 96.

35 Freud, *Jokes*, 97.

36 Freud, *Jokes*, 99.

37 Freud, *Jokes*, 100.

38 Freud, *Jokes*, 173.

39 Cook, "The Sign and Semblance of Her Honor," 75–103. I am indebted to Cook's application of Freud's theory of the joke in her text and have put it to the test in the Scala scenarios.

40 Scala does not specify which Boccaccian tale Graziano recites to the guests gathered at the country villa in act 1, 77, but it is close to the plot of the Seventh Day, Fifth Tale, in which a jealous husband guards the door only to have his wife admit her lover through the roof (Boccaccio, *The Decameron*, 542–50).

41 Beijer and Duchartre, *Recueil de plusieurs fragments des premières comédies italiennes*. For reprints of several woodcuts and engravings, see Duchartre, "Pictorial Supplement," 315–48.

42 Buckley, "Eloquent Action," 255–6.

43 Buckley, "Eloquent Action," 276.

44 The famous Harlequin, Tristano Martinelli, and other troupe members have been identified through their mannerisms and appearance. See Gambelli, *Arlecchino a Parigi*, 1.189–91.

45 Mastropasqua, "Lo spettacolo della Collezione Fossard,"91–125. In a later article, "Pantalone ridicola apparenza – Arlecchino comica presenza," Mastropasqua states that the order he had proposed was only one possible order, but that changes would not substantially alter the basic narrative structures that had been established.

46 See Katritzky, "The Recueil Fossard," for a discussion of the scholarly debate over establishing an order for a probable plotline; see also Katritzky, *The Art of Commedia*, 107–14.

47 "The Recueil Fossard," 105.

48 Katritzky references the four sets of continuous blocks of all of the five woodcuts in the consecutive order of the first five pictures of act 3 found at the Yale School of Drama, the Bodleian Library in Oxford, in Rome, and in Berlin (*The Art of Commedia*, 113).

49 Alba Ceccarelli Pellegrino sets out several questions about ways to read the images and the gestures and postures of the characters, and the accompanying text as part stage direction, part dialogue ("Gravures et légendes du Recueil Fossard," 129–59). I am indebted to both Mastropasqua's and Pellegrino's analyses of the complex theatrical meanings that emerge from the dialectic the images set in motion.

50 If the male actor Battista Amorevoli da Treviso, who was with the Confidenti in Paris in the 1580s, played the role, did he wear female prostheses? Gambelli notes that Beijer, struck by Francisquina's feminine appearance, insisted that the actress Silvia Roncagli (who later replaced Amorevoli as Franceschina with the Gelosi) must have played her (*Arlecchino a Parigi,* 1:152–3).

51 English translations of the *Recueil Fossard* verses are by Christine McWebb.

52 Scala, *Il finto marito,* in *Commedie dei comici dell'arte,* ed. Laura Falavolti, 261.

53 Although maidservants are never eligible to make marriages that will raise their social class, it often happens that their masters will arrange marriages for them with other servants. In *Il finto marito,* Ruchetta manages to force Demetrio to allow her to marry another servant, Trapola.

3 Iconic Prima Donnas

1 As Pamela Benson notes, the designation *donna di palazzo* rather than the logical *cortigiana* (courtesan) implies that these women's sphere of influence remained within the court, where their newly acquired skills in making witty conversation to entertain their lovers operated as "socially sanctioned public flirtation [where] sexuality is replaced with speech" (The Invention of the Renaissance Woman," 80, 90).

2 Taviani and Schino, *Il segreto,* 336. This argument has been regarded as credible on the ground that women below a certain class did not have access to an elite education.

3 There are many studies available on the careers of the famous courtesans. Two important ones are Masson, *Courtesans of the Italian Renaissance,* and Rosenthal, *The Honest Courtesan.*

4 Taviani and Schino, *Il segreto,* 336–7 (original emphasis).

5 Taviani and Schino, *Il segreto,* 341.

6 Valerini, *Oratione,* in Marotti and Romei, *La commedia dell'arte,* 37. There is less information about Flaminia, who reputedly came from Rome, but she is also celebrated by Leone de' Sommi, the Jewish impresario, who was knowledgeable about the Mantuan theatrical scene.

7 de' Sommi, *Quattro dialoghi*, 44–5, translation in "The Dialogues of Leone de' Sommi," in Nicoll, *The Development of Theatre*, 268.
8 D'Ancona, *Origini*, 2:452 (original emphasis).
9 D'Ancona, *Origini*, 2:449 (his note for location of San Andrea).
10 Armani's relationship with Signor Federigo da Gazuolo was of sufficient public interest that the details of a street fight that broke out between them made it into the records, which describe how on 7 July 1567 Gazuolo – in response to Armani's negative treatment of him – screamed back at her as if he were "a woman of the streets" (D'Ancona, *Origini*, 2:453).
11 D'Ancona, *Origini*, 2:449.
12 D'Ancona, *Origini*, 2:447.
13 The rivalry between them may have been trumped up for marketing purposes, since their reputations led to an invitation the following year (in April 1568) from Guglielmo Gonzaga, the duke of Mantua, to join together to form a single company: "his Excellency has a comedy given by the two companies: one by Pantalone, the other by Ganaza. His Excellency wished them to merge as one and took the best: this was Signora Vincenza and Signora Flaminia who performed most excellently, and dressed so well that none could do better" (D'Ancona, *Origini*, 2:455). This united company became the I Gelosi of enduring fame. However, lack of evidence renders it impossible to confirm whether or not Flaminia played with them. Vincenza never had the opportunity, as she was poisoned in 1569.
14 Rojek, *Celebrity*, 18.
15 D'Ancona, *Origini*, 2:451.
16 Benjamin, "Work of Art," 221–3.
17 Gell's theory about artistic enchantment outlines how artists who exhibit technical mastery of their art form have the power to enchant their audiences through their abilities to transform the materials they are working with in original ways ("Technology of Enchantment," 51–2).
18 D'Ancona refers to the two possible sources as *Didone* by Venetian Lodovico Dolce, published in 1547, or by Giambattista Giraldi Cintio, published in Ferrara in 1583, but probably written much earlier (*Origini*, 2:449n2).
19 Frances K. Barasch notes that Flaminia's impersonation of Dido as an *innamorata* fell into the tradition of the famous women poets like Gaspara Stampa and Tullia d'Aragona who had "appropriated the classics to redefine heroics within the emotional world of women" ("Italian Actresses in Shakespeare's World," 19). Additionally, Henke observes that the "erotic rhetoric of pastoral drama would have well suited Flaminia in performing the role of Dido, especially in composing a pastoral-style lamento excoriating her perfidious lover" (*Performance and Literature*, 88).

20 Eric Nicholson argues that this lurid tale of Drusilla's revenge was a perfect piece to showcase Flaminia's heroic ability to "mask and unmask feminine roles for a male audience" ("Romance as Role Model," 259–62).

21 D'Ancona, *Origini*, 2:451. This stoning incident was echoed by an offstage incident in which Flaminia is recorded as throwing rocks at the followers of Prince Cesare Gonzaga when a brawl broke out between them and her troupe. Such a scandalous event helped feed the gossip she attracted as a celebrity figure. For details, see Nicholson, "Romance as Role Model," 246n1.

22 Roach, *It*, 12, 39–40.

23 Valerini, *Oratione*, 37. Further citations to this work appear in the text.

24 Barthes, "Garbo," 56.

25 Max Weber defined "charisma" as "a certain quality of an individual personality by virtue of which [a person] is considered extraordinary and treated as endowed with supernatural, superhuman, or a least specifically exceptional powers or qualities" (*Economy and Society*, 244).

26 This belief aligns closely with elements of neoplatonic doctrine that gave the idealized court lady – as Castiglione describes her – the power to refract the gaze of those who desire her and, "by her merits and virtuous behavior, by her charm and grace, instill in the minds of all those who look upon her the true love that loveable things deserve" (*The Book of the Courtier*, 264).

27 Henke, "Virtuosity and Mimesis," 70–1.

28 Carlson, The Haunted Stage, 7–9.

29 Valerini completes his neoplatonic conceit on the nature of love with an affirmation of the eternal "joy that never ends" that his departed lover has bestowed on him and on his profession. This state of eternal joy and reunion after death is described by Giorgio Agamben as achievable through the composition of neoplatonic love conceits such as those improvised by Armani. See Agamben, *Stanzas*, 124–31.

30 Garzoni, *La piazza*, 754, in Marotti and Romei, *La commedia dell'arte*, 12–13.

31 Garzoni, *La piazza*, 754, in Marotti and Romei, *La commedia dell'arte*, 13.

32 Anne MacNeil supplies many interesting details about the illustrious careers of Piissimi and her husband Giovanni Pellesini (Pedrolino) with a special emphasis on her skill in singing and his in acrobatics (*Music and Women of the Commedia dell'Arte*, 8–24).

33 Scala, *Il teatro*, 2:397–409.

34 Andrews wonders if it was written to blacken Vittoria's reputation (*The Commedia dell'Arte of Flaminio Scala*, 249–50). Given the number of references to the character Vittoria's sexual activities, he may be right.

35 For another scenario that deals with different levels of theatrical illusion occurring when actors appear as characters, see Anonymous, "La commedia in commedia." It also contains an actor character, Graziano, a visiting *capocomico* who stands both inside and outside the action as he observes the *innamorata* Lidia drop her glove, which is picked up by a peripheral male lover, Lelio, who is not quite a cast member himself and who appears wearing a false beard as a disguise. Graziano's function as a *capocomico* is underlined when he tries to get Lidia and Lelio to pay for the play, but he also becomes involved in the action when Capitano, whom Graziano has raised, is discovered to be Pantalone's long-lost son.

36 Andrews denies the full metatheatricality of "Il ritratto" on the ground that it does not include a play within a play (*The Commedia dell'Arte of Flaminio Scala*, 249). A broader definition of "metatheatricality" as theatre that draws attention to its illusory mechanisms would include it.

37 Quinn, "Semiotics," 156.

38 Elizabeth Cropper argues that the conventions behind this very special class of miniature paintings tend to elide the distinctions between the representation of beauty and the beauty represented, with the result that "the portrayal of a beautiful woman also came to function as a synecdoche for the beauty of painting itself" ("The Beauty of Woman," 176).

39 Lacan outlines how the gaze operates: "generally speaking, the relationship between the gaze and what one wishes to see involves a lure. The subject is presented as other than he is, and what one shows him is not what he wishes to see. It is in this way that the eye may function as *objet a*, that is to say, at the level of lack" (*The Four Fundamental Concepts*, 104).

40 Quinn, "Semiotics," 158.

41 As noted above, Andrews suggests that the scenario may have been intended to blacken Piissimi's reputation.

42 Flaminio Scala, as the company director of the Confidenti, was familiar with the scandals that could arise when actresses misbehaved. Kathleen M. Lea recounts the case of an actress named Celia and her interfering mother and brother. The company lost their licence when Celia's brother was assaulted in the street for obstructing the performance of his sister's rival. Most interesting for our purposes was the discovery that some of her problems arose from her holding card games in her quarters, which led certain of her patrons to believe that they should not have to pay to attend her performances, since they had already spent a lot of money while gambling with her. The game of riffe was a perfect way to swindle gifts from players, since it involved competitive betting on the value of a trinket supplied by the actress and usually ended in her being rewarded handsomely

for having put it up in the first place (*Italian Popular Comedy*, 1:298–9). See also Ottonelli, who describes how the game was played, in Taviani, *La commedia dell'arte*, 365.

4 Transvestite Heroines

1 Jones and Stallybrass, "Transvestism," 217.

2 Laura Giannetti's description of the fluidity of gender categories in early modern Italy supports this argument. She claims "that the different social roles assigned to men and women were based on a patriarchal social order much more than on any natural differences" (*Lelia's Kiss*, 15).

3 Jardine, "Twins and Travesties," 27–38. As *Gl'ingannati* (*The Deceived*) is a source play for *Twelfth Night*, her argument is applicable.

4 Jardine, "Twins and Travesties," 28 (original emphasis).

5 Herlihy interprets the statistical evidence in fifteenth-century Florence, noting that "the richest households tend to gather in both boys and girls as they age, from birth up to their middle teens. At exactly age 15, the 25 per cent of wealthy households contain 45 per cent of the boys and 43.5 per cent of the girls (as opposed to 39 per cent and 35 per cent respectively of the cohort of babies, age 0–2). This drift of children primarily means that wealthy households were taking in orphaned relatives ... If we had data on servants and apprentices we would undoubtedly observe an even more massive drift of young persons in and out of the homes of the wealthy" (*Medieval Households*, 153).

6 Vecellio, *Habiti antichi*, quoted in Lawner, *Lives*, 20.

7 Aretino, *The Letters of Pietro Aretino*, 249.

8 In fact, since female transvestism became one of the most popular features of Italian and continental public stages, it cannot be claimed that actresses were introduced onto the stage in predominantly Roman Catholic countries to avoid the charge that boy actors encouraged the practice of sodomy. Such arguments are based on the well-known debates that raged in England over the practice of using boy actors in female roles on the Shakespearean stage. See J.W. Binns for information about the most famous debates that took place during 1593–4 between William Gager, a leading scholarly dramatist at Oxford who defended the value of theatrical performances, and his highly critical opponent, the learned Puritan Dr John Rainolds. Supporting Gager was the brilliant professor of civil law Alberico Gentili, an Italian Protestant who by no means supported the presence of women on the Italian stage, but did admit that the fact they were performing women's roles meant that the laws of Deuteronomy 22:5

were not being violated. "But this cannot much harm actors, who have female mimers and actresses, so that they do not need to don the clothing of the opposite sex." Surprisingly, however, he failed to mention that the actresses were playing transvestite roles ("Women or Transvestites," 111–12).

9 According to Daston and Park, female transvestite disguise was becoming increasingly associated with hermaphroditism, tribadism, and female presumption, as male fears about the challenge that early modern women were presenting to male authority culminated in the cultural construct of the monstrous mannish woman. In particular, they observe that sexual behaviours considered to be impediments to marriage, especially on the part of women, came under increasing scrutiny after the Council of Trent ("Hermaphrodite," 430–1).

10 Tyler notes that since class, race, and gender are complexly articulated, the different discourses they institute will have class, race, and sexual meanings all at once (*Female Impersonation*, 50).

11 Traub, "(In)significance," 156.

12 Lacan, "The Meaning of the Phallus,"56.

13 Tyler, *Female Impersonation*, 50. I am indebted to her treatment of the relationship between transvestism and fetishism and have used it in my readings of the scenarios featuring Isabella as Fabrizio.

14 Scala, *Il teatro*. The fifteen comic examples are: "La fortuna di Flavio" (Day 2), where Alissa appears as Turchetto; "La finta pazza" (Day 8), with Flaminia as Bigolo; "Il marito" (Day 9), with Franceschina as Cornelio; "La sposa" (Day 10), with Isabella as a male servant; "Il pellegrino fido amante" (Day 14), with Isabella as Fabrizio; "Lo specchio" (Day 16), with Isabella as Fabrizio; "Li tragici successi" (Day 18), with Isabella in male disguise; "Li tre fidi amici" (Day 19), with Flaminia in male disguise; "Il finto Tofano" (Day 24), with Isabella as Tofano; "La gelosa Isabella" (Day 25), with Isabella as Fabrizio; "Li tappeti alessandrini" (Day 26), with Isabella as Fabrizio; "La mancata fede" (Day 27), with Isabella in male disguise; "Li finti servi" (Day 30), with Isabella as Fabrizio; "Il ritratto" (Day 39), with Silvia Milanese as Lesbino; "Il giusto castigo" (Day 40), with Isabella in male disguise. Further, the transvestite figure is not restricted to comedy but also assumes tremendous importance in seven of the ten serious mixed genre final scenarios: "Gli avvenimenti, comici, pastorali e tragici" (Day 42), with the nymph Fillide as the shepherd Coridone; "L'Alvida" (Day 43), with the Amazonian warrior Brandino; "L'innocente persiana" (Day 45), with the Amazonian warrior Teodora; "Parte I – Dell'Oreseida" (Day 46), with the princess Eurilla as a shepherd; "III Parte – Dell'Orseida" (Day 48), with the Amazonian warrior Alvida; "L'arbore

incantato" (Day 49), with the nymph Fillide as the shepherd Lesio, and "La fortuna di foresta prencipessa di Moscovia" (Day 50), with the princess Lucella in male disguise.

15 Marjorie Garber sees the practice as reflecting changes in the fabric of society: "Transvestism was located at the juncture of 'class' and 'gender,' and increasingly through its agency gender and class were revealed to be commutable, if not equivalent. To transgress against one set of boundaries was to call into question the inviolability of both, and of the set of social codes – already demonstrably under attack – by which such categories were policed and maintained. The transvestite in this scenario is both terrifying and seductive precisely because s/he incarnates and emblematizes the disruptive element that intervenes, signaling not just another category crisis, but – much more disquietingly – a crisis of 'category' itself" (*Vested Interests*, 32).

16 Jane Tylus comments on the frequent appearance of women in upper-storey windows in the Scala scenarios – evidence that they were not allowed to move freely in public spaces ("Women at the Windows," 325).

17 Dekker and van de Pol, *The Tradition of Female Transvestism*, 55.

18 Stoller, *Observing the Erotic Imagination*, 176.

19 Andrews, *The Commedia dell'Arte of Flaminio Scala*, 77.

20 Roach, *It*, 39–40.

21 Quinn explains that since audiences recognize them, celebrities can never be conflated with their roles, giving them a larger-than-life presence. "Semiotics," 155.

22 Roach, *It*, 11.

23 He describes it as "the subject who is supposed to know" ("Semiotics," 158).

24 Scala, *Il teatro*, 1:149–58. Further citations of this work appear in the text.

25 Dubrow, *Echoes of Desire*, 55.

26 *Gl'ingannati* (*The Deceived*), in Giannetti and Ruggiero, *Five Comedies*. Further citations of this work appear in the text.

27 Robert C. Melzi, in "From Lelia to Viola," traces the many variations that the *Gl'ingannati* plot spawned during the seventy years separating it from Shakespeare's *Twelfth Night*, noting that, in addition to being translated into several languages, it also inspired several plays and novellas that may have provided Shakespeare with his models. His particular interest in the transvestite *innamorata* role confirms the enduring dramatic appeal of this transgressive figure.

28 Tyler, Female Impersonation, 50.

29 Jones and Stallybrass, "Transvestism," 217.

30 The dialogue between Fabrizio, Virginio, and Gherardo runs as follows:

> VIRGINIO. [To FABRIZIO] I only want to have a word with you.
> FABRIZIO. You can have it out here.
> GHERARDO. No, out here is not the place! This house is yours because you're going to be my wife.
> FABRIZIO. What wife? Why, you old bugg– ... you humbugger!
> GHERARDO. Your father has betrothed you to me.
> FABRIZIO. What are you thinking? Do you think I'm one of those pansy boys that you can ... eh? (*The Deceived*, 256)

31 The plot also resembles that of another erudite comedy, Ariosto's *I suppositi* (*The Pretenders*), in which the young lady of the household disgraces herself by becoming pregnant by someone who appears to be a lowly servant. While Ariosto's comedy is eventually resolved by the discovery that the young man in question was impersonating his own servant in order to infiltrate the household, Scala raises the stakes by making the imposter a young woman.

32 Traub, "(In)significance," 156.

5 Isabella Andreini: The Making of a Diva

1 Although the first record of Isabella and Francesco co-directing the Gelosi dates from 1583, the evidence that Isabella quickly rose to *prima donna* status after she joined the company in 1576 is not contested, for Francesco Andreini provides a list that names her amongst the other great members of the Gelosi company at its peak, claiming that their achievements had never been surpassed by any company that followed ("Ragionamento 14," in *Le bravure del Capitano Spavento*; in Marotti and Romei, *La commedia dell'arte*, 255–6).

2 The most comprehensive treatment of Isabella Andreini's life and works in English is Anne MacNeil, "Music and the Life and Work of Isabella Andreini. Also valuable is MacNeil's "The Divine Madness of Isabella Andreini." See also Erenstein, "Isabella Andreini," 37–49. One hundred of Andreini's poems have been translated in *Selected Poems of Isabella Andreini*, ed. Anne MacNeil, trans. James Wyatt Cook. Her pastoral *La Mirtilla* (1588) has been issued in a modern Italian edition by Maria Luisa Doglio and in an English translation by Julie D. Campbell.

3 Roach, *It*, 3.

4 Dyer defines authenticity as "both a quality necessary to the star phenomenon to make it work, and also the quality that guarantees the authenticity

of the other particular values a star embodies. It is the effect of authenticating authenticity that gives the star charisma" ("A Star Is Born," 133).

5 Quinn, "Semiotics," 157.

6 Dyer notes that there is always a certain instability in maintaining the notion that the star really is as she seems. What inevitably arises is a "rhetoric of authenticity," which will also be a mix of hype and artifice ("A Star Is Born," 137).

7 Rojek, *Celebrity*, 18.

8 Giovan Battista Andreini's birth and baptism were recorded on 9 February 1576 (Florence, Archivio dell'Opera del Duomo, Registro dei battezzati maschi dal 1571 al 1577, letter G. fo.172^{v}; see MacNeil, *Music and Women*, 199).

9 *La ferza*, in Marotti and Romei, *La commedia dell'arte*, 509.

10 Francesca Romana de' Angelis notes that it was a mark of prestige for upper-class women to bear large families and to be praised for undertaking the perils of childbirth. This may not have been the case for the Andreinis, who had to work very hard as theatre practitioners (*La divina Isabella*, 78).

11 Roach, *It*, 36–7.

12 See MacNeil for additional information about her daughter Lavinia's religious life. A complaint by the nuns regarding lack of payment for Lavinia's (Suor Fulvia's) expenses since her entry into the monastery recognized that an original dowry of three hundred lire had been paid by Eleanora de' Medici (Notarile, notaio Battaleoli Cristofor, 26 July 1627, Mantua, Archivio di Stato, cited in *Music and Women*, 48n28).

13 Copies of the two letters, dated 14 January and 5 April 1587, are located in Mantua, Archivio di Stato, Gonzaga, Autografi, b. 10, fos. 54–5; repr. in MacNeil, *Music and Women*, 276–7. Francesco Bartoli notes Lavinia's joining the Monestero della Cantelma, and adds that the three other sisters also lived in a Mantuan cloister (*Notizie istoriche*, 1:33). The fact that we do not know the names of three of the four daughters is unfortunate, and points to the difficulties of providing for female children.

14 For a list of these anthologies see MacNeil, introduction to Andreini, *Selected Poems*, 9–12.

15 For details of her admission as the only female member, see Maylender, *Storia delle Accademie d'Italia*, 3:320–1.

16 Vittorio Amedeo Arullani describes the much older Borgogni (who was in his sixties in the late 1580s, when he was acquainted with Isabella) as "someone suspiciously more than a simple admirer and fan of the famous actress: in my opinion, he was a true lover, a typical suitor, perhaps encouraged a little bit by the coquetry conceivable in an actress, but

reciprocated only – presumably as much as the same remarkable woman's honesty and marital status would permit" (*Di Gherardo Borgogni*, 12).

17 Arullani, *Di Gherardo Borgogni*, 10, quoting from Borgogni's *La fonte del disporto*.

18 Gamman and Makinen note that diva worship arises when a performer is given godlike powers by fans who turn her into a cult and fetishize every aspect of her life and being (*Female Fetishism*, 18–27).

19 This foundational article sifts the evidence in order to separate the mythology from the facts. See also my "The Imprint of Genius."

20 The first thirteen lines of the poem that Solerti referenced are: "Se già del vago Aminta / Tra ninfe e tra pastori / Cantasti i vaghi amore / Canta or, Tasso, la bella / Mi dolce pastorella, / Perché, di lei cantando, / Di mille andrai scemando / I pregi, e sarà Filli / Più degna ch'Amarilli / Più vaga ch'Amaranta. / Tu dunque Filli canta / Al suon di quella cetra / Che sì gran nome qui fra noi t'impetra." (Since you've already sung of the delightful love of the charming Aminta, / amidst the nymphs and shepherds, / then sing to me now, Tasso, of the beautiful / sweet shepherdess, because, in singing of her / you will lessen the praise of thousands / and Filli will be more worthy than Amarillus, / more beautiful than Amaranta. / Sing then of Filli, / I implore you, to the sound of your lyre, / you who are such a great name among us) (Borgogni, *Nuova scelta di rime*, 67–9, quoted in Solerti, *Vita di Torquato Tasso*, 1:757). Taviani notes the important fact that Solerti quoted only the first thirteen lines of the poem and hence missed out on the connection between Isabella and Tasso's sonnet. He explains that perhaps Solerti failed to recognize that Borgogni's name for Isabella was "Filli," despite his frequent use of it in his poetry to her. The poem written out in full includes the last four lines, where Borgogni spells out that he will help Tasso achieve his crowning in Rome in exchange for the sonnet ("Bella d'Asia," 67–8n44). See the following note for the important lines that refer to Tasso's desire for the laurel crown.

21 "Non ti sia dunque a sdegno / Cantar di Filli il pellegrino ingegno, / che di Castalia al fonte / Avrai di sacr'allor cinta la fronte" (Don't then fail to sing of the rare genius of Filli, / So that at the fountain of Castalia / you will have your sacred crown) (quoted in Taviani, "Bella d'Asia," 67n44).

22 Bartoli, *Notizie istoriche*, 1:37. Bartoli relies for his information on Giovan Battista Andreini's *La ferza*. The passage is in Marotti and Romei, *La commedia dell'arte*, 521.

23 Solerti denied that it ever took place, basing his dismissal of Isabella's being crowned in Rome on the argument that neither Andreini nor Gabriello

Chiabrera (whose name was added in a later account) were in Rome at the time (*Vita di Torquato Tasso,* 1:754–6).

24 He notes that the source of this information, Giovan Battista's *La ferza,* was written in 1625 and hence was close enough to the 1594 event to be remembered accurately. He also shows that in the fall of 1594 the Gelosi were on route from Naples to Florence, and could have easily come to Rome. Taviani, "Bella d'Asia," 36.

25 The effigy is an important concept for Roach, who argues that "effigies produce the uncanny effect of lifelikeness: just because such icons exist only in other people's imagination of them doesn't mean they are unreal" (*It,* 17).

26 One of the main reasons why skeptics refuse to believe it was written for Isabella was the puzzling fact that it was the only one of the tributes that did not explicitly name her. Furthermore, Francesco had added an editorial note to explicitly say that Tasso had written it for her, which many take as evidence that he was lying (reprinted in Luigi Rasi, *I comici italiani,* 1:138). Taviani points out that "Bella d'Asia" can be easily rearranged to read "(Isa)bella d'A: Isabella delli Andreini." This form of their last name appeared on Giovan Battista's horoscope, where he was designated "Lelio delli Andreini" ("Bella d'Asia," 46).

27 Bartoli included this version, originally printed in her *Lettere,* in *Notizie istoriche,* 1:36. Solerti, unable to find any references to Isabella in the sonnet, concludes that Bartoli randomly selected it because it offered such an apt description of Isabella (*Vita di Torquato Tasso,* 1:77n4) (*"Bella d'Asia,"* 46).

28 Tasso had written a treatise on the *impresa, Il conte, overo de l'imprese,* published in 1594. Robert Klein notes that by the end of the fifteenth century, the *impresa* "was by far the most important and widespread exercise of the 'symbolic faculty' ... because it was by definition a manifesto of the mind rather than a symbol to be deciphered. The beauty of the work is the beauty of the *ingegno* – ingenuity: the very word *concetto,* used at first to describe the initial idea, came to signify a cunning form of expression" ("The Theory of Figurative Expression in Italian Treatises on the Impresa," 16).

29 Tasso names "la bellezza de l'ingegno poetico" as the ability of the poet to recognize what defines the beautiful (*Il Minturno overo de la bellezza* [*Dialogue on Beauty*], 204).

30 Gell, "Technology of Enchantment," 44–7.

31 In Marotti and Romei, *La commedia dell'arte,* 12.

32 *Notizie istoriche*, 1:31–3.

33 The two volumes from 1601 and 1605 contain five hundred poems, including sonnets, madrigals, tercets, and canzonette. See MacNeil, introduction to Andreini, *Selected Poems*, 1–28.

34 Beyond the poems she wrote to Henri IV, Marie de' Medici, and other nobles in France are the eight poems she wrote praising "Madamoisella Maria de Beaulieu," a lady-in-waiting to Marguerite de Valois. The close ties between them and the treatise that Beaulieu wrote in defence of Andreini and the Gelosi in 1603 reveal the extent to which Andreini had become the darling of the French court (Campbell, "Querelle," 52–3).

35 My translation, in consultation with Professor Enrico Musacchio.

36 Introduction to Andreini, *Selected Poems*, 2.

37 William Kennedy outlines how Petrarchan poetry is intended to be shared by the speaker and the audience in a way that sets up an intimate dialogue between them ("Petrarchan Audiences," 1–20).

38 One common form was the *capitoli* that required the insertion of a line from Petrarch every third line. The three *capitoli* in the *Rime* are "capitolo 1, con ogni terzo verso del Petrarca," *Rime* 1:44–7; "capitolo 2, con ogni terso verso del Petrarca," *Rime* 1:164–7; and "capitolo 3, con ogni terzo verso del Petrarca," *Rime* 1:189.

39 The first is "Chi pensò mai veder far terra oscura" (*centon* 1, *Rime* 1:125). Written to commemorate the death of the noblewoman playwright Laura Guidiccioni Lucchesini, the first *centone* stands as a testimonial of Andreini's deep affection for a fellow female artist as well as showing great inventiveness in reconfiguring Petrarch's Laura to become Andreini's lost friend. The second one, "Amor m'ha posto come segno a strale" (*centon* 2, *Rime* 1:152) is dedicated, as is the entire volume, to her literary patron, Cardinal Cinthio Aldobrandini, and is a typical lament for the pain that love brings.

40 Innamorati, "Il riuso della parola," 163–85.

41 Individual line translations are taken from Durling, *Petrarch's Lyric Poems*. See Innamorati's line-referencing to Petrarch's sonnets in "Il Riuso," 172–3n23.

42 Alexander, "The Celebrity Icon," 325.

43 Cook, translator's foreward to Andreini, *Selected Poems*, x.

44 Ray labels Andreini "hermaphroditic" because she presents herself as both male and female (*Writing Gender*, 159). MacNeil had previously applied this term, describing Andreini's "hermaphroditic persona [as] credible within both masculine and feminine authoritative spheres" (*Music and Women*, 89).

45 Marshall defines celebrity as "a voice above others, a voice that is channeled into the media systems as being legitimately significant ... In its simultaneous embodiment of media construction, audience construction, and the real, living and breathing human being, the celebrity sign negotiates the competing and contradictory definitions of it own significance ... The power of the celebrity, then, is to represent the active construction of identity in the social world" (*Celebrity and Power*, x, xi).

46 Editions of *La Mirtilla* in the decades after its composition were many and frequent, including Verona: Girolamo Discepolo, 1588, 1599; Ferrara: Baldini, and Venice: Bonibello, 1590; Bergamo: Comin Ventura, 1594; Venice: Bonibello, 1598; Verona: Delle Donne e Varignano, 1599; Venice: Spineda, 1602; Milan: Bordone e Locarni, 1605; and Venice: Imberti, 1616. The play was also translated into French as *Myrtille bergerie* (Paris, 1602). Further citations from the Doglio edition and Campbell translation hereafter appear in the text.

47 Virginia Cox, who notes that Maddalena Campiglia's *Flori* was published in the same year as *La Mirtilla*, provides a list of the surviving seven pastoral plays by women that appeared in the 1580s and early 1590s. Of the seven, Barbara Torelli's *Partenia*, written in 1586, survived only in manuscript. After Andreini's and Campiglia's in 1588, there are two from the 1590s: one, the anonymous *Tragicomedia pastorale*, is located in the Biblioteca Marciana in Venice, and the other, Valeria Miani's *Amorosa speranza*, was written in 1598 and published in 1604. The author of *Tragicomedia pastorale* has been possibly identified as Leonora Bernardi, a gentlewoman from Lucca. The final two works, Isabetta Coreglia's *Dori* (1634) and *Erindo il fido* (1650), fall into a later time period (*The Prodigious Muse*, 92–3). See Lisa Sampson for additional examples, including ones that are lost (*Pastoral Drama*, 103).

48 Sampson concedes that *La Mirtilla* stands as the "first and only known one [pastoral drama] by a female actor" (*Pastoral Drama*, 119).

49 *Canzone* "Alla Signora Isabella Andreini, comica gelosa," in Borgogni, *Rime di diversi illustri poeti*, 145. Quoted in Taviani, "Bella d'Asia," 7.

50 If Andreini wrote her pastoral for purposes of legitimation, it should be noted that her profession as an actress who played in comedies on the public stage was a mark against her reputation as a writer. This prejudice against performing in comedies as a sign that actresses were not respectable is voiced by Ingegneri when he praises the pastoral as a genre that, in "admettendo le vergini in palco e le donne oneste, quello che alle comedie non lice, danno luogo a nobili affetti, non disdicevoli alle tragedie istesse" (permitting young maidens and honest women on the stage, something

that is forbidden in comedy, gives a place for noble sentiments, which are not improper in tragedies themselves) (*Della poesia rappresentativa*, 276).

51 Quinn further notes that a celebrity often "make[s] frequent recourse to the combination of normal artistic functions as a way to multiply the empowerment of his or her own image" ("Semiotics," 157).

52 The evidence that she also played Venus comes from a poem by Pantaleo Murassana, a Savonese friend of Chiabrera, who saw her perform and wrote about it in his dialect, referring to her as "Venere altera e doçe pastorella," which implies that she played both Venus and the nymph Filli (quoted in Franco Vazzoler, "Le pastorali dei comici dell'arte, 284).

53 Quinn describes how the rapt spectator, dreaming about an erotic union with the apparently present celebrity, "projects the self onto and into the celebrity to produce a vivid attention only partially ascribable to the fictional events of the art work" ("Semiotics," 158).

54 For Doglio, Andreini's creation of Filli and her ability to express the torments of love situates her within the tradition of lyrical female poets such as Veronica Gambara, Gaspara Stampa, and Veronica Franco, each of whom possesses "un riconosciuto spazio di autonomia intellettuale " (a recognized space of intellectual autonomy) combined with "un senso che implica però una profonda comprensione, quasi una fraterna solidarietà per chi soffre" (a sense that also carries with it a profound comprehension, an almost fraternal solidarity with those who suffer) (Introduction to Andreini, *Mirtilla*, 9).

55 MacNeil describes the musical contest in detail, explaining how Andreini exceeds her Virgilian model not only by making references not only to the forms that the songs must take but also by providing cues for the instrumental parts that are to accompany them (*Music and Women*, 38–45).

56 Their legendary rivalry has already been referenced in "Il ritratto"; it was documented again at the Medici wedding that took place a year later, in in 1589. Vazzoler suggests that the actresses' separate appearances in acts 1 and 2 of *La Mirtilla* was deliberate on Andreini's part, intended not only to recognize their individual stature but also to mirror their appearances in Aminta, where Andreini is not likely to have played Silvia because Piissimi had claimed that role, which left Aminta for Andreini ("Le pastorali dei comici dell'arte," 285)

57 MacNeil notes that Andreini has paired the stanzas in such a way "to offer numerous opportunities for ornamentation and competitive interpretation of specific words or images" (*Music and Women*, 44).

58 In *Il sacrificio* the nymph Melidia manages to talk her way out of the satyr's trap by appealing to her extra-human skills and getting him to untie her.

59 The satyr incident in *Il pastor fido* involves Corsica's use of trickery and physical force against the satyr, but is more about her escaping than confronting him. Leaving her golden wig behind is highly theatrical and comical but overall not as thematically central as it is in *Mirtilla*. Virginia Cox describes the decorous handling of the satyr scene by three of the female playwrights (Campiglia, Torelli, and Bernardi), as falling more closely in line with the male-authored pattern, which makes less mention of the satyr's sexual intent (*The Prodigious Muse*, 113–15).

60 Miani's treatment involves two scenes. In the first, the nymph Tirenia tricks the old satyr Elliodoro into retrieving an arrow for her, leaving him tied up by his feet to a tree. In the second, when he comes after her, her shepherd lover rescues her, ties the satyr up again, and leaves him to be tortured by Tirenia. She not only plucks his beard as Filli does, but actually cuts it all off, in addition to breaking off one of his horns (*The Prodigious Muse*, 112).

61 Quinn, "Semiotics," 158.

62 Crucial insights into the treatment of the nymph who falls in love with her own reflection are revealed by Emily Wilbourne's article "*Amor nello specchio*," where she deals with this trope in Giovan Battista's *Amor nello specchio*. Wilbourne reads the play to capture the "sounding body of Virginia Andreini" (who played Florinda) and to listen for the "persistent articulation of sexuality through vocality." What she discovers is that Virginia/Florinda expresses her explicit sexual passion through changing vocal patterns in both speech and sound (56.)

63 Doglio, introduction to Andreini, *Mirtilla*, 14. Wilbourne, on the other hand, argues that the expression of lesbian (or deviant) sexual practice brings it into focus as a possibility ("Amor nello specchio," 64–5).

64 Vazzoler argues that for Andreini and the commedia dell'arte performers who had to fight accusations of immorality because of their chaotic lifestyle, marriage unions might have had a more utopic value ("Le pastorali," 298).

65 Pavoni, *Diario descritto*, in Scala, *Il teatro*, appendix 2, 1:lxxii. Further citations of this work appear in the text.

66 The main theatrical event, *La pellegrina*, a "grave" comedy by Girolamo Bargagli performed by the highly esteemed young aristocratic members of the famous Sienese academy Gl'Intronati, was carefully chosen by the grand duke and by the brilliant team of artists, designers, and musicians behind the event. *La pellegrina* was tailored for the occasion and had been edited by Scipione Bargagli to suit the duke's wishes: the saintly pilgrim heroine Drusilla's nationality was changed from Spanish to French; her

birthplace became Lyon, and her long sea journey matched Christina's exact route from Marseilles. A conscious tribute to Christina, whose piety and commitment to religious good works were well known, the script was geared towards sacralizing her as a worthy partner for the former cardinal Ferdinando in an effort to glorify their union as presaging a new, golden age of enlightened rule (Newman, "The Politics of Spectacle," 95–113).

67 Five of the six *intermedi* were reconstructed in *Una stravaganza dei Medici*, produced by Thames Television/Raven/Framestore for Channel 4 (first broadcast December 1990). The six scenes stress Ferdinando's central role in bringing harmony to his realm through his association with the gods. The vast extraterrestrial worlds of the six *intermedi* mutate from the heavenly firmaments to a mountain filled with wood nymphs judging a singing contest; a fire-spewing Python in a rocky cave, defeated by Apollo; a three-headed Lucifer eating souls in Hell; and an undulating sea where the queen of the ocean blesses the fertility of the royal couple. In the finale, the Olympians send down Apollo and Bacchus to accompany Harmony and Rhythm to earth; they are joined by a chorus of mortals who sing an epithalamium to the royal couple, announcing a return to a golden age. Molinari describes the power of the *intermedi* as arising from the prince's ability to suggest that he was capable of moving easily between everyday and eternal time. Precisely this effect is captured in de' Rossi's description of the lightning-swift transitions between each act as the realistic Pisan cityscape, complete with smoking chimneys and workable doors, was made to disappear and reappear – as if by magic – as the great flying machines transformed the stage into one scene after another to suit the varied panoramas required by the *intermedi* (Molinari, *Commedia*, 120).

68 For further commentary see Andrews, *Scripts and Scenarios*, 233–7.

69 Although there was so much publicity about their being given separate performances to star in, it is likely that they did appear in each other's plays, taking the *seconda donna* role, with Andreini as Angelica and Piissimi as Flaminia. See Jaffe-Berg, *The Multilingual Art*, 64.

70 Barasch, referencing Zorzi, describes ways in which she had to speak badly, swallow *r*s and *l*s, lisp like a child, and make bird-like twitter sounds ("Italian Actresses," 6).

71 See MacNeil's "Divine Madness" for a wonderful description of Andreini's referencing of the *Phaedrus*.

72 Since its full title was *La Pazzia d'Isabella*, scholars sometimes mistake it for the Scala scenario of the same title, ("The Madness of Isabella," Day 38), partly because it contains some actual "mad" dialogue full of the brilliant inversions of logical concepts and language that were part of An-

dreini's subversive trademark. The mad speeches included in "La pazzia d'Isabella" were composed of a variety of *non sequiters* and patterned nonsense, for instance: "Io mi ricordo l'anno non me lo ricordo, che un Arpicordo pose d'accordo una Pavaniglia spagnola con una Gagliarda di Santin da Parma, per la qual cosa poi le lasagne, i maccheroni e la polenta si vestirono a bruno, non potendo comportare che la gatta fura fusse amica delle belle fanciulle d'Algieri; pure, come piacque al califfo d'Egitto, fu concluso che domattina sarete duo messi in berlina" (I remember, in the year I don't remember, the honorable member tried to dismember the membrane from a vain Jane from Spain: and so the lasagna, the macaroni and the polenta all dressed in black because they couldn't stand that the sly puss should befriend the pretty girls in Algiers; all the same, on the orders of the Caliph of Egypt, it was decreed that tomorrow morn you'll both be publicly shorn) (act 3, 394–5; in Andrews, *The Commedia dell'Arte of Flaminio Scala*, 232).

73 Rojek, *Celebrity*, 75.

74 Roach, *It*, 16.

75 Jaffe-Berg includes a discussion of what Isabella's erratic actions would have signified on stage (*Multilingual Art*, 60–4) as well as commentary on whether Isabella was naked or wearing a cardboard breastplate (58).

76 Andreini's linguistic inventions, accompanied by sounds and gestures that mimicked the syntax and rhythms of the actual languages, with a few actual words thrown in now and then to make audiences understand what was going on, were a trademark device of the commedia dell'arte. Dario Fo and others have argued that it was the ability of the commedia dell'arte to create a language beyond words that made it revolutionary, not only inside Italy but in all the neighbouring European countries. In order to be understood by its very diverse audiences, "this grammelot or babel of sounds produces speech through an onomatopoeic flow of words that are articulated without rhyme or reason, but capable of transmitting, with the aid of particular gesture, rhythms and sounds, an entire, rounded speech" (Fo, *The Tricks of the Trade*, 56).

77 MacNeil discusses the kinds of French songs Andreini might have sung, noting that this 1589 reference means that they had already been introduced into Italy before Monteverdi (*Music and Women*, 72–6).

78 Molinari believes this second turn moves the performance to a darker place because Isabella's rapid transformations question the very possibility of achieving a stable sense of identity. Calling them "dynamic, protean and demonic," he sees them as undercutting the message of harmonious order under Medicean rule that the gala was intending to convey (*Commedia dell'arte*, 120–2).

79 MacNeil mentions the encomiastic poems Andreini wrote for Christina for presentation at the wedding. A copy written out in Isabella's own hand of a *canzone* and epithalamium is in Florence, Biblioteca Nationale Centrale, Magl. VII, 15 (*Music and Women*, 64–7).

80 Rojek, *Celebrity*, 77.

81 Charles Ruelens provides the full text of the letters they exchanged, and a commentary on their relationship (*Erycius Puteanus et Isabelle Andreini*, 1–31). MacNeil provides translations of all the letters in *Music and Women* (305–23).

82 See Baschet, *Les comédiens italiens*, 126–43. On 7 December 1603, Isabella mentions receiving two hundred écus a month as pay for a thirty-six-day engagement at Fountainebleau (Florence, Archivio di Stato, Mediceo, f. 920, fols. 513^{r-v}). Another letter dated 31 December 1603 mentions that the company received six hundred écus for five months of service (Baschet, *Les Comédiens italiens*, 137–8).

83 Matthieu, *Historie de France*, 1:186. All quotations below are from this page.

84 Henry IV's letter of 13 April to his foreign secretary of state, the Marquis de Villeroy, stressed: "so that you may not delay in sending them the passport that is necessary for their return: and that it be sufficient, in order that they can take their furniture, arms, baggage, rings, jewelry, together with the money of which they will tell you" (Lettres de Henry IV [Correspondance générale, t.VII, 176], in Baschet, *Comédiens italiens*, 145). Marie de' Medici had also written to her sister Eleonora de' Medici, the Duchess of Mantova, asking her to treat Isabella with great care and every honour, closing with a tribute to her time in France: "she and her troupe have given great pleasure to the King and to me. For this I recommend her to you affectionately" (Paris, Bibliothèque Nationale de France, Fonds des 500 Colbert, Registres du cabinet de la Reine Marie de Médicis, MS 86, fo. 166, in Baschet, *Comédiens italiens*, 145).

85 Barbieri, *La supplica*, 18–19.

86 "D.O.M. ISABELLA ANDREINA PATAVINA, mulier magna virtute praedita. Honestatis ornamentum, maritalisque pudicitiae decus, ore facunda, mente fecunda, religiosa, pia, musis amica, et artis scenicae caput, hic resurrectionem expectat. Ob abortum obiit 4 Idus Iunii 1604 annum agens 42. Francisus Andreinus conjux moestissimus posuit" (in Rasi, *Comici italiani*, 1:58).

87 "D.O.M. CARISSIMA UXOR, ISABELLA DULCISSIMA, FRANCISUS TUUS hoc tibi condere monumentum curavit, si caret gemmis, non caret lachrymis. Mecum fletu amarissimo Lugdenenses omnes ingemuerunt. Quiescat corpus in Tumolo, et anima quiescat in Deo. Anno Sal. 1604. Die

10 Junij." Rasi notes that this second one was printed in the new edition of her *Rime* (*Comici italiani*, 1:58).

88 *Mana*, the mysterious active power that belongs to some living people and is shared by the souls of the dead and all spirits, is a term taken from the Melanesian belief system. It is a key concept in Emile Durkheim's The Elementary Forms of Religious Life (1912). See Rojek, *Celebrity*, 55, 58.

89 Memorial coins were in fashion during the Renaissance as a means of commemorating the accomplishments of royal and noble family dynasties. The fact that Francesco chose to have one struck for Isabella implies an attempt on his part to equate her with them. It is likely he chose one of the noted medallists of the Dupré family to strike the coin according to his design. See Jean Tricou for different theories as to who commissioned it and where it was made ("La medaille d'Isabella Andreini," 285).

90 In Marotti and Romei, *La commedia dell'arte*, 521.

91 Francesco Andreini, "Corinto" and prefatory letter, *Le bravure*, in Marotti and Romei, *La commedia dell'arte*, 215–18.

92 Giovan Battista described them as lovebirds: "quasi tortorella alor c'ha perduta la compagna, perdutala in Lione, non mai più volle poggiar di teatro su'l verde e lieto ramo" (like a dove losing a partner, losing her in Lyon, he never wanted to set foot again on that green and happy branch of the stage) (*La ferza*, in Marotti and Romei, *La commedia dell'arte*, 509).

93 "Corinto," in Marotti and Romei, *La commedia dell'arte*, 215; translated by Clubb, *Italian Drama in Shakespeare's Time*, 258.

94 Isabella Andreini, *Lettere della signora Isabella Andreini.*

95 Andreini, *Lettere*, 6, unnumbered. Further citations of this work appear in the text, as do modernized versions of certain *Lettere* collected in Marotti and Romei, *La commedia dell'arte*, and in Stortoni and Prentice Lillie, *Women Poets*, 226–31.

96 The other letter, "Del dolore nella morte della moglie" (On the Grief over His Wife's Death), appears earlier in the collection and does not identify Isabella as the wife in question but expresses the same sentiments as "Corinto" (*Lettere*, 235–8).

97 Ray explains that literary reputations in this period required the publication of an author's *Lettere*, which "served as the apex of literary achievement and even celebrity" (*Writing Gender*, 180).

98 The only letter to an actual person is "Della morte di Signor Tasso" (On the Death of Tasso) (*Lettere*, 184–7).

99 Carlson discusses the circumstances in which memories of an actress's performance "ghost" her reputation (*The Haunted Stage*, 87). (My own examples in chapter 4 from the *Lettere* and *Fragmenti* that the malcontent

Fabrizio inserts into "his" performance are just such an imaginary reconstruction.)

100 Ray, *Writing Gender*, 17.

101 This sexual attraction, already discussed in relation to other diva moments, comes from the spectator's sense of the "illusion of presence" that they grant to the star (Quinn, "Semiotics," 158).

102 Ian Maclean suggests that "neoplatonism is influential in the promotion of new ideas on woman in two domains: the theory of love and politics. There can be no doubt that the respect and honour paid to the female sex in the love poetry and the pastoral of Renaissance Europe is closely connected to the neoplatonist theory of beauty and love" (*The Renaissance Notion of Woman*, 85).

103 The male perspective on forced marriages is also expressed in some of the letters but is less connected to the misfortune of being born a particular gender.

104 See Stortoni and Prentice Lillie, *Women Poets*, 226–31, which includes both the Italian original and the English translation. Further citations of this work in both languages appear in the text.

105 This letter stands in sharp contrast to a comparable one, "Della morte d'un figliuolo" (On the Death of a Son, *Lettere*, 152–4), which could also be assumed to come from Isabella's pen and is formulaic in its expressions of condolence best captured in her concluding remarks: "Egli è molto meglio a mio giuditio, pianger la morte del figliuol buono, e virtuoso, che sospirar la vita del cattivo, e vitioso" (It is much better in my opinion to be mourning the death of a good and virtuous son, than sighing over the life of a wicked and vicious one; 154). Whereas the discussion in "On the Death of a Son" is confined to a specific son, the birth of a daughter in "On the Birth of a Woman" becomes an occasion to write about the entire female sex as in need of justification.

106 Ray, *Writing Gender*, 180.

107 Andreini, *Fragmenti*, 9. Further citations of this work appear in the text, as do citations from modernized versions of certain *contrasti* collected in Marotti and Romei, *La commedia dell'arte*, and in Pandolfi, *Commedia*, vol. 2.

108 Ersilia never talks about being an actress, but she does mention travelling with the touring companies.

109 Andreini, *La ferza*, in Marotti and Romei, *La commedia dell'arte*, 521. For a detailed description, see Rasi, "Andreini, Francesco," in *Comici italiani*, 1:87.

110 In death, because of her *mana*, she can "illuminate the conditions of the present" by reminding all those who are still living of her importance to her family. See Rojek, *Celebrity*, 55.

6 Conclusion

1 In Marotti and Romei, *La commedia dell'arte,* 510.
2 Roach, *It,* 3.
3 Rojek, *Celebrity,* 17–18.
4 Quinn, "Semiotics," 158.
5 Campbell, "Querelle," 56.
6 Alexander Doty, "Introduction," 4.
7 Charles Sterling, "Early Painting," 20–1.
8 In Marotti and Romei, *La commedia dell'arte,* 167.

Bibliography

Ademollo, Alessandro. *I teatri di Roma nel secolo decimosettimo.* Bologna: Forni, 1888.

Agamben, Giorgio. *Stanzas: Word and Phantasm in Western Culture.* Translated by Ronald L. Martinez. Minneapolis: University of Minnesota Press, 1993.

Alberoni, Francesco. "The Powerless 'Elite': Theory and Research on the Phenomenon of the Stars." Translated by Denis McQuail. In *The Celebrity Culture Reader,* edited by P. David Marshall, 108–23. New York: Routledge, 2006.

Alexander, Jeffrey C. "The Celebrity Icon." *Cultural Sociology* 4, no. 3 (2010): 323–36.

Amariglio, Jack, and Antonio Callari. "Marxian Value Theory and the Problem of the Subject: The Role of Commodity Fetishism." In *Fetishism as Cultural Discourse,* edited by Emily Apter and William Pietz, 186–216. Ithaca: Cornell University Press, 1993.

Anderson, Michael. "Making Room: Commedia and the Privatisation of the Theatre." In Cairns, *The Commedia dell'Arte,* 74–97.

Andreini, Francesco. *Le bravure del Capitano Spavento.* Venice: Giacomo Antonio Somasco, 1607. Modern edition by Roberto Tessari. Pisa: Giardini, 1987. Excerpts in Marotti and Romei, *La commedia dell'arte.* 213–302.

– *Ragionamenti fantastici posti in forma di dialoghi rappresentativi.* Venice: Giacomo Antonio Somasco, 1612.

Andreini, Giovan Battista. *La ferza contra l'accuse date alla commedia.* Paris: Nicolao Callemont, 1625. Excerpt in Marotti and Romei, *La commedia dell'arte,* 489–534.

Andreini, Isabella. *Fragmenti di alcune scritture della signora Isabella Andreini Comica Gelosa, et Academia Intenta. Raccolti da Francesco Andreini Comico Geloso, detto il Capitano Spavento, e dati in luce da Flamminio Scala Comico, e da lui dedicati all'illustrissimo Sig. Filippo Capponi.* Venice: Gio. Battista Combi, 1620.

– *Lettere della signora Isabella Andreini padovana, comica gelosa e academica Intenta, nominata l'Accesa.* Venice: Marc'Antonio Zaltieri, 1607. Reprint, Gio. Battista Combi, 1620. Page references are to the 1620 edition.
– *La Mirtilla.* Verona: Girolamo Discepolo, 1588.
– *La Mirtilla.* Edited by Maria Luisa Doglio. Lucca: Fazzi, 1995.
– *La Mirtilla: A Pastoral.* Translated by Julie D. Campbell. Tempe: Arizona Center for Medieval and Renaissance Studies, 2002.
– *Rime. Parte prima.* Milan: Girolamo Bordone and Pietromartire Locarni, 1601.
– *Rime. Parte seconda.* Milan: Girolamo Bordone and Pietromartire Locarni, 1605.
– *Selected Poems of Isabella Andreini.* Edited by Anne MacNeil. Translated by James Wyatt Cook. Lanham: Scarecrow Press, 2005.
Andrews, Richard. "L'attrice e la cantante fra Cinquecento e Seicento. La presenza femminile in palscoscenico." In *Teatro e musica. Écritures vocale et scenique.* Actes du colloque international, 17–19 February 1998. Edited by Margherita Orsino, 27–43. Toulouse: Presses Universitaires du Mirail, 1999.
– *Scripts and Scenarios: The Performance of Comedy in Renaissance Italy.* Cambridge: Cambridge University Press, 1993.
– ed. and trans. *The Commedia dell'Arte of Flaminio Scala: A Translation and Analysis of 30 Scenarios.* Lanham: Scarecrow, 2008.
Anonymous. "La commedia in commedia." In the Corsini ms collection, *Raccolta dei scenari più scelti di istrioni.* Rome: Biblioteca Corsiniana Mss. 45, G.5, 178.
Apter, Emily, and William Pietz, eds. *Fetishism as Cultural Discourse.* Ithaca: Cornell University Press, 1993.
Aretino, Pietro. *I ragionamenti.* Edited by Alberto Moravia. Rome: Newton Compton, 1972.
– *The Letters of Pietro Aretino.* Translated by Thomas Caldecott Chubb. Hamden, CT: Archon, 1967.
– *The Ragionamenti.* Edited by Peter Stafford. London: Odyssey Press, 1970.
Ariosto, Lodovico. *Orlando furioso.* Edited by Lanfranco Caretti. Turin: Einaudi, 1992.
– *Orlando furioso.* Edited by Steward A. Baker and A. Bartlett Giamatti. Translated by William Stewart Ross. Indianapolis: Bobbs-Merrill, 1968.
– *The Pretenders.* In *The Comedies of Ariosto.* Translated and edited by Edmond M. Beame and Leonard G. Sbrocchi, 52–98. Chicago: University of Chicago Press, 1975.
Arullani, Vittorio Amedeo. *Di Gherardo Borgogni: Letterato Albese e delle relazioni di lui con alcuni poeti suoi contemporanei: Tommaso Stigliani, Isabella Andreini, e Torquato Tasso.* Alba: Libreria Sansoldi, 1910.

Baldesano, Guglielmo. "Del fuggire li teatri e le vanità de gli spettacoli." In *Stimolo alle virtù*. Rome: Aloisio Zannetti, 1592. Excerpt in Taviani, *La commedia dell'arte*, 96–106.

Barasch, Frances K. "Italian Actresses in Shakespeare's World: Flaminia and Vincenza." *Shakespeare Bulletin* 18, no. 4 (2000): 17–21.

– "Italian Actresses in Shakespeare's World: Vittoria and Isabella." *Shakespeare Bulletin* 19, no. 3 (2001): 5–9.

Barbieri, Nicolò. *La supplica discorso famigliare a quelli che trattono de' comici*. Venice: Marco Ginammi, 1634. Modern edition by Ferdinando Taviani. Milan: Il Polifilo, 1971.

Bargagli, Girolamo. *La Pellegrina*. Siena: I Florimi, 1518. Modern edition by Florindo Cerrata. Florence: Olschki, 1971.

– *The Female Pilgrim*. Translated by Bruno Ferraro. Ottawa: Dovehouse, 1988.

Barish, Jonas. *The Antitheatrical Prejudice*. Los Angeles: University of California Press, 1979.

Barthes, Roland. "The Face of Garbo." In *Mythologies*, translated by Annette Lavers, 56–7. London: Paladin, 1985.

Bartoli, Francesco. *Notizie istoriche de' comici italiani che fiorirono intorno all'anno MDC fino a' giorni presenti*. 2 vols. Padua: Conzatti, 1781–82. Reprint, Bologna: Arnaldo Forni Editore, 1978.

Bascapè, Carlo. "Della Settuagesima," 8 January 1606. In *Scritti publicati da mons. Reverendiss. D. Carlo Vescovo di Novara*. Novara: Gerolamo Sesalli, 1609. Excerpt in Taviani, *La commedia dell'arte*,, 54–63.

Baschet, Armand. *Les comédiens italiens à la cour de France sous Charles IX, Henri III, Henri IV, et Louis XIII*. Paris: E. Plon, 1882. Reprint, Geneva: Slatkine, 1969.

Beccari, Agostino. *Il sacrificio*. Ferrara: Alfonso Caraffa, 1587. In *Favole*, edited by Fulvio Pevere, 1–130. Turin: Edizioni Res, 1999.

Beecher, Donald, and Massimo Ciavolella, eds. *Comparative Critical Approaches to Renaissance Comedy*. Ottawa: Dovehouse, 1986.

Beijer, Agne, and Pierre Louis Duchartre. *Recueil de plusieurs fragments des premières comédies italiennes qui ont été représentées en France sous le regne de Henry III. Recueil dit de Fossard, conservé au Musée National de Stockholm*. Paris: Duchartre and Buggenhoudt, 1928.

Benjamin, Walter. "The Work of Art in the Age of Mechanical Reproduction." In *Illuminations*, translated by Harry Zohn, 217–51. New York: Shocken, 1968.

Benson, Pamela Joseph. *The Invention of the Renaissance Woman: The Challenge of Female Independence in the Literature and Thought of Italy and England*. University Park, PA: Pennsylvania University Press, 1992.

Bettella, Patrizia. *The Ugly Woman: Transgressive Aesthetic Models in Italian Poetry from the Middle Ages to the Baroque.* Toronto: University of Toronto Press, 2005.

Bhabha, Homi K. "The Other Question: Stereotype, Discrimination and the Discourse of Colonialism." In *The Location of Culture,* 66–84. London: Routledge, 1994.

Binns, J.W. "Women or Transvestites on the Elizabethan Stage?: An Oxford Controversy." *Sixteenth Century Journal* 5, no. 2 (1974): 95–120.

Blau, Herbert. *To All Appearances: Ideology and Performance.* New York: Routledge, 1992.

Boccaccio, Giovanni. *The Decameron.* Translated by G.H. McWilliam. London: Penguin, 1972.

Bonifacio, Giovanni. *Le arte de cenni.* Vicenza: Francesco Grossi, 1616.

Borgogni, Gherardo. *Delle Rime et Prose del Sig. Torquato Tasso nuovamente poste in luce. Parte Quarta.* Milan: Pietro Tini, 1586.

– *La fonte del disporto, dialogo del Sig. Gherardo Borgogni l' Errante Accademico Inquieto di Milano.* Bergamo: Comino Ventura, 1598. Reprint, 1602.

– *Nuova scelta di rime.* Bergamo: Comin Ventura, 1592.

– *Rime di diversi illustri poeti de' nostri tempi.* Venice: La Minima compagnia, 1599.

Borromeo, Carlo. *Lettere.* In G.B. Castiglione, *Sentimenti di S. Carlo Borromeo intorno agli Spettacoli, a sua altezza reverendissima monsignor cristoforo de' Migazzi Arcivescovo di Vienna e principe del S.R.I.* Bergamo: Pietro Lancellotti, 1759. Excerpts in Taviani, *La commedia dell'arte,*, 16–24.

– *Memoriale di Monsignor Illustrissimo e Reverendissimo Cardinale di Santa Prassede Arcivescovo al suo diletto popolo della Città, et Diocese de Milano.* Milan: Michel Tini, 1579. Excerpt in Taviani, *La commedia dell'arte,* 24–31.

Borsellino, Nino. "Tra testo e gesto: Drammaturgie di fine Cinquecento." In Chiabò and Doglio, *Origini della commedia,* 13–47.

Bosisio, Paolo. "Tecniche recitative dei comici dell'arte." In *La Commedia dell'Ate tra cinque e seicento in Francia e in Europa.* Atti del Convegno Internazionale di Studio, Verona-Vicenza, 19–21 October 1995. Edited by Elio Mosele, 111–28. Fasano: Schena, 1997.

Bossy, John. "The Counter-Reformation and the People of Catholic Europe." *Past and Present* 47 (1970): 51–70.

Brown, Beverley. "A Feminist Interest in Pornography – Some Modest Proposals," *m/f* 5/6 (1981): 5–18.

Brown, Pamela Allen, and Pater Parolin, eds. *Women Players in England, 1500–1660: Beyond the All-Male Stage.* Aldershot: Ashgate, 2008.

Bruni, Domenico. "Prologhi di Domenico Bruni comico. Parte seconda."

Biblioteca Nazionale Braidense di Milano. Excerpts in Marotti and Romei, 373–433.

Bruns, Gerald L. *Inventions: Writing, Textuality, and Understanding in Literary History*. New Haven: Yale University Press, 1982.

Bruster, Dougas. "Female-Female Eroticism and the Early Modern Stage." *Renaissance Drama* 24, no. 9 (1993): 1–32.

Buckley, Matthew. "Eloquent Action: The Body and Meaning in Early Commedia dell'Arte." *Theatre Survey* 50, no. 2 (2009): 251–315.

Bullough, Vern L., and Bonnie Bullough. *Crossdressing, Sex, and Gender*. Philadelphia: University of Pennsylvania Press, 1993.

Burattelli, Claudia. *Spettacoli di corte a Mantova tra Cinque e Seicento*. Florence: Le Lettere, 1999.

Buratelli, Claudia, Domenica Landolfi, and Anna Zinanni, eds. *Comici dell'arte: corrispondenze*. 2 vols. Florence: Le Lettere, 1993.

Burgin, Victor, James Donald, and Cora Kaplan, eds. *Formations of Fantasy*. London: Routledge, 1986.

Butler, Judith. *Bodies That Matter: On the Discursive Limits of "Sex."* London: Routledge, 1993.

– *Gender Trouble: Feminism and the Subversion of Identity*. London: Routledge, 1990.

Cairns, Christopher, ed. *The Commedia dell'Arte from the Renaissance to Dario Fo*. Lewiston, NY: Edwin Mellen, 1989.

Campbell, Julie D. "Francesco Andreini: 'On Taking a Wife.'" In *In Dialogue with the Other Voice in Sixteenth-Century Italy: Literary and Social Contexts for Women's Writing*, edited by Julie D. Campbell and Maria Galli Stampino, 265–87. Toronto: IterBooks, 2011.

– Introduction to *La Mirtilla* by Isabella Andreini, xi–xxvii. Translated by Julie D. Campbell. Tempe: Arizona Centre for Medieval and Renaissance Studies, 2002.

– "The *Querelle* over Sylvia: *La Mirtilla* and *Aminta* in Dialogue." In *Literary Circles and Gender in Early Modern Europe*, 51–72. Aldershot: Ashgate, 2006.

Campiglia, Maddalena. *Flori, a Pastoral Drama*. Edited by Virginia Cox and Lisa Sampson. Translated by Virginia Cox. Chicago: University of Chicago Press, 2004.

Carlson, Marvin. *The Haunted Stage: The Theatre as Memory Machine*. Ann Arbor: University of Michigan Press, 2001.

Castagno, Paul. *The Early Commedia dell'Arte: The Mannerist Context*. New York: Peter Lang, 1994.

Castiglione, Baldessare. *Il libro del cortigiano*. Venice: Aldo Manuzio, 1528.

– *The Book of the Courtier.* Translated by Charles S. Singleton. New York: Doubleday, 1959.

Cecchini, Pier Maria. *Brevi discorsi intorno alle comedie, comedianti, e spettatori.* Naples: Roncagliolo, 1616.

– *Frutti delle moderne comedie ed avisi a chi le recita.* Padua: Guareschi, 1628.

Chiabò, Maria, and Federigo Doglio, eds. *Origini della commedia improvvisa o dell'arte.* Atti del convegno internationale di Roma-Anagni. Rome: Torre d'Orfeo, 1996.

Cixous, Hélène, and Catherine Clément. *The Newly Born Woman.* London: I.B. Taurus, 1996.

Clivio, Gianrenzo P. "The Languages of the Commedia dell'Arte." In *The Science of Buffoonery: Theory and History of the Commedia dell'Arte,* edited by Domenico Pietropaolo, 209–37. Ottawa: Dovehouse, 1989.

Clubb, Louise George. *Italian Drama in Shakespeare's Time.* New Haven: Yale University Press, 1989.

– "Italian Stories on the Stage." In *The Cambridge Companion to Shakespearean Comedy,* edited by Alexander Leggatt, 32–46. Cambridge: Cambridge University Press, 2002.

– "Theatregrams." In *Comparative Critical Approaches to Renaissance Comedy,* edited by Donald Beecher and Massimo Ciavolella, 14–33. Ottawa: Dovehouse, 1986.

Cocco, Esther. "Una compagnia comica nella prima metà del secolo XVI." *Giornale storico dell letteratura italiana* 65 (1915): 55–70.

Colie, Rosalie L. *The Resources of Kind: Genre Theory in the Renaissance.* Edited by Barbara Kiefer Lewalski. Berkeley: University of California Press, 1973.

Connolly, Joy. *The State of Speech: Rhetorical and Political Thought in Ancient Rome.* Princeton: Princeton University Press, 2007.

Cook, Carol. "The Sign and Semblance of Her Honor: Reading Gender Differences in *Much Ado About Nothing.*" In *Shakespeare and Gender: A History,* edited by Deborah Barker and Ivo Kamps, 75–103. London: Verso, 1995.

Coryate, Thomas. *Coryates's Crudities.* 2 vols. London: William Stansby, 1611. Reprint, Glasgow: James MacLehose and Sons, 1905.

Cousin, J. "Une scène des *Gelosi*: Isabella Andreini et sa troupe (Tableau du Musée Carnavalet)." *Bulletin des Musées de France* 2 (1890): 67–70.

Cox, Virginia. *The Prodigious Muse: Women's Writing in Counter-Reformation Italy.* Baltimore: Johns Hopkins University Press, 2011.

Croce, Benedetto. *Poesia popolare e poesia d'arte: studii sulla poesia italiana dal tre al cinque-cento.* 4th ed. Bari: Laterza, 1957.

Cropper, Elizabeth. "The Beauty of Woman: Problems in the Rhetoric of Renaissance Portraiture." In *Rewriting the Renaissance: The Discourses of Sexual

Difference in Early Modern Europe, edited by Margaret W. Ferguson, Maureen Quilligan, and Nancy Vickers, 175–90. Chicago: University of Chicago Press, 1987.

D'Ancona, Alessandro. *Origini del teatro italiano*. 2 vols. Turin: Loescher, 1891. Reprint, Rome: Bardi, 1971.

Daston, Lorraine, and Katharine Park. "The Hermaphrodite and the Orders of Nature: Sexual Ambiguity in Early Modern France." *GLQ: A Journal of Lesbian and Gay Studies* 1, no. 4 (1995): 419–38.

Dawson, Olivia. "Speaking Theatres: The 'Olimpico' Theatres of Vicenza and Sabbioneta, and Camillo's Theatre of Memory." In *Design, Image, and Acting*, vol. 2 of *The Renaissance Theatre: Texts, Performance, Design*, edited by Christopher Cairns 85–92. Aldershot: Ashgate, 1999.

de' Angelis, Francesca Romana. *La divina Isabella: Vita straordinaria di una donna del Cinquecento.* Florence: Sansoni, 1991.

Debord, Guy. *The Society of the Spectacle.* Translated by Donald Nicholson-Smith. New York: Zone, 1994.

Dekker, Rudolf M., and Lotte van de Pol. *The Tradition of Female Transvestism in Early Modern Europe.* London: Macmillan, 1989.

Della Casa, Giovanni. *Galateo*. Translated by Konrad Eisenbichler and Kenneth R. Bartlett. Toronto: Centre for Reformation and Renaissance Studies, 1986.

– *Il Galateo*. Florence: Jacopo e Bernardo Giunti, 1561.

de Mendoza, Pedro Hurtado. *Scholasticae, et morales disputationes*. Salamanticae: Iacintho Taberniel, 1631. Excerpts in Taviani, *La commedia dell'arte*, 86–9.

de Pineda, Juan. *Discorso del danno che cagionano le comedie, et lascivi spettacoli. Raccolto dall'opere del P.F. Giovanni di Pineda dell'ordine di S. Francesco. Tradotto dalla lingua spagnuola dal Commend. Fra Giulio Zanchini da Castiglionchio, Cavaliere di San Giovanni, Spedalingo di Santa Maria Nuova di Firenze.* Florence: Giorgio Marescotti, 1599. Excerpt in Taviani, *La commedia dell'arte*, 120–3.

de' Rossi, Bastiano. *Descrizione dell'Apparato e dell'Intermedi fatti per la commedia rappresentata in Firenze, nelle Nozze de' Serenissimi Don Ferdinando de' Medici e Madama Christina di Lorena Gran Duchi di Toscana.* Padua: Antonio Padovani, 1589.

de' Sommi, Leone. *Quattro dialoghi in materia di rappresentazioni sceniche.* Edited by Ferruccio Marotti. Milan: Il Polifilo, 1968.

– "The Dialogues of Leone di Somi." In Allardyce Nicoll, *The Development of Theatre*, 251–78. Revised 5th ed. New York: Harcourt, Brace, 1966.

Doglio, Maria Luisa. Introduction to *La Mirtilla*, by Isabella Andreini, 5–30. Edited by Maria Luisa Doglio. Lucca: Fazzi, 1995.

Dotoli, Giovanni. "La rivoluzione della commedia dell'arte." In *La commedia dell'arte tra Cinque e Seicento in Francia e in Europa*. Atti del convegno internazionale di studio, Verona-Vicenza, 19–21 October 1995. Edited by Elio Mosele, 21–42. Fasano: Schena, 1997.

Doty, Alexander. "Introduction: There's Something about Mary." *Camera Obscura* 22, no. 65 (2007): 1–9.

Dubrow, Heather. *Echoes of Desire: English Petrarchanism and its Counterdiscourses.* Ithaca: Cornell University Press, 1995.

Duchartre, Pierre Louis. *The Italian Comedy.* Translated by Randolph T. Weaver. New York: Dover, 1966.

During, Simon. *Modern Enchantments: The Cultural Power of Secular Magic.* Cambridge, MA: Harvard University Press, 2002.

Dyer, Richard. "*A Star Is Born* and the Construction of Authenticity." In *Stardom: Industry of Desire,* edited by Christine Gledhill, 132–40. London: Routledge, 1991.

– *Heavenly Bodies: Film Stars and Society.* 2nd ed. New York: Routledge, 2004.

Eamon, William. "The Secrets of Nature in Popular Culture." In *Science and the Secrets of Nature: Books of Secrets in Medieval and Early Modern Culture,* 234–66. Princeton: Princeton University Press, 1994.

Edinger, Edward F. *The Mystery of the Coniunctio: Alchemical Image of Individuation.* Transcribed and edited by Joan Dexter Blackmer. Toronto: Inner City Books, 1994.

Eisenbichler, Konrad, and Philip Sohm, eds. *The Language of Gesture in the Renaissance.* Toronto: University of Toronto Press, 1986.

Eisenstadt, S.N., ed. *Max Weber on Charisma and Institution Building.* Chicago: University of Chicago Press, 1968.

Epstein, Julia, and Kristina Straub, eds. *Bodyguards: The Culture of Gender Ambiguity.* London: Routledge, 1991.

Erenstein, Robert. "Satire and the *Commedia dell'Arte.*" In *Western Popular Theatre,* edited by David Mayer and Kenneth Richards, 28–47. London: Methuen, 1977.

– "Isabella Andreini: A Lady of Virtue and High Renown." In *Essays on Drama and Theatre: Liber Amicorum Benjamin Hunningher,* 37–49. Antwerp: Standaard, 1973.

Evangelista, Annamaria. "Le compagnie dei comici dell'arte nel teatrini di Baldracca a Firenze: Notizie dagli epistolari (1576–1653)." *Quaderni di Teatro* 6 (1984): 50–72.

Falavolti, Laura, ed. *Il finto marito.* In *Commedie dei comici dell'arte,* 225–365. Turin: Unione Tipgrafico Editrice Torinese, 1982.

Ferris, Lesley, ed. *Crossing the Stage: Controversies on Cross-Dressing.* London: Routledge, 1993.

Ferrone, Siro. *Attori mercanti corsari. La commedia dell'arte in Europa fra Cinque e Seicento.* Turin: Einaudi, 1993.

– "La vendita del teatro: tipologie europee tra Cinque e Seicento." In Cairns, *The Commedia dell'Arte*, 35–72.

Fitzpatrick, Tim. *The Relationship of Oral and Literate Performance Processes in the Commedia dell'Arte: Beyond the Improvisation/Memorization Divide.* Lewiston, NY: Edwin Mellen, 1995.

Fo, Dario. *The Tricks of the Trade.* Edited by Stuart Hood. Translated by Joe Farrell. Turin: Methuen Drama, 1987.

Fradenburg, Louise, and Carla Freccero, eds. *Premodern Sexualities.* London: Routledge, 1996.

Freedman, Barbara. *Staging the Gaze: Postmodernism, Psychoanalysis, and Shakespearean Comedy.* Ithaca: Cornell University Press, 1991.

Freud, Sigmund. "Fetishism." In *The Standard Edition of the Complete Psychological Works of Sigmund Freud*, translated and edited by James Strachey, 21:147–57. London: Hogarth, 1927.

– "The Splitting of the Ego in the Defensive Process." In *The Standard Edition of the Complete Psychological Works of Sigmund Freud*, translated and edited by James Strachey, 23:275–328. London: Hogarth, 1938.

– "Freud and Fetishism: Previously Unpublished Minutes of the Vienna Psychoanalytic Society." Edited and translated by Louis Rose. *Psychoanalytic Quarterly* 57 (1988): 147–66.

– *Jokes and Their Relation to the Unconscious.* Translated and edited by James Strachey. New York: Norton, 1960.

Gallop, Jane. *The Daughter's Seduction: Feminism and Psychoanalysis.* Ithaca: Cornell University Press, 1982.

Gambelli, Delia. *Arlecchino a Parigi: Dall'inferno alla corte di Re Sole.* Vol. 1. Rome: Bulzoni, 1993.

Gamman, Lorraine, and Merja Makinen. *Female Fetishism.* New York: New York University Press, 1995.

Garber, Marjorie. *Vested Interests: Cross-Dressing and Cultural Anxiety.* London: Routledge, 1997.

Garzoni, Tommaso. *La piazza universale di tutte le professioni del mondo.* Venice: G.B. Somascho, 1585. Excerpts in Marotti and Romei, *La commedia dell'arte*, 11–19.

Gell, Alfred. "The Technology of Enchantment and the Enchantment of Technology." In *Anthropology, Art and Aesthetics*, edited by Jeremy Coote and Anthony Shelton, 40–63. Oxford: Clarendon, 1992.

Giannetti, Laura. *Lelia's Kiss: Imagining Gender, Sex, and Marriage in Italian Renaissance Comedy.* Toronto: University of Toronto Press, 2009.

Giannetti, Laura, and Guido Ruggiero, trans. and eds. *Gl'ingannati (The Deceived).* In *Five Comedies from the Italian Renaissance,* 205–84. Baltimore: Johns Hopkins University Press, 2003.

Gilder, Rosamond. *Enter the Actress: The First Women in the Theatre.* London: George G. Harrap & Co., 1931.

Goldberg, Jonathan, ed. *Queering the Renaissance.* Durham: Duke University Press, 1994.

Goodden, Angelica. *Actio and Persuasion: Dramatic Performance in Eighteenth-Century France.* Oxford: Clarendon, 1986.

Gordon, Mel. *Lazzi: The Comic Routines of the Commedia dell'Arte.* New York: Theatre Library Association, 1983.

Gori, Domenico. *Trattato contra alle comedie lascive.* Biblioteca Riccardiana di Firenze, cod. 2236. Excerpt in Taviani, *La commedia dell'arte,* 136–43.

Grazzini, Antonio Francesco. "Canto di Zanni e di Magnifichi." In *Tutti I trionfi, carri, mascherate o canti carnascialeschi.* Vol. 2, 449–501. Lucca: Pel Benedini, 1750. Excerpt in Richards and Richards, *The Commedia dell'Arte,* 53–4.

Grossberg, Laurence. "Is There a Fan in the House? The Affective Sensibility of Fandom." In *The Celebrity Culture Reader,* edited by P. David Marshall, 581–90. New York: Routledge, 2006.

Guarini, Giovanni Battista. *Il pastor fido.* Venice, 1590. Edited by Ettore Bonara. Milan: Mursia, 1977.

Guarino, Raimondo. "Performing Theatre: On Acting in the Early Renaissance." In *Design, Image, and Acting,* vol. 2 of *The Renaissance Theatre: Texts, Performance, Design,* edited by Christopher Cairns, 102–14. Aldershot: Ashgate, 1999.

– *Teatro e mutamenti. Rinascimento e spettacolo a Venezia.* Bologna: Il Mulino, 1995.

Günsberg, Maggie. *Gender and the Italian Stage from the Renaissance to the Present Day.* Cambridge: Cambridge University Press, 1997.

Haskell, Molly. *From Reverence to Rape: The Treatment of Women in the Movies.* 2nd ed. Chicago: University of Chicago Press, 1987.

Heck, Thomas. *Commedia dell'Arte: A Guide to the Primary and Secondary Literature.* New York: Garland, 1988.

– ed. *Picturing Performance: The Iconography of the Performing Arts in Concept and Practice.* Rochester, NY: University of Rochester Press, 1999.

Heiss, Ursula. "Transvestism and the Stage Controversy in Spain and England. 1580–1680." *Theatre Journal* 44, no. 3 (1992): 357–74.

Henke, Robert. *Performance and Literature in the Commedia dell'Arte.* Cambridge: Cambridge University Press, 2002.

– "Virtuosity and Mimesis in the Commedia dell'arte and *Hamlet*." In *Italian Culture in the Drama of Shakespeare and His Contemporaries: Rewriting, Remaking, Refashioning*, ed. by Michele Marrapodi, 69–81. Aldershot: Ashgate, 2005.

– "The Italian Mountebank and the *Commedia dell'Arte*." *Theatre Survey* 38, no. 2 (1997): 1–29.

– "Towards Reconstructing the Audiences of the *Commedia dell'Arte*." *Études Théâtrales Essays in Theatre* 15 (1997): 207–20.

Hennessy, Rosemary. *Profit and Pleasure: Sexual Identities in Late Capitalism*. London: Routledge, 2000.

Herlihy, David. *Medieval Households*. Cambridge, MA: Harvard University Press, 1985.

Hetherington, Kevin. *Expressions of Identity: Space, Performance, Politics*. London: Sage, 1998.

Ingegneri, Angelo. *Della poesia rappresentativa & dell'arte di rappresentare le favole sceniche*. Ferrara: V. Baldini, 1598. In *Lo spettacolo dall'umanesimo al manierismo*, edited by Ferruccio Marotti, 271–311. Milan: Feltrinelli, 1974.

Innamorati, Isabella. "Il riuso della parola: Ipotesi sul rapporto tra generici e centoni." In Chiabò and Doglio, *Origini della commedia*, 163–85.

Irigaray, Luce. "Love of the Other." In *An Ethics of Sexual Difference*, translated by Carolyn Burke and Gillian C. Gill, 133–50. Ithaca, NY: Cornell University Press, 1993.

– "Women on the Market." In *This Sex Which Is Not One*, translated by Catherine Porter with Carolyn Burke, 170–91. Ithaca: Cornell University Press, 1985.

Jacobs, Fredrika H. *Defining the Renaissance Virtuosa: Women Artists and the Language of Art History and Criticism*. Cambridge: Cambridge University Press, 1999.

Jaffe-Berg, Erith. *The Multilingual Art of Commedia dell'Arte*. Ottawa: Legas, 2009.

Jardine, Lisa. "Twins and Travesties: Gender, Dependency and Sexual Availability in *Twelfth Night*." In *Erotic Politics: Desire on the Renaissance Stage*, edited by Susan Zimmerman, 27–38. New York: Routledge, 1992.

Jones, Ann Rosalind. *The Currency of Eros: Women's Love Lyric in Europe, 1540–1620*. Bloomington: Indiana University Press, 1990.

– and Peter Stallybrass. "Transvestism and the 'Body Beneath': Speculating on the Boy Actor." In *Renaissance Clothing and the Materials of Memory*, 207–19. Cambridge: Cambridge University Press, 2000.

Jonson, Ben. *Volpone*. In Ben Jonson, *Four Comedies*, edited by Helen Ostovich, 59–227. New York: Routledge, 2013.

Jordan, Constance. *Renaissance Feminism: Literary Texts and Political Models.* Ithaca: Cornell University Press, 1990.

Katritzky, M.A. *Women, Medicine and Theatre, 1500–1750: Literary Mountebanks and Performing Quacks.* Aldershot: Ashgate, 2007.

– *The Art of Commedia: A Study in the Commedia dell'Arte 1560–1620 with Special Reference to the Visual Records.* Amsterdam: Rodopi, 2006.

– "Mountebanks, Mummers and Masqueraders in Thomas Platter's Diary (1595-1600)." In *The English and Italian Theatre,* vol. 1 of *The Renaissance Theatre: Texts, Performance, Design,* edited by Christopher Cairns, 12–44. Aldershot: Ashgate, 1999.

– "Was *Commedia dell'Arte* Performed by Mountebanks? *Album amicorum* Illustrations and Thomas Platter's Description of 1598." *Theatre Research International* 23, no. 2 (1998): 104–25.

– "The Recueil Fossard 1928–88: A Review and Three Reconstructions." In Cairns, *The Commedia dell'Arte,* 99–116.

– "A Renaissance Commedia dell'Arte Performance: Towards a Definitive Sequence of Sieur Fossard's Woodcuts?" *Nationalmuseum Bulletin* 12, no. 1 (1988): 37–53.

– "Italian Comedians in Renaissance Prints." *Print Quarterly* 4, no. 3 (1987): 236–54.

Kennedy, William. "Petrarchan Audiences and Print Technology." *Journal of Medieval and Renaissance Studies* 14, no.1 (1984): 1–20.

– *The Site of Petrarchism: Early Modern National Sentiment in Italy, France, and England.* Baltimore: Johns Hopkins University Press, 2003.

Kerr, Rosalind. "The Italian Actress and the Foundations of Early Modern European Theatre: Performing Female Sexual Identities on the Commedia dell'Arte Stage." *Early Theatre* 11, no. 2 (2008): 181–97.

– "Isabella Andreini (Comica Gelosa 1560–1604): Petrarchism for the Theatre Public." *Quaderni d'italianistica* 27, no. 2 (2006): 71–92.

– "Tra(ns)vesting the Laws of Gender and Genre in Flaminio Scala's *Il Marito.*" In *Queer Italia: Same-Sex Desire in Italian Literature and Film,* edited by Gary Cestaro, 105–16. New York: Palgrave, 2004.

– "The Tragic Death of Carnival: Treatments of Romeo and Juliet in Scala and Shakespeare." In *Intertestualità shakespeariane: Il Cinquecento italiano e il rinascimento inglese,* edited by Michele Marrapodi, 183–206. Rome: Bulzoni, 2003.

– "The Imprint of Genius: Tasso's Sonnet to Isabella Andreini. A Commentary on Ferdinando Taviani's 'Bella d'Asia, Torquato Tasso, gli attori e l'immortalità.'" *Quaderni d'italianistica* 22, no. 2 (2001): 81–96.

Klein, Robert. "The Theory of Figurative Expression in Italian Treatise on the *Impresa.*" In *Form and Meaning: Essays on the Renaissance and Modern Art.*

Translated by Madeline Jay and Leon Wieseltier. New York: Viking Press, 1979.

Krips, Henry. *Fetish: An Erotics of Culture.* Ithaca: Cornell University Press, 1999.

Lacan, Jacques. "The Meaning of the Phallus." In *Feminine Sexuality: Jacques Lacan and the École Freudienne*, edited by Jacqueline Rose and Juliet Mitchell, translated by Jacqueline Rose. New York: Norton, 1982.

– *The Four Fundamental Concepts of Psycho-Analysis.* Edited by Jacques-Alain Miller. Translated by Alan Sheridan. New York: Norton, 1981.

– *Écrits: A Selection.* Translated by Alan Sheridan. New York: Norton, 1977.

Lacour, Léopold. *Le premières actrices françaises.* Paris: Librairie française, 1921.

Laplanche, Jean, and Jean-Bertrand Pontalis. *The Language of Psycho-Analysis.* Translated by David Nicholson-Smith. New York: Norton, 1973.

Laqueur, Thomas. "Sexual Desire and the Market Economy during the Industrial Revolution." In *Discourses of Sexuality: Aristotle to AIDS*, edited by Domna C. Stanton, 185–215. Ann Arbor: University of Michigan Press, 1992.

Lawner, Lynne. *Lives of the Courtesans.* New York: Rizzoli, 1987.

Lea, Kathleen Marguerite. *Italian Popular Comedy: A Study in the Commedia dell'Arte, 1560–1620 with Special Reference to the English Stage.* 2 vols. New York: Russell and Russell, 1962.

Lechner, Sister Joan Marie. *Renaissance Concepts of the Commonplaces.* New York: Pageant Press, 1962.

Licino, Battista, ed. *Rimi di diversi celebri poeti dell'età nostra nuovamente raccolte e poste in luce.* Bergamo: Comino Ventura e Compagni, 1587.

Luckhurst, Mary, and Jane Moody, eds. "Inroduction." In *Theatre and Celebrity in Britain, 1660–2000.* Houndsmill: Palgrave MacMillan, 2005.

Maclean, Ian. *The Renaissance Notion of Woman: A Study in the Fortunes of Scholasticism and Medical Sciences in European Intellectual Life.* Cambridge: Cambridge University Press, 1980.

MacNeil, Anne. Introduction to *Selected Poems by Isabella Andreini*, edited by Anne MacNeil, translated by James Wyatt Cook, 1–28. Lanham: Scarecrow, 2005.

– *Music and Women of the Commedia dell'Arte in the Late Sixteenth Century.* Oxford: Oxford University Press, 2003.

– "The Divine Madness of Isabella Andreini." *Journal of the Royal Music Association* 120 (1995): 195–215.

– "Music and the Life and Work of Isabella Andreini: Humanistic Attitudes toward Music, Poetry, and Theatre during the Late Sixteenth and Early Seventeenth Centuries." PhD diss., University of Chicago, 1994.

Mamone, Sara. *Firenze e Parigi, due capitali dello spettacolo per una regina: Maria de'Medici.* Milan: Silvana, 1987.

Marotti, Ferruccio, and Giovanna Romei, eds. *La commedia dell'arte e la società barocca.* Vol. 2, *La professione del teatro.* Rome: Bulzoni, 1991.

Marshall, P. David. *Celebrity and Power: Fame in Contemporary Culture.* Minneapolis: University of Minneapolis Press, 1997.

Marx, Karl. *Capital: A Critique of Political Economy.* Vol. 1. 1867. Reprint, translated by Ben Fowkes, New York: Vintage, 1977.

Masson, Georgina. *Courtesans of the Italian Renaissance.* London: Secker and Warburg, 1975.

Mastropasqua, Fernando, "Lo spettacolo della Collezione Fossard." In *Ruzante e Arlecchino. Tre saggi sul teatro popolare del Cinquecento,* edited by Fernando Mastropasqua and Cesare Molinari, 91–125. Parma: Studium Parmense, 1970.

– "Pantalone ridicola apparenza – Arlecchino comica presenza." In *Alle origine del teatro moderno. La commedia dell'arte.* Atti del convegno di studi di Pontedera, 28–30 may 1976. Edited by Luciano Mariti, 97–103. Rome: Bulzoni, 1980.

Matthieu, Pierre. *Historie de France et des choses memorable avenues aux Provinces durant sept années de paix du régne du Roy Henry IIII, Roy de France & de Navarre. Divisee en sept livres.* Vol. 1. Paris: Chez I. Metayer, 1606.

Maylender, Michele. *Storia delle Accademie d'Italia.* Bologna: Licinio Cappelli Editore, 1926–30.

Mazzoni, Stefano. "Genealogia e vicende della famiglia Andreini." In Chiabò and Doglio, *Origini della commedia,* 107–52.

McCallum, E.L. *Object Lessons: How to Do Things with Fetishism.* Albany: State University of New York, 1999.

McClure, George W. *The Culture of Profession in Late Renaissance Italy.* Toronto: University of Toronto Press, 2004.

McConachie, Bruce A. "Using the Concept of Cultural Hegemony to Write Theatre History." In *Interpreting the Theatrical Past,* edited by Thomas Postlewait and Bruce A. McConachie, 37–58. Iowa City: University of Iowa Press, 1989.

McGill, Kathleen. "Women and Performance: The Development of Improvisation by the Sixteenth Century Commedia dell'Arte." *Theatre Journal* 43, no.1 (1991): 59–69.

Melzi, Robert C. "From Lelia to Viola." *Renaissance Drama* 9 (1966): 67–81.

Miani, Valeria. *Amorosa speranza, favola pastorale.* Venice: Francesco Bolzetta, 1604.

Mirollo, James V. *Mannerism and Renaissance Poetry.* New Haven: Yale University Press, 1984.

Molinari, Cesare. *La commedia dell'arte.* Milan: Mondadori, 1985.

– "L'altra faccia del 1589: Isabella Andreini e la sua 'Pazzia.'" In *Musica e spettacolo, scienze dell'uomo e della natura,* vol. 2 of *Firenze e la Toscana dei Medici nell'Europa del '500,* 565–73. Florence: Olschki, 1983.

Moryson, Fynes. *Shakespeare's Europe: A Survey of the Condition of Europe at the End of the 16th Century, Being Unpublished Chapters of Fynes Moryson's Itinerary (1617).* Edited by Charles Hughes. New York: Benjamin Blom, 1967. First published 1903. Page references are to the 1967 edition.

Moss, Ann. "The *Politica* of Justus Lipsius and the Commonplace-Book." *Journal of the History of Ideas* 59, no. 3 (1998): 421–36.

Moulton, Ian Frederick. *Before Pornography: Erotic Writings in Early Modern England.* Oxford: Oxford University Press, 2000.

Nagler, Alois Maria. *Theatre Festivals of the Medici 1539–1637.* New Haven: Yale University Press, 1964.

Newman, Karen. "The Politics of Spectacle: *La Pellegrina* and the *Intermezzi* of 1589." *MLN* 101, no. 1 (1986): 95–113.

Nichol, Allardyce. *The World of Harlequin: A Critical Study of the Commedia dell'Arte.* Cambridge: Cambridge University Press, 1963.

Nicholson, Eric. "Romance as Role Model: Early Female Performances of *Orlando furioso* and *Gerusalemme liberata.*" In *Renaissance Transactions: Ariosto and Tasso,* edited by Valerie Finucci, 246–69. Durham: Duke University Press, 1999.

Ong, Walter J., S.J. *Rhetoric, Romance and Technology.* Ithaca: Cornell University Press, 1971.

Orgel, Stephen. *Impersonations: The Performance of Gender in Shakespeare's England.* Cambridge: Cambridge University Press, 1996.

– "Nobody's Perfect: Or Why Did the English Stage Take Boys for Women?" *South Atlantic Quarterly* 88 (1989): 7–29.

Ottonelli, Giovan Domenico. *Della Christiana Moderatione del Theatro.* 6 vols. Firenze: Giovanni Antonio Bonardi, 1655. Excerpt in Taviani, *La commedia dell'arte,* 315–526.

Pandolfi, Vito, ed. *La commedia dell' arte. Storia e testi.* 6 vols. Florence: Sansoni, 1957–61.

Park, Katharine. "The Rediscovery of the Clitoris: French Medicine and the Tribade, 1570–1620." In *The Body in Parts: Fantasies of Corporeality in Early Modern Europe,* edited by David Hillman and Carla Massio, 171–93. New York: Routledge, 1997.

Parkins, Ilya. "Notes on a Relationship: Fetish Object, Femininity, Historian." *Tessera* 31 (2002): 90–9.

Pavis, Patrice. *Dictionary of the Theatre:Terms, Concepts, and Analysis.* Translated by Christine Shantz. Toronto: University of Toronto Press, 1998.

Pavoni, Giuseppe. *Diario descritto da Giuseppe Pavoni delle feste celebrate nelle solennissime nozze delli Serenissimi Sposi il Sig. Don Ferdinando Medici e la Sig. Donna Christiana di Loreno Gran Duchi di Toscana*. Bologna: Giovanni Rossi, 1589.

Pellegrino, Alba Ceccarelli. "Gravures et legends du *Recueil Fossard:* essai d'analyse sémiologique." In *La commedia dell'arte tra Cinque e Seicento in Francia e in Europa*. Atti del convegno internazionale di studio, Verona-Vicenza, 19–21 October 1995. Edited by Elio Mosele, 129–70. Fasano: Schena, 1997.

Pérez Pastor, Cristóbal. *Nuevos datos acerca del histrionismo español en los siglos XVI y XVII*. Madrid: Fortanet, 1905.

Perrucci, Andrea. *A Treatise on Acting, from Memory and by Improvisation (1699)*. Translated and edited by Francesco Cotticelli, Anne Goodrich Heck, and Thomas F. Heck. Lanham: Scarecrow, 2008.

– *Dell'arte rappresentativa premeditata ed all'improviso*. Naples: Michele Luigi Mutio, 1699. Modern edition by Anton Giulio Bragaglia. Florence: Sansoni, 1961.

Peters, Julie Stone. *Theatre of the Book 1480–1880: Print, Text, and Performance in Europe*. Oxford: Oxford University Press, 2000.

Petrarch, Francesco. *Petrarch's Lyric Poems*. Translated by Robert M. Durling. Cambridge, MA: Harvard University Press, 1976.

Pieri, Marzia. *La nascita del teatro moderno in Italia tra XV e XVI secolo*. Turin: Bollati Boringhieri, 1989.

Pietropaolo, Domenico, ed. *The Science of Buffoonery: Theory and History of the Commedia dell'Arte*. Ottawa: Dovehouse, 1989.

Pietz, William. "The Problem of the Fetish, I." *Res* 9 (Spring 1985): 5–17.

– "The Problem of the Fetish, II." *Res* 13 (Spring 1987): 23–45.

– "The Problem of the Fetish, IIIa." *Res* 16 (Autumn 1988): 105–23.

– "Fetishism and Materialism: The Limits of Theory in Marx." In *Fetishism as Cultural Discourse*, edited by Emily Apter and William Pietz, 119–51. Ithaca: Cornell University Press, 1993.

Procacci, Giuliano. *History of the Italian People*. Translated by Anthony Paul. London: Penguin, 1970.

Quinn, Michael L. "Celebrity and the Semiotics of Acting," *New Theatre Quarterly* 6, no. 22 (1990): 154–61.

Rasi, Luigi. *I comici italiani*. 3 vols. Florence: Fratelli Bocca, 1897–1905.

Ray, Meredith Kennedy. *Writing Gender in Women's Letter Collections of the Italian Renaissance*. Toronto: University of Toronto Press, 2009.

– "*La castità conquistata:* The Function of the Satyr in Pastoral Drama." *Romance Languages Annual* 9 (1998): 312–28.

Re, Emilio. "Comedianti a Roma nel secolo XVI." *Giornale storico della letterature italiana* 63 (1914): 291–300.

Reulens, Charles. *Erycius Puteanus et Isabelle Andreini: Lecture faite à l'Académie d'Archéologie le 3 Février 1889*, 1–31. Anvers: Van Merlen, 1889.

Riccoboni, Luigi. *L'Histoire du Théâtre Italien depuis la decadence de la Comédie Latine, avec un catalogue des Tragédies et Comédies italiennes imprimées depuis l'an 1500 jusqu'à l'an 1660 et une dissertation sur la tragédie moderne.* Paris: Delormel, 1728. Reprint, Bologna: Forni, 1969.

Richards, Kenneth, and Laura Richards. *The Commedia dell'Arte: A Documentary History.* Oxford: Basil Blackwell, 1990.

Roach, Joseph. *It.* Ann Arbor: University of Michigan Press, 2010.

Rocke, Michael. *Forbidden Friendships: Homosexuality and Male Culture in Renaissance Florence.* Oxford: Oxford University Press, 1996.

Rojek, Christopher. *Celebrity.* London: Reaktion, 2001.

Rosenthal, Margaret. *The Honest Courtesan: Veronica Franco, Citizen and Writer in Sixteenth-Century Venice.* Chicago: University of Chicago Press, 1992.

Ruggiero, Guido. *The Boundaries of Eros: Sex Crime and Sexuality in Renaissance Venice.* Oxford: Oxford University Press, 1985.

– *Binding Passions: Tales of Magic, Marriage and Power at the End of the Renaissance.* New York: Oxford University Press, 1993.

Russo, Mary. *The Female Grotesque.* London: Routledge, 1994.

Sampson, Lisa. *Pastoral Drama in Early Modern Italy: The Making of a New Genre.* Oxford: Legenda, 2006.

Sanuto, Marino. *I diarii.* Edited by Rinaldo Fulin et al. 58 vols. Venice: Deputazione Veneta di Storia Patria, 1879–1903.

Saslow, James. *The Medici Wedding of 1589: Florentine Festival as* Theatrum mundi. New Haven: Yale University Press, 1996.

– *Ganymede in the Renaissance: Homosexuality in Art and Society.* New Haven: Yale University Press, 1996.

Scala, Flaminio. *Il finto marito.* Venice: Andrea Baba, 1618. In *Commedie dei comici dell'arte*, edited by Laura Falavolti, 225–365. Turin: Unione Tipgrafico Editrice Torinese, 1982.

– *Il teatro delle favole rappresentative.* Venice: Giovan Battista Pulciani, 1611. Modern edition by Ferruccio Marotti. 2 vols. Milan: Il Polifilo, 1976.

Scher, Stephen K., ed. and curator. *The Currency of Fame: Portrait Medals of the Renaissance.* New York: H.N. Abrams in Association with the Frick Collection, 1994.

Scott, Virginia. "*La Virtu et la volupté:* Models for the Actress in Early Modern Italy and France." *Theatre Research International* 23, no. 2 (1998): 152–8.

– "In the Beginning: '12 livres per year.'" In *Women on the Stage in Early Modern France: 1540–1750*. Cambridge: Cambridge University Press, 2010.

Segre, Cesare. *Semiotica filologica*. Turin: Einaudi, 1979.

Seneca, A. *De comicis spectaculis tollendis, 1597*. In G.B. Castiglione, *Sentimenti di S Carlo Borromeo intorno agli Spettacoli*. Excerpt in Taviani, *La commedia dell'arte*,, 109–16.

Senelick, Laurence. *The Changing Room: Sex, Drag and Theatre*. London: Routledge, 2000.

Smith, Winifred. *Italian Actors of the Renaissance*. New York: Coward-McCann, 1930.

– *The Commedia dell'Arte*. New York: Columbia University Press, 1912.

Solerti, Angelo. *Vita di Torquato Tasso*. 2 vols. Turin: Loescher, 1895.

Stallybrass, Peter, and Allon White. *The Politics and Poetics of Transgression*. Ithaca: Cornell University Press, 1986.

States, Bert O. "The Actor's Presence: Three Phenomenal Modes." In *Acting (Re)Considered: Theories and Practices*, edited by Phillip B. Zarrilli, 22–42. London: Routledge, 1995.

Sterling, Charles. "Early Paintings of the Commedia dell'Arte in France." *Bulletin: The Metropolitan Museum of Art*, new series, 2, no. 1 (1943): 11–32.

Stoller, Robert. *Observing the Erotic Imagination*. New Haven: Yale University Press, 1985.

Stortoni, Laura, and Mary Prentice Lillie, eds. and trans. *Women Poets of the Italian Renaissance: Courtly Ladies and Courtesans*. New York: Italica Press, 1997.

Stratton, Jon. *The Desirable Body: Cultural Fetishism and the Erotics of Consumption*. Manchester: Manchester University Press, 1996.

Tasso, Torquato. *Aminta*. Venice: Aldo Manuzio, 1583. Edited and translated by Charles Jernigan and Irene Marchegiani Jones. New York: Italica Press, 2000.

– *Il conte, overo de l'imprese*. 1594. Edited by Bruno Basile. Rome: Salerno Editrice, 1993.

– *Il Minturno overo de la bellezza*. 1593–4. In *Tasso's Dialogues: A Selection with the Discourse on the Art of the Dialogue*. Translated by Carnes Lord and Dain A. Trafton. Berkeley: University of California Press, 1982.

– *Le rime di Torquato Tasso*. In *Edizione critica su i manoscritte e le antiche stampe*. Vol. 4, *Rime d'occasione e d'encomio*. Edited by Angelo Solerti. Bologna: Romagnoli dell'Acqua, 1902.

Taviani, Ferdinando. "Bella d'Asia: Torquato Tasso, gli attori e l'immortalità." *Paragone Letteratura* 35 (1984): 3–76.

– ed. *La commedia dell'arte e la società barocca.* Vol. 1, *La fascinazione del teatro.* Rome: Bulzoni, 1969.

Taviani, Ferdinando, and Mirella Schino. *Il segreto della commedia dell'arte.* Florence: La Casa Usher, 1982.

Tessari, Roberto. *La commedia dell'arte nel Seicento: "Industria" e "arte giocosa" nella società barocca.* Florence: Olschki, 1969.

– *Commedia dell'arte: La maschera e l'ombra.* Milan: Mursia, 1989.

– "Sotto il segno di giano: La commedia dell'arte di Isabella e di Francesco Andreini." In Cairns, *The Commedia dell'Arte,* 1–33.

– "Francesco Andreini e la Stagione d'Oro." In Chiabò and Doglio, *Origini della commedia,* 85–105.

– "O diva o 'Estable à tous chevaux.' L'ultimo viaggio di Isabella Andreini." In *Viaggi teatrali dall'Italia a Parigi tra Cinque e Seicento.* Atti del convegno internazionale di Torino, 6–8 April 1987. Edited by Roberto Alonge, 28–142. Genoa: Costa and Nolan, 1989.

Toschi, Paolo. *Le origini del teatro italiano.* Turin: Einaudi, 1955.

Traub, Valerie. *Desire and Anxiety: Circulations of Sexuality in Shakespearean Drama.* London: Routledge, 1992.

– *The Renaissance of Lesbianism in Early Modern England.* Cambridge: Cambridge University Press, 2002.

– "The (In)significance of 'Lesbian' Desire in Early Modern England." In *Erotic Politics,* edited by Susan Zimmerman, 150–69. New York: Routledge, 1992.

Tricou, Jean. "La medaille d'Isabella Andreini." *Extrait de la Revue Numismatique,* 6th series, 2 (1959–1969): 283–7.

Troiano, Massimo. *Dialoghi di Massimo Troiano: Ne' quali si narrano le cose più notabili fatte nelle Nozze dello Illustriss. & Eccell. Prencipe Gvglielmo VI. Conte Palatino del Resno, e Duca di Bauiera: e dell'Illustriss. & Eccell. Madam Renata di Lorena ...* Venice: Zaltieri, 1569. In Pandolfi, *Commedia,* 2:79–83.

Turchetti, Piero. "Luoghi teatrali dell'arte a Firenze tra il XVI e il XVII secolo." In Chiabò and Doglio, *Origini della commedia,* 415–22.

Tyler, Carole-Anne. *Female Impersonation.* London: Routledge, 2003.

Tylus, Jane. "Women at the Windows: *Commedia dell'Arte* and Theatrical Practice in Early Modern Italy." *Theatre Journal* 49, no. 3 (1997): 323–42.

Valerini, Adriano. *Oratione D'Adriano Valerini Veronese, in morte della divina signora Vincenza Armani, comica eccellentissima.* Verona: [1570]. In Marotti and Romei, *La commedia dell'arte,* 31– 41.

Vecellio, Cesare. *Habiti antichi e moderni di tutto il mondo.* Venice: Damiano Zenaro, 1590.

– *Vecellio's Renaissance Costume Book.* 1598. New York: Dover, 1977.

Ubersfeld, Anne. *Reading Theatre.* Translated by Frank Collins. Toronto: University of Toronto Press, 1999.

Una stravaganza dei Medici. First broadcast December 1990 by Thames Television/Raven/Framestore. Conducted by Andrew Parrot. Written by Christofano Malvezzi (1547–99).

Vazzoler, Franco. "Le pastorali dei comici dell'arte: *La Mirtilla* di Isabella Andreini." In *Sviluppi della drammaturgia pastorale nell'Europa del Cinque- Seicento,* edited by Maria Chiabò and Federigo Doglio, 281–99. Viterbo: Centro Studi sul Teatro Medioevale e Rinascimentale, 1992.

Weber, Max. *Economy and Society: An Outline of Interpretive Sociology.* Vol. 1, edited by Guenther Roth and Claus Wittich, translated by a number of scholars. Berkeley: University of California Press, 1978.

Wiesner, Merry E. *Women and Gender in Early Modern Europe.* Cambridge: Cambridge University Press, 1993.

Wilbourne, Emily. "*Amor nello specchio* (1622): Mirroring, Masturbation, and Same-Sex Love." *Women and Music: A Journal of Gender and Culture* 13, no.1 (2009): 54–65.

Williams, Linda. *Hard Core: Power, Pleasure, and the "Frenzy of the Visible."* Berkeley: University of California Press, 1989.

Wilshire, Bruce. *Role Playing and Identity: The Limits of Theatre as Metaphor.* Bloomington: Indiana University Press, 1982.

Zampelli, Michael A. "The 'Most Honest and Most Devoted of Women': An Early Defense of the Professional Actress." *Theatre Survey* 42, no. 1 (2001): 1–23.

Zimmerman, Susan, ed. *Erotic Politics: Desire on the Renaissance Stage.* London: Routledge, 1992.

Zorzi, Ludovico. *L'attore, la commedia, il drammaturgo.* Turin: Einaudi, 1990.

– *Il teatro e la città.* Turin: Einaudi, 1977.

Zorzi Pugliese, Olga. "Variations on Ficino's *De Amore:* The Hymns to Love by Benivieni and Castiglione." In *Ficino and Renaissance Platonism,* edited by Konrad Eisenblicher and Olga Zorzi Pugliese, 113–21. Ottawa: Dovehouse, 1986.

Index

Page numbers that appear in *italics* refer to figures.